HIDDEN TUSCANY

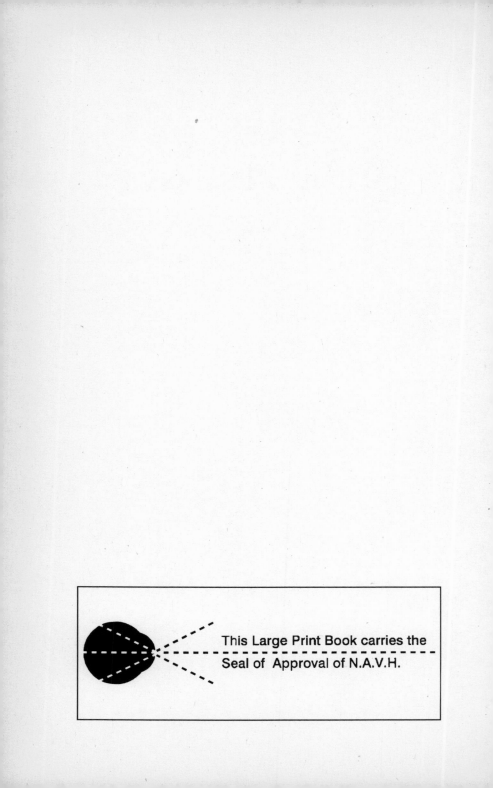

This Large Print Book carries the
Seal of Approval of N.A.V.H.

HIDDEN TUSCANY

DISCOVERING ART, CULTURE, AND MEMORIES IN A WELL-KNOWN REGION'S UNKNOWN PLACES

JOHN KEAHEY

THORNDIKE PRESS

A part of Gale, Cengage Learning

GALE
CENGAGE Learning®

Farmington Hills, Mich • San Francisco • New York • Waterville, Maine
Meriden, Conn • Mason, Ohio • Chicago

GALE
CENGAGE Learning®

LIBRARY OF CONGRESS CATALOGING-IN-PUBLICATION DATA

Keahey, John.
  Hidden Tuscany : discovering art, culture, and memories in a well-known
region's unknown places / by John Keahey. — Large print edition.
    pages cm — (Thorndike press large print nonfiction)
    "Unabridged"—Title page verso.
    ISBN 978-1-4104-7243-4 (hardcover) — ISBN 1-4104-7243-4 (hardcover)
    1. Tuscany (Italy)—Description and travel. 2. Keahey, John—Travel—
Italy—Tuscany. 3. Tuscany (Italy)--History, Local. 4. Coasts—Italy—Tuscany.
5. Tuscany (Italy)—Social life and customs. 6. Arts, Italian—Italy—Tuscany.
7. Cooking—Italy—Tuscany. 8. Large type books. I. Title.
DG734.23.K425 2014
945'.5—dc23   2014023779

Published in 2014 by arrangement with St. Martin's Press, LLC

Printed in Mexico
1 2 3 4 5 6 7 18 17 16 15 14

To the memory of
Kathlyn Eliza Turgeon Keahey,
Joe Judson Keahey,
and Todd Judson Keahey

CONTENTS

7

PREFACE

Water should always be nearby. I like being around it, on it, close enough to catch occasional glimpses of gray-blue sea bubbling with whitecaps. I don't necessarily like being *in* it, unless I am merely sitting close to the surface on a rock or on cool, soft sand, and not moving around a lot. I have my reasons for my unreasonable dislike of immersion. I experienced three near-drowning experiences, once during toddlerhood when I fell into a canal and was saved by my older brother, once during childhood in a YMCA pool, and once as an impetuous twenty-something off the beach at Malibu, California. Each time fate intervened by placing my brother or a couple of strangers next to me who would make sure I survived.

When I decided to visit western Tuscany to discover places most Americans either quickly pass through en route to somewhere else or never even think about while standing, elbow to elbow, in hours-long lines in Florence or Siena, I figured I wanted to be close to the sea, both of them: the Ligurian and the Tyrrhenian. This 180-mile-long western coastline has numerous beaches for all degrees of sunbather, from plebeians like myself with a few euros in their pockets to royalty with their much-deeper pockets. It has islands where visitors, after reasonably short ferry rides *on* the water, can take long walks through Mediterranean shrubs and forests, through vast swaths of wildflowers, the likes of which are not seen in North America. There are ruins to abruptly discover and explore, some going back to the Middle Ages, some to the Romans, some to the Etruscans, and some well beyond, back to protohistory and even farther into prehistory.

Of course, those travelers who do not possess my fear of floating can have remarkable adventures *in* the sea. They are able to observe a multitude of creatures and reefs while snorkeling or scuba diving around the edges of the tops of subterranean mountain ranges that poke out of those two seas between Tuscany and Corsica.

So why did western Tuscany become the subject of a travel narrative? It began with a conversation with Anna Camaiti Hostert, a former government official in Tuscany and a film and literature professor at various U.S. and Italian universities. She had helped me with my third book, *Seeking Sicily: A Cultural Journey Through Myth and Reality in the Heart of the Mediterranean,* and spoke with me often of her home in Tuscany's Maremma. She suggested more than once that its story deserved to be told. Time went by, and with her recommendation in mind I eventually proposed a book examining Maremma and other little-known places in what may be Italy's best-known region.

I knew, and the publisher agreed, that it had to go beyond Maremma — the southernmost area, and perhaps one of the most unique areas, of western Tuscany. We settled on the western part of the famous region simply because many guidebooks skim over it, and because we sensed it is generally unknown among Americans. We would studiously avoid writing about the whole of Tuscany, concentrating on the coastal area, its islands, and a handful of its inland villages — never straying far from the sea — that Americans seem to seldom visit.

Americans know well the eastern half of Tuscany and places such as Pinocchio's birthplace of Collodi (for the kids), Pistoia, Florence, Siena, San Gimignano, and Montepulciano. Few of the places along Tuscany's western coast make it into guidebooks. The big ones are there: Carrara and its marble. Pietrasanta usually gets a mention, along with Pisa and its Leaning Tower, Livorno and its canals, Grosseto and nearby Etruscan sites. Some of the seven major islands of the Tuscan Archipelago also get a few paragraphs.

What are missed are the small villages in between these tourist havens, each with its own festivals and customs. Many have some of the most spectacular scenery in all of Tuscany and offer food unique only to the particular village, as I found, for example, in Santa Fiora, a tiny hill town virtually unknown to outsiders.

I don't expect travelers who read this book to follow in my footsteps. This is not a traditional guidebook with must-do itineraries, hotels, and restaurants. My goal is to engender a spirit of discovery, to get folks who consider themselves more traveler than tourist to rent a car, invest in a detailed road map, pick places that look intriguing, and make spontaneous stops. Learn some history, find something out about the Etruscans, and pick a few of the little-known sites to visit. It would burn out all but the hardiest etruscologist to try to hit them all.

And it doesn't matter what time of year the traveler chooses. While some major coastal destinations could be booked solid by European and Asian tourists during July and August, smaller beach communities and tiny inland villages just a few miles from the coast are worth using as a base for daylong forays.

This book is the result of several trips around Tuscany during the spring, summer, and early fall of 2012. For purposes of economy, parts of some journeys are blended in with others, and, to avoid confusion, some traveling companions during two trips were not mentioned.

Except for a few weeks, I mostly traveled alone, enjoying the freedom of movement such solitariness provides and not having to make compromises or explain why I suddenly wanted to go in this direction and not that one. Late in the day, or in the midst of some great discovery that I instantly wanted to share with someone who wasn't there, were the loneliest times. But there was always one thing I could count on to take me out of such a feeling: conversations with Tuscans. This was true whether they happened to be the waiter who patiently explained to me why a dish I wanted calls for tagliatelle, not spaghetti, or the clerk in a bookstore describing her island's flowers and birds. Or perhaps it was the clerk in a small one-star hotel who asked me each evening what I experienced that day in his beloved corner of western Tuscany and then, with growing excitement, would describe other places I absolutely should not miss experiencing. "Experiencing is much better than just seeing," he told me one evening.

Little things like that keep the traveler's soul charged.

CHRONOLOGY

BC

c.a. 1000 — The earliest indication of Etruscans in what today is known as Tuscany. Seventeenth-century historians began referring to the area by the name Etruria. It included portions of today's northern Lazio and western Umbria regions. Ancient Greek writers referred to these early peoples as Tyrrhenians. Of course there were protohistoric and prehistoric peoples in the area who preceded the Etruscans, but little is known about them.

c.a. 900 — Populonia, in today's western Tuscany, begins to be established along with other Etruscan centers. Eventually, these early peoples expanded as far south as Rome and as far east as the Adriatic Sea coast, where they established Adria and Spina as trading ports.

509 — Rome removes its Etruscan king, launching the Roman Republic.

358 — Etruria is swallowed up by Rome, which then establishes its own colonies, usually at sites previously occupied by Etruscans and their predecessors.

AD

476 — Western Roman Empire ends. While the end was a gradual process and not entirely sudden, this is the date cited by eminent English historian Edward Gibbon.

568 — Germanic Lombard rulers conquer Tuscany. By 700, it had become a Lombard dukedom. The name for the region during this period was Tuscia. This lasted until 773, when Charlemagne, soon to become Holy Roman Emperor, moved down from France into Italy, extending Frankish rule to the southern border of Tuscany.

Early 1100 — Countess Matilda of Tuscany orders construction of the Ponte della Maddalena over the Serchio River. It later becomes known as the Devil's Bridge.

1050 — City-states ascend; Pisa becomes a dominant naval power. Over the next several

16

centuries, Pisa battles with Florence and Genoa, and even pirates and Saracens, for domination of Mediterranean trading routes.

1348–1352 — The Black Death claims as many as 60,000 of Tuscany's 110,000 souls.

1397 — The Medici family in Florence begins its ascent.

1406 — Pisa becomes a Florentine port. Later, in the fifteenth century, Pisa's influence declines as its port on the Arno River silts up. In ancient times, the Ligurian Sea was two miles from the city, and ships sailed up the Arno. Today, the sea is six miles west of Pisa's historic center.

1569 — Tuscany becomes a dukedom under the Medici ruler Cosimo I.

1737 — The Grand Duchy of Tuscany falls to the Habsburg-Lorraine upon the death of the last male Medici of the Grand Ducal line, Gian Gastone.

1799 — Napoleon occupies Tuscany and much of northern Italy.

1814 — The government begins draining some of the swamps that have consistently plagued western Tuscany with malaria, leading to hundreds of thousands of deaths since ancient times. (Centuries earlier, Countess Matilda also had attempted to drain swamps, but Fascist Duce Mussolini had the most success, accomplishing significant land reclamation in the 1930s.)

1848 — Tuscany produces its first constitution and, within a year, declares itself a republic.

1861 — Tuscany joins the newly formed Kingdom of Italy under Vittorio Emanuele II as part of the long process of unifying the country. It took an additional nine years for all of Italy to come under the national flag.

1870 — With the fall of Rome's papal forces, all of Italy is united.

1920 — Mussolini comes to power; Fascism begins its rise.

1936 — Hitler-Stalin Pact.

1939 — The Rome-Berlin Axis becomes a military alliance.

1941 — Italy and Germany declare war on the United States following the December 7 Japanese attack on Pearl Harbor, Hawaii.

1943–1945 — During the Italian Campaign, the war between the Allies and Germany in and around Italy, Tuscan cities such as Pisa and Livorno are devastated, along with numerous towns and villages, as Allies drive Germans northward from Pisa and toward the Po Valley that runs east–west across northern Italy. The Allies' routes north include the western Tuscany coastline and through the Serchio River Valley.

1943 — Italy surrenders to the Allies on September 8, 1943. Mussolini is deposed and arrested, but German commandos rescue him from his mountain prison in central Italy. After meeting with Hitler, he sets up a new government, the Repubblica Sociale Italiana (RSI), on Lake Garda in northern Italy.

1944 — On July 19, Allies take over the heavily bombed port of Livorno, which becomes a supply base for the Italian Campaign's drive toward the Po Valley. On August 12, 560 citizens — elderly people, women, teenagers, children, and infants —

are massacred in the western Tuscan village of Sant'Anna di Stazzema.

1945 — On May 2, German and RSI forces in Italy surrender. On May 7, Germany surrenders to the Allies, ending World War II in Europe. The instruments of surrender are signed the following day.

1946 — The Kingdom of Italy is dissolved by popular vote, King Vittorio Emanuele III and his family are deposed, and the Italian Republic begins.

1948 — Tuscany, at 8,900 square miles, becomes one of the country's regions, which today number twenty.

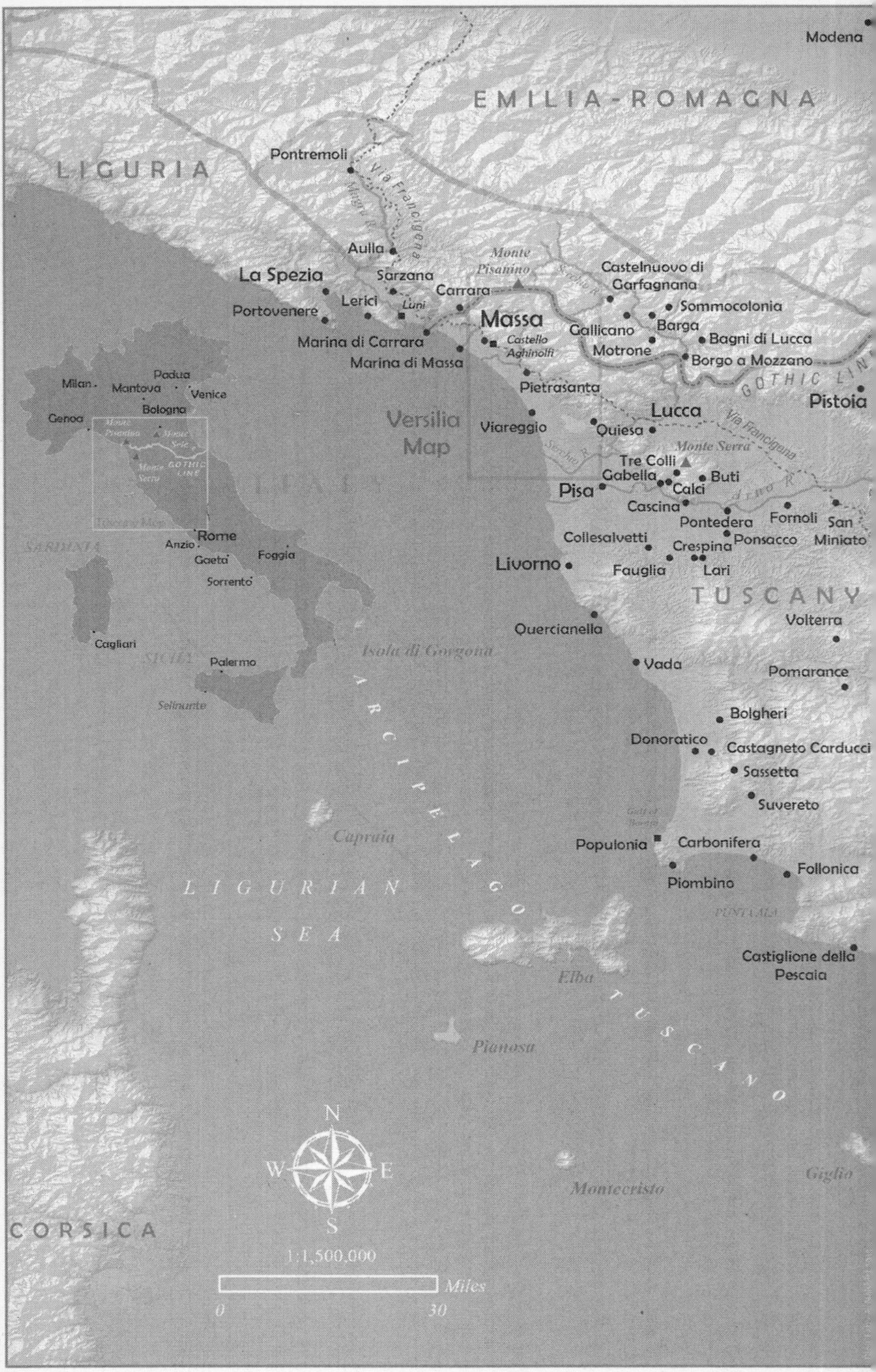
Modena
EMILIA-ROMAGNA
LIGURIA
Pontremoli
Via Francigena
Magra R.
Aulla
Monte Pisanino
La Spezia
Sarzana
Castelnuovo di Garfagnana
Carrara
Lerici
Luni
Sommocolonia
Portovenere
Massa
Gallicano
Barga
Castello Aghinolfi
Bagni di Lucca
Marina di Carrara
Motrone
Marina di Massa
Borgo a Mozzano
GOTHIC LINE
Pietrasanta
Pistoia
Versilia Map
Lucca
Viareggio
Quiesa
Via Francigena
Monte Serra
Serchio R.
Tre Colli
Gabella
Buti
Pisa
Calci
Arno R.
Cascina
Fornoli
Pontedera
San Miniato
Collesalvetti
Ponsacco
Crespina
Livorno
Fauglia
Lari
TUSCANY
Quercianella
Volterra
Isola di Gorgona
Vada
Pomarance
Bolgheri
Donoratico
Castagneto Carducci
Sassetta
Suvereto
Capraia
Populonia
Carbonifera
Piombino
Follonica
LIGURIAN SEA
ARCIPELAGO TUSCANO
Elba
Castiglione della Pescaia
Pianosa
Montecristo
Giglio
CORSICA
N
W
E
S
1:1,500,000
Miles
0
30
Milan
Padua
Mantova
Venice
Bologna
Genoa
GOTHIC LINE
Tuscany Map
Rome
Anzio
Gaeta
Foggia
Sorrento
Cagliari
Palermo
Selinunte

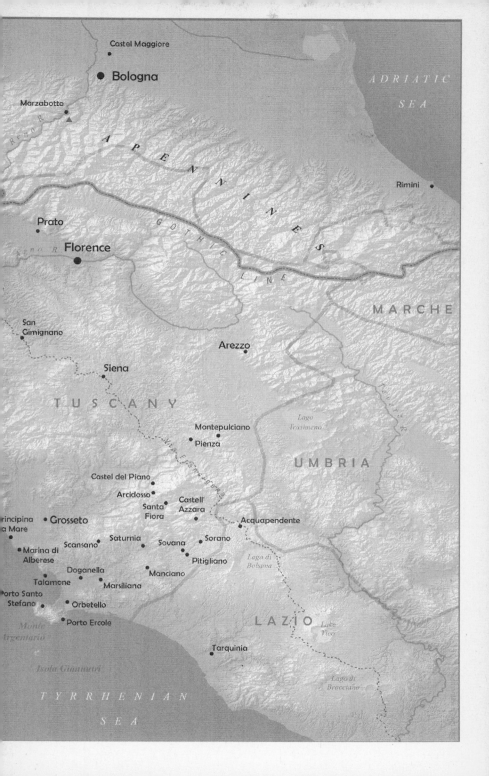

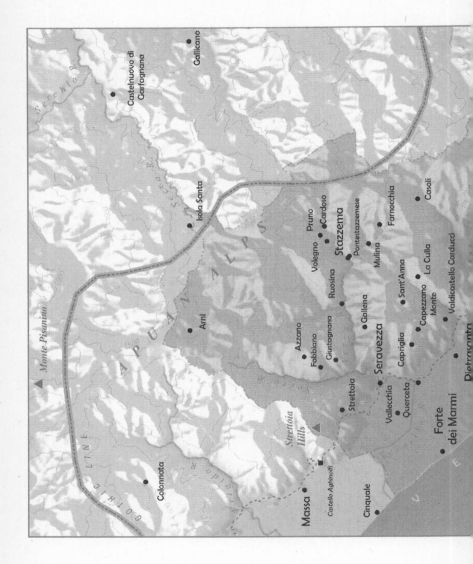

Motrone

LIGURIAN

SEA

Lido di Camaiore

Viareggio

Camaiore

Montemagno

Luciano

Piano di
Mommio

Massarosa

Quiesa

Tripoli
Massaciuccoli

Migliarino

Serchio

V E R S I L I A

N
W   E
S

1:275.000

Miles
0   5

ONE:
A STARTER

The greatest legacy of the old tenant-farming system is what is now — all too fashionably — called the *cucina povera* — the poor kitchen. *Cucina povera* is a misnomer. Tuscan food may be simple but it isn't poor. It can be amazingly imaginative, occasionally even innovative, and always based on the freshest local produce. The cooking is still well available in rural *trattorie* and unpretentious restaurants throughout the region.

> — Beth Elon, *A Culinary Traveller*
> *in Tuscany: Exploring and Eating*
> *Off the Beaten Track* (2009)

The tall, slender man, fashionably dressed in black slacks and a knitted shirt and with hair cropped close to his head, set a bone-white bowl in front of me. It was half full of something pureed. He reached for the bottle of mineral water to fill my glass. This, I thought to myself, is something I can eat. Finally. The meal was supposed to be a simple one — my first major sit-down after arriving in western Tuscany three days earlier. A bug I apparently picked up in Spain had laid me low, curbing my usual robust appetite and forcing me to seek a doctor's help in Naples.

Armed with proper medication and after an overnight rest, I had left Naples via coastal train for Pietrasanta, a six-hour journey through Rome and Pisa. A few hours after arriving, I met my landlady, signed a six-month lease, paid lots of euros for two months' advance rent, and settled into my two-room apartment — three if you count the bathroom. I spent the next few days in light spring rain wandering the small town's half-dozen or so streets and lounged under an umbrella in the piazza in front of the Duomo. On day three, I felt ready for a regular meal — a dish of lasagna sounded just right. Along one of Pietrasanta's pedestrian-only streets just off the main piazza there appeared a cheery place with a half-dozen tables tucked into a medieval-era building. Its small sign simply read FIL-IPPO. Surrounded by a few clusters of mothers, fathers, grandparents, and children, I ordered the *lasagna al ragú.*

The man walked away, and I examined the contents of the bowl more closely. In the center, on top of the puree, was a bright green ring of something else, along with other embellishments here and there. Its taste was remarkable. I hastily downed the concoction with a few swipes of my large spoon. The bowl disappeared, and a new bowl, this one holding a large square of lasagna, was put in its place.

This version of something I grew up with in a non-Italian home was different: the pasta squares were not overcooked like I had experienced over most of my life. Filippo's version was lightly *al dente,* with a creamy cheese infused between tender slices of pasta and doused appropriately with a meat sauce like I never had, even long ago when I was in Bologna, a city famous for its ragú. It simply melted in my mouth.

Sipping strong Italian coffee afterwards, I got the man's attention and asked his name. It was Filippo himself, Filippo di Bartola. He spoke good English — better than I spoke basic Italian — so I asked him about that strange dish I had at the beginning of the meal.

Filippo seemed surprised by the question. He shrugged. "It has no name. It is simply a starter." He said its ingredients were heavily pureed potato; celery and zucchini, also heavily pureed; plus touches of pesto and fennel.

I wanted to talk to him some more about his food and about western Tuscan culture, but it was 3 P.M. and the restaurant was closing — I was the last to leave — and he had had a long day. Two English tourists walked in, and Filippo politely directed them down the street. He told them it was late in the day on a Sunday for a restaurant to be open, but they might find a pizza seller farther along.

"Let us meet in three days," he told me. "I would like to talk to you; it will help me practice my English."

I had arrived, shaky from the Spanish bug, in Pietrasanta in mid-April 2012, and was prepared to use this near-coastal town in northwestern Tuscany as a base for a six-month visit to the region's western coast. At an elevation of only forty-six feet, Pietrasanta is about a mile and a half from the sea, with nearby beach communities — Marina di Pietrasanta, Forte dei Marmi, Lido di Camaiore, and Viareggio — getting the sun-seeker action by European tourists and Italians alike. Pietrasanta, close to the marble quarries of Carrara, Massa, and

Seravezza, is famous as a center where artists live and work. It is home particularly to sculptors from all over the world, because the town of some twenty-five thousand souls backs up onto the foothills of the marble-rich Alpi Apuane, or Apuan Alps.

Pietrasanta is positioned, between Genoa and Pisa, along the major north–south routes of the A12 *autostrada* and the parallel state highway SS1, known locally as "Via Aurelia." In addition, Pietrasanta sits on the ancient narrow pathway known as Via Francigena, which, in the age of growing tourism, is clearly marked along Tuscany's entire length for walkers and bicyclists. The Via Francigena is the route that pilgrims from all over Europe once followed to Rome, the capital of Christendom. From there, many would move on by land and boat to the holy city of Jerusalem.

These ancient routes along Tuscany's west coast still draw travelers, but this part of Italian tourism's most popular region is not as well known as its more famous eastern half. The 180-mile-long coastal area, from Carrara in the north to Grosseto and Orbetello in the south, draws European travelers but few Americans.

The part of western Tuscany where I am living — the area around Pietrasanta, the

Apuan Alps — is known as Versilia. It generally includes Pietrasanta, Forte dei Marmi, Seravezza (which plays heavily in the area's marble-quarry history), Stazzema, and Camaiore. There are other villages included in this mini region, most notably Sant'Anna di Stazzema, the village tucked in the hills a few miles above Pietrasanta. It was this village where German soldiers, on August 12, 1944, executed 560 men, women, and children.

Most Americans visiting Italy, of course, know "classical" Tuscany: Florence, Siena, San Gimignano, and the Chianti area where Chianti Classico wine is produced. And many go to Italy's picturesque coastal villages in the Cinque Terra region of southern Liguria, south of Genoa. But western Tuscany remains largely unknown to U.S. travelers who zip through it on high-speed trains from Milan to Rome or along the *autostrada,* stopping only to eat a cafeteria lunch at an Autogrill, Italy's most common type of roadside service area.

A bed-and-breakfast owner on the outskirts of Pietrasanta near Camaiore, Tuscany native Riccardo Barsottelli, told me that the largest numbers of visitors include the English, Germans, Swiss, and Austrians. Then come the Dutch, Belgians, Swedes, and Norwegians. Finally, a few Americans, French, Australians, and, perhaps, some Spanish, make up the third group.

Barsottelli said that in his experience, the Americans who come are sons and daughters of parents who brought them as children. "Most have an earlier tie to the coastal area, or perhaps they are second- or third-generation people who emigrated to America from here," he said.

Pietrasanta, while a few miles inland and with its own vibrant nightlife, has been around since the thirteenth century. Its geographical position seems to have been the key to its founding. In 1255, the *podestà* of Lucca, its governing magistrate, was Guiscardo da Pietrasanta. In 1255, he decided to move inhabitants of two nearby villages into the area and create a town that would sit along a road network to Genoa in the north and then to France.

Just as important, the new village would be a clear shot to the village of Motrone, just a short distance to the southwest of Pietrasanta and on the coast. Motrone was the primary trading port for the area in the early fourteenth century, so most of the Tuscan merchants dealing in Mediterranean trade ended up living in Pietrasanta.

Historian M. E. Bratchel quotes a letter

sent by a Pietrasantese official to the Duke of Milan in 1431, where Pietrasanta was described as "the noblest place in our territory, and in a special sense our port [Motrone] through which we obtain provisions." Pietrasanta also became a mining center through the fifteenth century, and marble from an array of quarries was being processed there. A century later, Michelangelo was there signing contracts for marble.

Bratchel said the town possessed a complicated society in the early 1430s because of

the very large number of resident and visiting foreigners: members of the Genoese garrison; artisans from Liguria, Lombardy, and all over Tuscany; merchants from Genoa and Pisa; and scions of the great feudal families like the Cattani of Massa and Malaspina of Lunigiana.

A good many of the beach resorts along this western stretch of land flanking the Mar Ligure and Mar Tirreno were developed only after World War II, rebuilt from ruins of the war. For example, much of Forte dei Marmi, once a tiny village of fishermen, did not exist then as a tourist destination. During World War II, medieval buildings were destroyed as a result of fierce fighting between the retreating Germans and Italians still loyal to Mussolini, and advancing Americans. After the war, particularly during the 1950s and '60s, developers created a coastal resort town from the rubble. This new town, located a few miles west and a bit north of Pietrasanta, is a wealthy enclave. Its array of exclusive stores, hotels, and apartment/condominium buildings is ensconced in those beautiful postwar buildings.

Today, Pietrasanta remains a town of *negoziante* (shopkeepers) and artists. There are few chain stores here. Those are found far to the east in Siena and Florence.

There are art galleries for the well-heeled, jewelry stores with items behind immaculately shined windows worth hundreds, if not several thousands, of euros each. They are alongside smaller shops selling fruit or dozens of varieties of pasta, or providing services, such as one tiny shop where an elderly man sits, wreathed in the rich smell of leather and glue, repairing shoes.

Finally, I have a chance to sit down with Filippo di Bartola, a native Pietrasantese, now in his forties. The noon-hour rush nearly over, we sit amongst a small group of diners topping off their three-course lunches with small cups of espresso and interesting-looking *dolce,* or desserts. Filippo brings me a wonderful concoction of cream over light-as-air fondant topped with various berries *dai boschi,* from the woods: currants, raspberries, blueberries. He starts the conversation with a geography lesson.

"We have the mountains and the sea, and generally the weather is not too hot, not too cold. It is *clima mite* [mild climate]."

Filippo believes that the high value of the euro compared to the dollar is what has kept many Americans away from Pietrasanta and Tuscany's western coast. They would rather spend their money seeing the more well-known parts of Italy, and a two-week vacation does not lend itself to much time for exploring. Although the euro declined during the summer of 2012, it did not happen soon enough to boost American tourism here.

He says the largest group of visitors, besides Riccardo Barsottelli's English, Germans, Swiss, and Austrians, are northern Italians, including those from classical Tuscany in the east. They have been coming here for decades as vacationers or as artists. Since the nineteenth century, Florentines, for example, anxious to escape the summer heat of Tuscany's deep interior, have kept second homes along its coast, a tradition now also taken up by the English and Germans.

During my talk, a few days later, with Riccardo Barsottelli, he points out that only starting in the 1990s has the land just a few kilometers from the sea become a desirable location for vacation homes for non-Italians. His upscale bed-and-breakfast, Locanda al colle, for example, is located in the hills above Capezzano Pianore between coastal Pietrasanta and inland Camaiore, and is surrounded by groves of olive trees.

"Well into the 1970s property on the hills was worth very little. Now there is a boom here," he says, gesturing at the tree-studded hillsides surrounding his restored eighteenth-century house with its modern addition.

Both Riccardo and Filippo describe the food of their Versilia as being a different variation of what tourists are used to farther east. Their claims are backed up by the authors of *The Appetite Comes Through Eating: A Brief Journey in "Gourmet" Versilia,* a book praising Versilian cuisine: ". . . the Versilia is a sort of gastronomic movement, a laboratory of new trends and rediscoveries . . . between the coast and plain, the hills and the mountains."

Filippo di Bartola says the way Versilians

use meat is one distinction. For example, the meat sauce for the *lasagna al ragú* I had during that first meal is a combination of beef and pork. Farther east, he says, Florentine cooks would typically use only beef.

"Very common here," he says. "Not so common in the rest of Italy." I can't challenge his remark, since I have not eaten everywhere in Italy, but I do know that I have never had the likes of the lasagna I had that Sunday, or the *tordelli* I ate a few days later.

With the local dish known as *Versiliese tordelli,* according to *Gourmet Versilia,* pouches are made from thinly rolled pasta cut into circles using a wide-mouth drinking glass. These disks are then filled with a combination of meats blended with sausage, egg, Parmesan and pecorino Romano cheeses, and wild thyme. These are folded in half with the outer edges sealed by the slight pressure of a finger, and covered with meat sauce. The recipes vary from town to town and restaurant to restaurant, the secrets guarded by tight-lipped cooks. Traditionally, *tordelli* is served during special occasions, but today's Versilian *ristoranti* and *trattorie* usually have one type or another on their daily menus.

A week later, Filippo surprises me with

another unique dish with a long name: *testaroli della Lunigiana all'olio extra vergine, Parmigiano e basilica.* It is from an area north and a bit east of Pietrasanta, from villages in the marble-rich mountains above Carrara. It is a kind of "pasta" I had never heard of. In checking various cookbooks and regional guides, I discovered this pasta is often served with a pesto sauce made of basil, pine nuts, and garlic, but Filippo's version does not incorporate the pesto — instead it was just drizzled with olive oil and sprinkled generously with Parmesan and basil leaves.

This so-called pasta is made with the simple marriage of wheat flour — some recipes simply call for "flour" — and water. That's it. Mix in a bit of olive oil and pour it like pancake batter, a quarter-inch thick, into a cast-iron skillet that also has a light skim of oil on its surface.

To create that skim, writer Beth Elon recommends cutting off the end of a potato, dipping the tuber into olive oil, and rubbing it onto the skillet's surface. You then cook the mixture for a few minutes and flip it over for another few minutes.

Before the *testaroli* was served, another "starter with no name" magically appeared before me: a pureed mixture of tomato, potato, and carrot served warm with three small toasted bread cubes. "All unique to here," Filippo declared. And I couldn't argue with him; I had never seen such starters elsewhere.

Riccardo, meanwhile, goes into greater detail about the food unique to coastal Tuscany. He points to a dish — *spaghetti con arselle* — found only in villages along the sea because of the type of tiny mussel the sauce contains. Each serving is peppered with those tiny mollusks found by the tens of thousands clinging to rocks and piers along the shoreline.

Simplicity seems to reign here. There is *tagliata de tonno,* made up of a generous slice of baked tuna coated with crushed pistachios. Or a hungry seafood lover can choose a bread soup with clams. The bread, usually a day or two old, is laid on the bottom of the bowl, clams are placed on top, and a broth is poured over the concoction.

This simplicity in preparation follows me throughout western Tuscany. In the region's southeast corner, in the village of Pitigliano located about thirty miles east of the coast at Orbetello, I came across the best tomato sauce for pasta I have ever eaten. Light and with chunks of tomatoes pressed through a strainer, this sauce, the owner of Ristorante

Guastini told me, uses only well-chopped basil, onion, and celery, cooked together in a splash of olive oil before the strained tomatoes are added. "*Utilizzare gli ingredienti a vostro gusto* [Use the ingredients to your taste]," she advised me. *"Molto semplice!"*

But one of northwestern Italy's best snack foods — and one with a great story behind it — is *la cecina*. With chickpea flour as its main ingredient, the dish follows the pattern of *molto semplice.* (A variety of approaches can be found on the Internet and in many Italian cookbooks.) The chickpea flour is mixed with water, salt, and some olive oil. Most cooks let the mixture sit for an hour or so, then pour a portion into the center of a well-oiled round pizza pan, letting it spread out on its own to the edges. In northwestern Italy, there are large pans, called *teglie,* that are used exclusively for making *la cecina,* but fourteen-inch-diameter pizza pans do the job as well, a friend advised me.

What comes out of the oven is a large, round, yellow, slightly moist concoction that can be liberally sprinkled with pepper. It looks like a very thin pizza, but it is nothing like the Neapolitan-inspired dish. *La cecina* is found along the coast from the French city of Nice, once a part of Italy but ceded to France in 1860, to Pisa, just twenty miles south of Pietrasanta. It can be purchased by the slice from street-food sellers, either in carts or those tiny shops in city centers that specialize in pizza by the slice.

The story, or perhaps one should call it "legend," of how *la cecina* came about is a curious one: In the thirteenth century, long before a "unified" Italy existed, Genoa and Pisa were warring city-states. In a naval battle fought in August 1284 near a rocky islet called Meloria, located off the coast from Livorno and a few miles southwest of the Arno River's mouth, Genoa nearly wiped out the Pisan fleet and took hundreds of prisoners.

On the way back to Genoa, with the prisoners locked away deep in ships' holds, a storm tossed the vessels around, spilling jars of olive oil and chickpea flour around the prisoners' quarters. The contents mixed together along with the salt water that had seeped in from the Mediterranean. The Genoese, so the legend goes, didn't want to waste the ingredients, so they said the prisoners could eat the mixture.

The Pisans, being proud folks, refused to eat it, and let their plates sit out in the sun for a day or two. When hunger finally won over pride, they discovered that the sun-baked concoction was really quite good. It is the salt water that apparently gives the chickpea flour its fine taste.

Many of these easily prepared dishes are considered "peasant" food. Yet when travelers today sit in the grandest *ristorante* or the tiniest *osteria,* or inn, they eat various versions of these dishes and usually pay a lot of money for them. These days, finely executed and presented food like this (with the exception of snack food like *la cecina*) is what most of us come to expect when ordering "Italian."

Such basic ingredients, particularly in small towns and villages, come from the local *fattorie,* or farms, or a family's own small plot of land. And during times of great strife — wars, periods of famine or plagues — the magnificent dishes that make up what we consider wonderful Italian food simply were not available.

In the midst of such strife, waste was unheard of. Every bread crumb, every bit of leftover meat, every part of an animal's organs was used, and wild herbs plucked from hillsides and fields were sought out. These traditions are hard to shake. In current days of plenty, I have seen well-dressed Italians from the Veneto to Sicily gathering wild herbs while waiting for a bus or, outside of Rome, in a field in the shadow of a Roman viaduct's ruins just off the Appian Way. War and poverty create such habits that are passed on to subsequent generations who hear an older generation's stories of the extreme privation that Italians have gone through from ancient times through twentieth-century wars.

Pamela Sheldon Johns, in her classic *Cucina Povera: Tuscan Peasant Cooking,* tells stories of such privations. In Pietrasanta — today a city of beauty and art, of massive public displays of sculpture great and small, of hotels and B and Bs, jammed restaurants and bars filled with Europeans, Italian tourists, and Pietrasantesi — times were incredibly difficult during World War II, especially during the occupation by retreating Germans following Italy's 1943 surrender to the Allies.

German soldiers would come into houses and demand wine. Once, Johns relates, soldiers slaughtered a family's cow, hauling off the meat but leaving the head.

"We were hungry at home; I started dragging the head down the road, and a couple of boys tried to take it," Johns quotes her storyteller, Ilvana Corsi Tognocchi of Pietrasanta. "A German officer saw what was happening and ran them off. I made it home with the head, and my mother made soup."

Ilvana said meat was very scarce during the war, despite her father being a butcher. So the family ate only what they had: polenta with olive oil and pecorino cheese. "I remember eating spaghetti and beans a lot," she told Johns. They made cooking pots out of empty bomb casings, and because the Germans did not like corn, they would put grain in containers with corn sprinkled on top so the soldiers would leave them alone.

Other families, when they harvested grapes for wine for themselves and with the hope of selling to others, "would save the seeds from the pressings, and [they] roasted and ground them to make a hot drink," Johns describes. It was a poor substitute for espresso, a quintessentially Italian drink that either was not available or the price was too dear for many families. And sometimes, the innocent civilians in the war-torn land were reduced even more to basics, living off old bread and dried chestnuts.

The outstanding and varied dishes found in restaurants and in many Italian homes today were, as Johns tells us, "born in frugality and innovation." People, whether caught up in the privations during the many wars that swept through Tuscany and elsewhere in Italy or simply because they were poor, used only what was locally available, scouring the landscape for whatever they could find, such as chestnuts lying on the ground, which they would dry and eat or make into flour.

Living near the sea was a blessing because folks could go out in small boats and catch their daily meals. But during most of 1944, Germans forbid locals to go out in boats "for military security reasons." Occasionally, brave locals would slip down to the shore and fill a bucket with seawater so they could boil it down for the salt.

Stories of such privations are slipping away as older generations leave us and because the Italian peasant class disappeared after World War II ended in 1945. People at all levels of society now have the ability to make a variety of dishes their forebears never could have dreamed of having, except in few-and-far-between times of plenty.

The food part of my journey along Tuscany's Mediterranean coast taught me that the uniqueness of certain dishes, region to region, village to village, comes out of what is available in each local spot. For example, in the north, including Tuscany, chestnuts are plentiful, so they end up in various dishes or as flour. Farther along in west-central Tuscany, in the heart of wheat country famous for its flours, chestnuts might only be sold on street corners hot off a charcoal grill. Polenta, a type of cornmeal boiled into porridge, is common in the north of Italy and particularly in western Tuscany, but is seldom seen in the south. *La cecina* might be big along the coast north of Pisa, but unheard of in Rome and towns farther south. Those places have their own urban legends about certain dishes that have become uniquely Roman or Neapolitan or Palermitani.

Other examples abound. Pesto, usually made with crushed basil and garlic, is mildly garlicky in Italy's north, particularly in western Tuscany, and heavily garlicky in the south. Tomato sauces on pasta are quite subtle and light in the western Tuscan villages I frequented, a bit creamier in Rome, and heavily dominated by chunky tomatoes in Naples and far to the southern end of the peninsula and Sicily.

Meanwhile, back in Pietrasanta, the type of pasta covered in meat sauce is different than, say, pasta Bolognese in Bologna far to the east. There the only pasta used for that famous sauce is tagliatelle, long, flat ribbons similar to fettuccine but common only in Emilia-Romagna and Umbria. Using any other pasta for that dish, say spaghetti or Versilia's flat, square-cut testarolli pasta, would be sacrilege in those regions.

But Tuscany's wild west is not all about food. Art, old and new, and the people who make it are a big part, particularly in the area around where Michelangelo selected his marble.

Two:
ART AND THE CITY

Man had discovered marble — or rather, the marble had found him. Cold stone had become a living presence, a subterranean angel leading humankind out of darkness.
— Eric Scigliano, *Michelangelo's Mountain: The Quest for Perfection in the Marble Quarries of Carrara* (2005)

Roberta Giovannini Onniboni, a sixty-something lifelong Pietrasantese artist, remembers well, and with great joy, when she was in her mid-twenties, and sculptors young and old from all over the world came to her town to make art. One of those artists was Colombian Fernando Botero. Others were Lithuanian Jacques Lipchitz, Pole Igor Mitoraj, and American Jeff Koons, who came there for a few years in the early 1990s with his then-wife, Italian parliamentarian and porn star Ilona Staller. (Ilona went by the film name Cicciolina.) These artists, plus many others, made up a swirling stew that kept bubbling over a flame of creativity and was composed of interesting ingredients. Roberta knew all of them and worked with most as an *artigiana,* or sculptor's assistant.

"It was a remarkable time," she recalled. Pietrasanta was not well known to the outside, non-artist world. The English upper crust in particular had, in the late nineteenth century and again following World War II, discovered the nearby beach community Forte dei Marmi, and a curious few drifted into Pietrasanta.

But the town was on the artists' radars. Mentors in colleges and art schools everywhere advised their students that if they wanted to learn how to be sculptors, they should go to Pietrasanta. Its proximity to Carrara and Massa meant there was plenty of marble of all shapes, colors, and sizes nearby, plus Pietrasanta had its own even nearer quarries, found above Seravezza, just down the road and up into the foothills.

"Forty years ago," she explained, "Pietrasanta was a 'medieval' country. A few students from Canada and the United States were here, and they were very poor when they came. They were eighteen or twenty years old — just young people interested in art. Then, many more-famous sculptors came" — people like Lipchitz in the 1960s, then Botero in the 1970s — "and things began to change; it got more expensive.

"At that time there were [few] restaurants, for example. Nothing. No tourists. It was a desert. Now it is like a show."

Today, as fourth-generation Pietrasantese sculptor Spartaco Palla had told me earlier, there are only two or three studios in Pietrasanta proper. When more tourists began to visit, most studios were pushed to relocate because of the dust and the noise of power hammers against stone in a town that now needed more space for shops and restaurants.

What forced the issue was when heavy machinery — marble saws and power hammers — began to dominate in the mid-twentieth century. The studios either closed or moved to the suburbs. The spaces that once were filled with more than one hundred studios became high-end clothing stores, art galleries, and eating establishments.

The artists who "discovered" Pietrasanta in the post–World War II period and those working there today amble along the same streets used by many earlier artists, including the Florentine sculptor Michelangelo. There is not much evidence that he actually made art in this part of Versilia. He was there only as a buyer of marble — primarily in Pietrasanta and Seravezza — for a three- or four-year period in the mid-sixteenth century. His lifelong patrons, the Medici of Florence, under the leadership of the Medici Pope Leo X, controlled these mountains above Seravezza, but not the white-marble quarries above Carrara.

Michelangelo had spent three years designing the façade for the Medici church, San Lorenzo, in Florence, and the family wanted it to be faced with *their* marble, not marble from the peaks above Carrara. Michelangelo undertook the task of developing the Medici quarries, but grudgingly. He had always preferred the *marmo carrarese* and had well-established relationships with the *cavatori,* or marble workers, there.

Essentially, he wasted nearly a half decade of his creative life; his design for San Lorenzo's façade never was used, and today the church still exhibits the unfinished, rough-brick exterior of the eleventh-century Romanesque structure. He made little, if any, art during his years in Pietrasanta-Seravezza. It is clear, in Eric Scigliano's well-documented book *Michelangelo's Mountain,* that despite what many people in those two towns would like to believe, the great artist never used local marble for any of his creations, using only *marmo carrarese.*

There are two buildings in the heart of Pietrasanta with plaques indicating that Michelangelo signed marble contracts there in the spring of 1518. Locals would like to think he did more for their town, however. This wish gave rise to a legend maintained by generations of Pietrasantesi that the great artist designed the unique stairway inside the 120-foot-high bell tower that sits alongside Pietrasanta's Duomo di San Martino.

Originally, the tower's exterior was faced in white stone. Today, only the rough brick surface remains. The stairs, whether designed by the great artist or not, are what make this structure interesting. Winding upward like a tight corkscrew against the interior walls of this rectangular tower, these stairs are now closed to the public and can be observed while standing on the rectangular ground floor. In a way, it is reminiscent of the concept of the Giuseppe Momo double-helix staircase that leads to the exit of the Vatican Museum in Rome.

In Pietrasanta's bell tower, however, the steps are narrow, and there are no handrails.

It indeed must have been a gut-tingling climb for anyone forced to creep along the wall's edge. One slip, and the visitor would plummet to the stone floor below.

Michelangelo's time here did leave physical evidence of his presence in these mountains more than five hundred years ago. On a bright Saturday in June, a friend and I drove the few miles from Pietrasanta to Seravezza in search of that presence. He likely spent a lot of time in Seravezza, which is higher up and offers a clear shot to the Medici quarries — perhaps more time than he spent in Pietrasanta.

Seravezza, with its charming folklore and marble industry museum in the Medici palace alongside the Serra River, is as inviting as Pietrasanta, just three miles away. But it has a decidedly different feel to it. While Seravezza is a narrow, stone-quarry town, as rough-hewn as the tall mountains that close in around it, Pietrasanta is an artist community with softer, gentler hues that blend in with the rolling coastal hills it sits against. The Serra and Vezza rivers merge here and become the Versilia River, which cuts through the town's center and ultimately flows to the sea, three or four miles to the southwest.

In his unhappy quest to develop marble quarries for the Medici family, Michelangelo would have ridden mules or horses from Seravezza up the valley toward the summit of Monte Altissimo and the village of Azzano. He would have passed tiny villages such as Giustagnana and Fabbiano on his way to inspect the site of a marble quarry high on the mountain overlooking Azzano, which sits in the midst of a sloping hardwood forest. Today, where the road curves, a sign points to a dirt track leading to the bottom of Michelangelo's quarry. The main road loops back toward Seravezza, giving the traveler a route through a forest valley with small stone villages dotting the upper flanks. These hamlets, strung above the narrow roadway, like colored bits of stone on a giant's necklace, are where many *cavatori* live.

It was along this valley that Michelangelo had to direct workers to build bridges over streams and the Serra River, and lay out a stone road that ran straight up the valley toward the face of Monte Altissimo.

Remnants still exist of that original steep road ordered by Michelangelo. One section runs just outside of Azzano alongside a thousand-year-old Romanesque parish church, the Pieve della Cappella. Locals have their own legend involving the artist. They credit him with the design of the church portico, now just tumbled remains, along with a circular stained-glass window high above the sanctuary door. Like the belief of folks in Pietrasanta that Michelangelo designed the bell tower stairs, this claim has no proof to support it.

Just below the church, on the edge of a wide gully, that steep section of medieval stone road sits across from an abandoned quarry still littered with chiseled blocks of stone, most likely broken out of the mountain a few centuries ago. This is not Michelangelo's quarry. His was farther along, even higher than Azzano.

The presence of the great Florentine master and the spark of industry his presence promised created exciting times for locals. Previously, much of the marble from the Serra River Valley was merely collected from the riverbed. Roads and bridges allowed for more large-scale marble extraction. Today, small pieces of white and gray marble, remains of what has been lopped off in modern industrial operations or bits that wash down in the torrential rains that often sweep through Versilia, can still be found in the river all the way to the coast.

From Azzano, Michelangelo's mountain

— the quarry he attempted to open for the Medici — looms high up to the northeast. Its exposed flanks do not blaze white like those above Carrara, but dark streaks along the high faces of the mountain's steep marble slabs and lack of fresh cuts show it has been a long time since that particular quarry was worked.

A local writer, Peter Rosenzweig, said it ceased operations in the 1970s, yielding to unbeatable competition from quarries at Carrara. Not much has come out of the quarry over the centuries; it appears to have been closed longer than it was open. Rosenzweig said there was a flurry of activity in the eighteenth century, when a vein of hardy white marble was exposed, but these episodes appear to have been brief and infrequent.

I cannot help but wonder what Michelangelo would have created if he had not spent those years trying to open that quarry above Azzano. Another magnificent ceiling, perhaps? More sculptures for the tomb of Pope Julius II? The marble his quarrymen sliced out of Monte Altissimo was "scattered like a trail of crumbs," Eric Scigliano tells us. One marble column carved out of Monte Altissimo apparently did make it to Florence and was deposited in front of San

Lorenzo. It sat there until the seventeenth century, said Scigliano, "when it was buried in a ditch along with other detritus from the unfinished façade."

So much for Michelangelo's mountain and his inability to say no to the Medici and to Pope Leo X. Leo died in 1522, four years after Michelangelo signed contracts in Pietrasanta. Interest in creating the façade of San Lorenzo in Florence diminished. Thankfully, Michelangelo would have another forty-two years to carve statues, paint such marvels as *The Last Judgment* in the Sistine Chapel, and, among several other projects, design the new St. Peter's in Rome.

Michelangelo may have preferred Carrara marble but he didn't discover it. Artisans, builders, and emperors alike have been drawn to the whiteness and durability of this stone through history, and quarrying it dates back to the prehistory of this popular region. The Etruscans first started slicing stone from the area around the more accessible base of the western slope of Monte Pisanino, located just above what became the towns of Carrara-Massa and to the north of Monte Altissimo. They used the stone sparingly, for such things as decorations and tombstones, likely because it was so difficult to move larger pieces. (It would be the Romans who would develop transport technology and use it to harvest stone higher up on the mountain.)

Carrara marble is not soft like the tufa formations these mysterious early Etruscans used for more important larger structures, such as their tombs, and for construction of villages throughout Tuscany and beyond. Once off the mountain, the marble had to be moved by boat to where it was needed. The Etruscans, and the Romans who succeeded them, based a deep-water port at the ancient mouth of the Magra River. Luni acted as the debarkation point for marble harvested in the area and eventually became a major Roman city. In later centuries, as a large population center, Luni would be the seat of Catholic bishops. But nature always has its way. Silt gradually deposited by the river dramatically expanded the coastline westward and turned the area around the crumbling city into a mosquito-laden marshland. The bishops moved their church farther up the Magra River to Sarzana, and the population followed. Luni, by the time Michelangelo arrived in Versilia three or four centuries later, had devolved into ruin.

There are walkways through the archaeologically revealed stones of Luni, which is now located just over the Tuscany boundary and in the modern region of Liguria. The paths lead to what must have once been the water's edge, a good mile or so inland from the Magra's present mouth. Over the centuries this coastline filled in bit by bit, generation by generation, much like the Mediterranean mouth of the Arno River moved, over the centuries, from near Pisa's historic center to a point perhaps six miles away today.

The Romans first started quarrying marble on a promontory across the Magra River, and while it was a beautiful white color, Scigliano tells us that its composition was inferior to the marble above Carrara. The Romans moved their quarrying operations a few miles to the east, into the Apuan basin. The earliest references place activity there in the first century BC.

In Rome, the massive Pyramid of Cestius, dated between 18 and 12 BC, apparently was constructed of Carrara marble. This was also about the time that Emperor Augustus started covering Rome's brick and local-stone buildings with marble slabs, giving us the image we carry in our heads today of that ancient city. Sometimes marble from eastern Greece was used in Rome, but stone from the closer Carrara was likely used more often.

Augustus merely clothed his city in veneer, or relatively thin sheets of marble. But the Greeks, Scigliano writes, had built their glorious cities with blocks of marble. The Romans only mimicked "the grandeur the Greeks achieved with solid marble."

Some pure-white stone comes from places like Georgia and Colorado in the United States. Even marble from the Greek island of Naxos is whiter than the stone found at Carrara. The difference, and the key to what makes Carrara stone so sought-after, is its hardness. Marble from Carrara is made up of fine, hard-to-see crystals. Some of the whiter stone found elsewhere is too soft, or it is coarser but with easily visible crystals, or it is too brittle, or it "lacks the translucence that makes Carrara's seem alive," said Scigliano.

The journey to Azzano and Michelangelo's mountain was a spur-of-the-moment drive recommended by a friend when we talked one afternoon about Scigliano's book. It was among the first of many such journeys from my comfortable base in Pietrasanta. People I met would tell me about places I'd never heard about and I would decide to see them for myself. Or, I would just rent a car and go, following narrow roads or walk-ing along a stretch of the pilgrims' route, the Via Francigena. Travelers with time on their hands — shouldn't all worthwhile travel be this easygoing? — would be well advised to set up a base in or around a place like Pietrasanta. Then take the narrow roads along the flanks of the Apuan range and visit village after village. Go to Azzano, have a coffee or a delightful meal in a small, family-run *trattoria,* and then head up the road to the gravel cutoff that leads to the walking trail to the base of Michelangelo's moun-tain.

Then, the adventurous travelers could head back down the road to the coastal highway, turn above the highway, and drive through Carrara.

Various valleys fan out from this promi-nent town, making Carrara the apex for all the marble that flows downhill; the slopes of these various valleys are spotted with vil-lages sitting near the giant white slabs of stone still waiting to be harvested. Choose any of those valleys and these tiny villages open up, each with their own unique feeling or aura.

One, the highest village above Carrara, is called Colonnata. It spills across a lower slope at the base of a series of imposing mountains with their faces sheared off to expose the marble for which the area around Carrara is famous. Standing on a walkway along the front of old stone houses and staring off toward quarries to the north and south, these stone walls seem almost close enough to touch.

If tourists visit here, it would be ironic, because there is no mention of the town in most Tuscany guidebooks in English. Scigliano posits that the village's name suggests that it might have started out as a *colonia* of Rome, an outpost with housing for slaves who were forced to work in the Roman quarries.

Marble produced from the Colonnata basin includes the "gray *bardiglio* and black *nero di Colonnata.*" Clearly, the variety of marble found in the quarries that are carved out of these mountains shows that the Carrara area produces more than just stunning white, translucent stone.

The people of Massa-Carrara Province have reputations for being strongly individualistic and politically left-leaning. The rigor of the work in quarries, I suspect, has helped create this individualism. Friends in Pietrasanta describe the people working in the mountains within and above those two towns as "rough and direct" in their speech. Among one another, they speak in dialect nearly undecipherable to outside Italians. They voice short, clipped-off words and phrases that writer Eric Scigliano described as sounding like "chisels tapping against stones."

The far left is not out of reach for many of these people today. It was in Carrara where, immediately after the end of the war in 1945, the Italian Anarchist Federation was founded. Roots of the movement go as far back in Italian history as 1869, on the eve of Italian Unification that was completed the following year.

Colonnata, for example, is home for many villagers with those tendencies. Mounted on a wall next to a small parking area, there is a modern plaque that states quite succinctly, *Ai compagni anarchio uccisi sulla strada della liberta* (To fellow anarchists killed on the road to freedom).

This plaque likely refers to late-August 1944 reprisals carried out by German SS troops and Italian black-shirt Fascists just days after the August 12 massacre at Sant'Anna several miles to the southwest. Mussolini's right-wing Fascists still loyal to their leader killed hundreds of Carraresi and people from villages around Carrara, includ-

64

ing Colonnata, either as part of German reprisals or long after Italy's September 1943 surrender to the Allies. Colonnata was burned.

The close-up views of white-marble peaks in the clear mountain air hang over the village and dominate the small square in front of the parish church dedicated to San Bartolomeo. There, a long, rectangular block of white marble shows off hand-carved miniatures of quarry workers scaling a cliff face, chipping away at slabs of the stone. Inside is a stunning carved relief of Mary ascending to heaven. The interior of this church, with its various marble carvings, along with the stone block honoring quarry workers out front and the 360-degree views of blazing white peaks from its tiny piazza are worth the journey to Colonnata.

Gourmands have another reason to come here. Colonnata is also known for its style of well-seasoned *lardo,* or pig fat, that *cavatori* devoured in great quantities for each noontime meal over the centuries — along with a tomato, perhaps an onion, and wine — to maintain their strength during incredibly demanding daily labor.

It comes in various colors. I am not the

first traveler to notice that in a way these changes in color are symbolic of the various shades of marble found in these mountains. *Lardo* is so important in this area that Colonnata's patron saint is not the Madonna, patron saint of *cavatori*. Instead it is Saint Bartholomew, the patron saint of butchers. There is even a *lardo* festival each year in this village.

I tried *lardo* a few times: a nicely seasoned sample from an outdoor vendor who set up his table outside the Medici palace in Seravezza, and at a restaurant in Capezzano Monte high on the slope above Pietrasanta. The taste was astounding — the seasonings of rosemary, pepper, and other herbs made it worth the experiment. And once I had a small crust of warm bread with a small slice of *lardo* melted on top. Delightful. But too much of this delicacy, I felt, could stop my heart cold, unless I was engaged daily in quarrying stone.

Carrara may produce highly sought-after marble in a market that will last for many decades longer, but the bulk of the artist community is primarily centered close to Pietrasanta. The foundries and shops may have moved out of the town center, but they are not far away. Still, those wonderful bohemian early years of the 1960s, when young artists from all over the world were coming there, remain a distinct memory for my artist friend and Pietrasanta native Roberta Giovannini Onniboni. A few days after our first meeting, where she reminisced about the town's artistic life in the '60s, we went on a walk through the town. It is small, and I had walked these streets many times in the weeks after my arrival, but I still knew nothing about their history.

We walked along Via Dei Piastroni, the street of the house of her birth. At its northern end, she pointed to Piazza Statuato, her primary playground as a child in the 1950s. "That was our space," she said. "We would play games all day long and climb on that statue." Today a fence surrounds the statue, a memorial to the soldiers of World War I. Children no longer play there. The piazza, a regular daytime pay lot for workers and visitors, is jammed with cars. But on Thursdays, cars are banished, and a huge market takes over. Dozens of vendors sell everything from underwear to toilet paper to strawberries to slabs of locally grown beef, pork, and heavily seasoned *lardo.*

Roberta's street, from Piazza Statuto on the northern edge of the city center to

Piazza del Duomo in the middle of the town, is perhaps fifteen hundred feet long. It is one of five north–south *stradi* found within what would have been the original medieval town surrounded by high stone walls. To the south of the Duomo, the extensions of those five streets bear different names.

As we walked, Roberta pointed to the façades of medieval-era structures that once housed sculpture studios. One, a large studio fifty years ago, is now broken down into three small shops and one restaurant. Another is an office for a political party's public-assistance office.

Today, no art is made along this street; it is sold in only a few shops. Its name, Via dei Piastroni, is only a reminder of its not-so-distant past. Translated literally, it refers to what artisans call a particular kind of decorative marble slab with a series of chiseled ridges — not art in a creative sense but a functional part of a decorative façade for a wall.

Roberta began her career as an *artigiana* at age twenty-five, about the same time that Colombian artist Fernando Botero, who had begun working in Florence, came to Pietrasanta to attend a memorial service for his friend, the artist Jacques Lipchitz. Botero, whose name has an Italian origin and means "boat-maker," liked what he saw in Pietrasanta, and its overwhelming atmosphere of contemporary art. He has been in the town ever since. Roberta said that Botero has told her: "When I die, I want to remain in Pietrasanta."

As she did with other artists, she became his assistant. They meshed so well together that Botero would trust her to finish his models, in clay, once he had decided on the image. He would mold half of the model to indicate how it should look and ask her to finish the other half and then see it through production.

Of her skill as an artist, she said she has this innate ability to see a work of art, whether Botero's or her own, "only in my mind and eye. I can put myself into the mind of Botero and others." For example, she would oversee the completion of the Colombian's work in the *fonderia* where his bronze figures, giant and small, are cast and put together by a series of craftspeople, and know exactly what he would accept or reject.

Early on, Roberta said it was difficult for women to become established in the artist culture of Pietrasanta.

"Eventually, foreigners would give me a lot of work, but the Italians were slow to accept a woman as a sculptor," she said matter-of-factly and without rancor. "It is just the way it was. But it has changed."

It has always been easy for her to support herself, until recent years. "Five years ago, there was no problem making money. Today it is more difficult because of the economy."

Many artists I spoke with in Pietrasanta told me the same thing: Sales are significantly down because of the financial woes of Europe and America.

When Roberta abandoned her role working as someone's assistant and struck out on her own as a sculptor, she said she would still get calls from Botero and others seeking her help.

"Botero is the only one I will do this for today," she told me over coffee one humid late-June afternoon. "I tell all others, no."

When I met her in the spring of 2012, Roberta was helping Botero prepare for his *mostra,* his huge exhibition in honor of his forty years in Pietrasanta and his eightieth year of life. Years earlier, he purchased a large house just a few hundred yards from the town's main square, and there he remains today with his wife, the Greek artist Sophia Vari. He is often seen wandering through the square or sitting in a wicker chair outside one of the five bars, sometimes

70

alone, sometimes with friends. Forty years later, he is Pietrasanta's most famous artist-resident, and his art depicting oversized people and animals is displayed throughout — from huge bronze statues to a pair of frescoes, on opposite walls of a tiny church on via Mazzini, that show Botero's visions of Hell and Judgment Day. This fresco work is much in the tradition, but modernized, of Michelangelo's masterpieces on the end walls of the Vatican's Sistine Chapel.

Roberta's own three-dimensional painting *Previsione* was hanging in the Church of St. Agostino as part of an exhibition that soon would be removed so Botero's could be set up. The painting, which also could qualify as sculpture, is created out of Plexiglas, resin, and an acrylic. The subject, a man in dark glasses, seems to be looking at the observer from all directions; his sharp, pointed face protrudes from the bottom panel, almost inviting the observer to rub noses with him. It is vibrantly colorful, figurative art.

Roberta has had major shows elsewhere in Europe, including the European Parliament building in Brussels. She spent a year in Singapore helping restore a church. In her Pietrasanta studio, she works in many different forms with her strong, large hands that completely envelop the hand of an acquaintance and exude overpowering strength. These are hands, arms, and broad shoulders that come from years of lifting, molding, and chipping marble with hammers and chisels.

As an *artigiana,* she would be handed all kinds of material — marble, clay, bronze, wax, plaster — and told to make the finished piece.

"Sometimes I work in marble, just for me, for my pleasure." Often, she will experiment with a type of Japanese clay, *raku,* or various resins, wood, Plexiglas, and terra-cotta.

When using marble, she might make clay or plaster models of her proposed work, but when transferring that image to the actual stone, she said she does not use a *pantographo,* a device used to keep the same relationships, say of eyes to nose, or breast to chin, to the work in stone that may be two, three, four, or more times larger than the plaster model. Some statues — for example a Lipchitz bronze that might have ended up more than sixty feet high — were made by *artigiani* who followed a significantly smaller model but kept the relationships precisely the same. Roberta said she visualizes those relationships; for her, the *pantographo* is unnecessary.

A visitor to a studio, shopping for a statue he or she may want in marble, can see how this process works. If the visitor wants a replica of Michelangelo's *David,* the studio would show a small model that is perhaps the size of a normal person, or even smaller. Then, the studio's artists can use that plaster model, along with a *pantographo,* to make the newly carved statue in marble any height the customer wants.

It is a good life, Roberta said, one that has evolved well past the marble-only culture that dominated at the time of her birth more than sixty years ago. Pietrasanta is still a haven for artists but has become much more expensive than it was forty years ago when her career began and before the creative people who toiled there became famous.

THREE:
WORKING IN STONE

Every block of stone has a statue inside it, and it is the task of the sculptor to discover it.

— Michelangelo di Lodovico
Buonarroti Simoni

In Pietrasanta and elsewhere in northwest Tuscany where art predominates, the people who work in stone — sculptors and *artigiani,* or assistants — are usually easily spotted. Their clothes are dusted with a powder that suggests they are either taking a coffee break from their job in the back room of a bakery or they just spent the morning chipping *marmo,* or granite, or shaping softer travertine.

A fine whiteness might smudge their faces and coat their hands. It can permeate their hair, unless the top of the head, for men and women alike, is wrapped in a turban of sorts. Some of the males, particularly among

74

the *artigiani,* tend to wear caps denoting favorite soccer teams or businesses. Several craftsmen whom I saw in various studios wore hats made of folded newspaper. These newspaper hats are reminders of what northern Italian quarry workers traditionally wore as a kind of badge of honor — and a way to distinguish themselves and their craft from other laborers.

Many of the powder-dusted workers are the assistants. The sculptors themselves, the artisans whose names go with massive works carved out of stone, typically do not perform a lot of the carving of those works. There are exceptions, of course. I met two acclaimed sculptors in Pietrasanta who do all of their own work, from designing and creating the model, to shaping the marble and polishing the final work.

When assistants are used, a sculptor will create the concept of an individual piece (large and small), design it, and create a plaster, clay, or wax model to guide the assistant, who will start chipping away on the marble block with power tools — sometimes the simple hammer and chisel will be hauled out — to define the margins of the piece. Usually, a four-inch margin of safety is left around the figure's rough outline.

In an essay, Anna Laghi, coauthor of *Pi-*

etrasanta: Work of Art, describes how the block is marked up by using a compass or pantograph to transfer reference points from the model to the roughed-out block.

In a small *laboratorio* in Valdicastello Carducci, about three miles southeast of Pietrasanta, I watched sculptor Stefano Pierotti having an intense conversation with his *artigiani* and working with a *pantographo* on his plaster model. Then he would move the locked-in device to the same points on the face of his marble work in progress. In the thirty minutes or so that I watched, he moved the device back and forth between plaster model and marble block dozens of times. Often, he would consult with his assistant before actually chipping away a few flakes from his statue's face, then pause again to use the *pantographo.*

In this case, the sculptor was doing the work and the *artigiano* was offering advice. But these consummate craftsmen and women might go further in executing the sculptor's concept and design. As the work takes on its final shape and form, the sculptor typically steps in and fine-tunes and polishes key elements. Or, if he or she trusts the *artigiani,* the assistants might even do some of the smoothing and polishing.

"It has been this way from the very beginning," asserts Nicola Stagetti, a forty-eight-year-old who began working as an *artigiano* at age sixteen at Basanti Art Center, one of the larger studio complexes, or *laboratori,* still in operation close to Pietrasanta's historic center.

"Even Michelangelo had assistants," Stagetti said.

Laboratori abound near Pietrasanta and its outlying areas. Big and small, they are spaces where art is being made by dozens of assistants and sculptors alike. The sounds of hammering and chiseling — cold steel against cold steel, steel against stone, pneumatic chisels grinding away — predominate in some surrounding neighborhoods throughout the day.

There is even a tiny, one-room shop across a narrow courtyard from where I lived for nearly six months in Pietrasanta. It was there that I would see seventy-four-year-old Franco Lombardi, who started sculpting at age eleven, inside his dark shop carving sprays of flowers on flat pieces of pure-white marble. His specialty: grave markers.

Marble isn't the only art form created here. During the summer months, a painter can often be seen with easel set up in a corner of Piazza del Duomo, oils in one hand, a brush in the other, and a steady gaze toward the hill above Pietrasanta and the tiny village of Capezzano Monte perched way up there. Since the 1970s, bronze art in particular has become more and more popular here. Some marble sculptors work in both forms; others specialize solely in bronze.

One incredibly humid morning in late July, Roberta Giovannini Onniboni took me on a tour of the various kinds of studios in and around the town. The first stop was Cervietti Studio, a large complex where *artigiani,* working on perhaps a dozen projects, were re-creating traditional statues of religious and mythological figures and a few new ones, either for clients or for sculptors. One massive project under way was a re-creation of the sculptures found in the giant fountain of Versailles outside of Paris. These sculptures were destined for Taiwan.

I watched as Franco Viviani gently works his *martello,* or specialized power chisel, to softly shape a piece of white marble, referring every few minutes to a plaster model, taking precise measurements, and then moving back to the actual stone to shave a bit here, a slight piece there.

Across the room in the modern, high-ceilinged studio, Moreno Cervietti was, in contrast to Franco's precise fine-tuning with a power tool, pounding away with hammer and chisel at the outer fringes of a new block of stone. Chips were flying. Seeing him with his noise-canceling headphones and his safety glasses made me wonder how ancient and medieval sculptors and their *artigiani* did it without any of today's modern protection.

Leaving Cervietti Studio, we moved on to a tiny studio, down the narrow road next to the railway line that connects all the towns of coastal Tuscany. Inside, we found Alessandro Pertrucci up to his elbows in wet plaster, preparing a mold of a woman's head made from a clay model. This mold could be used to make copy after copy of the head, obviously that of a modern woman but also in the tradition of the gods and goddesses from ancient Greece and Rome.

Alessandro, a professional modeler, or *formatore,* also had lined the interior of the mold with a thin layer of rubber, which allows the head to be cast in bronze if the client so wishes.

On this day, the model was being prepared for a plaster copy, and Alessandro's hands moved deftly around the interiors of the two halves, piling a bit of wet plaster here and there, evening out the depth, then smoothing the edges and removing the excess with a flat blade. Eventually, the two halves would be joined and, much later, taken apart, revealing a plaster model of the head. Small bits of excess hardened plaster would be trimmed and the head smoothed to the kind of sheen the client ordered.

The next stop was at the Fonderia Mariani, the foundry owned by Adolfo Mariani, a friendly, mustachioed, fifty-something whom I had regularly seen in CRO, the local workers' club in front of my apartment on Vicole Porta a Lucca.

His *fonderia* is truly a large industrial operation, specializing in casting and assembling bronze sculptures, from small to giant. The mysteriousness of the process of creating bronze captivated me. Like Alessandro's small shop, this foundry also had mold-makers who make rubber or silicone molds that are then filled with wax.

The model is wrapped in a fireproof material. When it goes into the kiln, the heat melts the wax, leaving empty spaces around the figure to be filled with molten bronze during the actual casting process.

I watched the casting of part of what would become a giant sculpture by Colombian artist Fernando Botero. Four men were wrapped in flameproof clothing and had shields of tinted plastic over their faces. They manipulated a caldron of molten bronze. One man operated a remote-control device to pull the caldron out of its raging furnace and move it over to the large box where the model was buried in mounds of coarse-grained sand, a funnel sticking out of the top to direct the bronze liquid down into the spaces left by the melted wax. Two other men, at either end of a long clamp gripping the caldron, held on to bars that allowed them to tip it for pouring into the funnel. A fourth man, armed with a long-handled hoe-type tool, stood on a box so he could see into the caldron as he stroked the liquid bronze out with the hoe's blade.

The process was a magnificent example of precise, beautifully choreographed work-manship; the four acted as one organism. Everyone knew what to do and when to do it — no words spoken, just impeccable tim-ing developed during years of working to-gether.

When the model is removed from deep in its sand box and cooled, craftsmen break the shell, and the sculpture emerges. It goes into the hands of the "chaser," who grinds away rough edges and cleans the piece to prepare it for coloring, or the application of its patina. For large bronze sculptures, individual pieces might be cast separately. The Botero piece I saw cast is only one small part of the whole. Once all the parts are done, craftsmen assemble and weld it together. To the eye, the finished piece looks smooth, complete, whole, with no lines showing where parts were joined.

You see these craftsmen, around the lunch hour, sitting with a friend or two, munching a *panino* of crusty bread jammed with salami and cheese, and supplementing the meal with a beer or a glass or two of wine, delivered in quarter-liter glass containers.

In one local workers' club on the south edge of Pietrasanta's historic center — CRO Porta a Lucca (CRO stands for Circolo Ricreativo Operai, literally "recreation club for workers") — *artigiani* drop by in the early morning before work for quick shots of espresso, sometimes fortified with a rich Italian liquor such as grappa, and *cornetti,* soft rolls that resemble a French croissant. Around lunchtime, this particular club serves a hearty three-course Italian meal, usually of soup or pasta as a *primo* and a substantial meat or fish dish, with vegetable, as a *secondo.* If the customer wants, a salad is included, plus *caffè* at the end. The price is remarkably low for Pietrasanta — ten euros — especially considering it includes a quarter liter of house wine or perhaps a beer, soft drink, or bottle of mineral water.

This particular club, located several hundred feet from one of Pietrasanta's largest sculpture centers where dozens of members are employed, costs eight euros a year to belong, if the member is retired, and ten euros if still working. It is where many also go on their days off and on Saturdays. They all know one another, having grown up in the same neighborhood and worked together at the highly creative and mostly anonymous craft of carving and polishing stone for well-known sculptors.

The most regular visitors — some seem implanted there for several hours out of each day — are *pensionati,* long retired from the various sculpture and bronze-foundry operations around the city. They engage in lively conversation with their lifelong friends and play hand after hand of cards in games that usually erupt into loud arguments that the uninitiated visitor might think could lead to violence. But those arguments never do.

"It is like to be in a family here," said the club's thirty-nine-year-old owner, Daniele Maretti, who in 2012 had owned the business for five years. His sister Manola works with him, along with other friends and family members.

The club first opened in 1945 as a Communist club — the second to open in Italy immediately after the war, at a time when the Fascists who survived were quickly switching their politics from the right to the left. Many clubs that began life under the influence of the far left still exist today. Driving through villages, a traveler can spot various buildings with the word *circolo* (club) in the name. On the Tuscan coast, it could be a club for fishermen; inland, it might be a club for the *contadini,* or farmers; elsewhere, it could be a club for teenagers or young adults.

Originally, the clubs were designed to help their clientele get jobs. The workers, all good Communist party members at the time, used it as a kind of patronage system that was prevalent at all levels in postwar Italy. Nearly two decades ago, the system changed. The state took over the job of helping people find jobs — ostensibly to level out the system for Italians of all political persuasions.

Daniele characterizes his members as perhaps "left-leaning, but not extreme." He guesses there are probably few Communists on his two-hundred-strong membership list.

That list also includes perhaps fifty women — something some other *circoli* might still not allow.

"When I came here, no women ever came inside. I changed that," he said proudly. "Now we have women teachers, office workers come here daily, especially for lunch." And many women *artigiane,* of course. While it exists to provide a low-cost setting for friends and acquaintances of all ages to socialize, the club is particularly important to those pensioners, giving them a friendly, inexpensive place to go to while away their days.

A visitor schooled in only the basics of the Italian language will not always recognize much of what is being said in CRO Porta a Lucca, particularly among the *pensionati.* These men and women speak in the dialect of their neighborhood — an emotional form of speech removed from the precise Tuscan speech that became Italy's national language after unification 150 years ago. These members can speak pure Italian, of course. Everyone learns that in school. But here, among lifelong friends, their unique, rapid-fire words bounce loudly off the unadorned walls and low ceiling.

Such clubs, while serving *caffè* and drinks, do not qualify as a typical Italian bar that serves anyone who walks through the doors. National laws forbid "bar" or drinks signs for such private clubs — except a small one placed in an out-of-the-way corner of a window.

This name of "CRO Porta a Lucca" is in black letters mounted flat on the mustard-colored outside wall, high above two awnings and plastic chairs lined up for smokers. A small box of artificial flowers sits among the chairs, along with two tall ashtrays. The windows have curtains, just like a home would. From the street, an unknowing passerby would have no idea there is a club inside — unless he hears the loud voices of the card players erupt from the front door or sees a few of the members standing outside with cigarettes, or perhaps glasses of wine in their hands, and engaged in intense discussions about the weather, European soccer, the faltering European economy, or how tough it is to live solely on a government pension after decades of hard work. I overheard one man mention that he and his wife live on nine hundred euros a month, roughly twelve hundred dollars.

When members arrive, "it is like somebody coming into your house," the ever-effervescent owner Daniele said. He will serve the occasional tourist who might stumble into the place, but if they come in more than twice, he will let them know that the club is private. For me, Daniele knew from my first visit that I would be working for several months in Pietrasanta. That makes me an *operai,* a distinction that, along with my ten-euro fee, allowed me entry. We have become friends. I eat lunch there every day when I am in town, and it is where I have my morning *caffè* and *cornetto.*

There are one hundred sculptors working in Pietrasanta at any given time. Some live there year-round, others come in year after year for two- or three-month stretches. I met three who share studio space with friends but who generally prefer to work alone, without any help from *artigiani.*

"I did that once: had someone do some polishing for me," said Doris Pappenheim, a Dutch sculptor from Edam, Holland. "It was not the way I wanted it. I won't do it again. People who don't sculpt don't see it. You get a special eye; you touch it by hand. That's how we make our work."

She rents a studio on the edge of Pietra-santa's historic center, near Daniele's CRO Porta a Lucca. This studio is in a cluster of smaller studios next to a larger firm known simply as SEM. Just east of Doris's is the studio of young American sculptor Richard C. Janes, who has lived in Pietrasanta for four years. He is carving, without assistants but with the help of an older mentor, two bigger-than-life statues of American soldiers for a war memorial outside of Chicago. Still emerging, slowly, from the stone, these figures are imposing, and they exude strong authority.

Through a gate next door is a long three-sided structure, the fourth side open to the fresh Tuscan air. At the far end, her clothes, face, and hands powdered white, is Elizabeth Page Purcell, a New Yorker who prefers the appellation of "stone carver" rather than sculptor because she works only with stone, principally marble. There are others of course, men and women working in this large industrial complex rattling with the overlapping sounds of many pneumatic hammers. Scattered around larger structures housing computerized stone-cutting machinery are tin-roofed workstations for rent-paying artists doing their own work and for SEM's *artigiani,* who are carving and polishing stone for others. They represent the tight community of artists and artisans in Pietrasanta who work long hours, five or six days a week, and who gather daily at CRO for its simple, inexpensive, but nourishing lunches.

I had first spotted Doris from across the room when she entered with a friend. Her hair was covered tightly in a light yellow turban, and her clothes were mottled with marble dust. A smudge of white powder covered the right side of her nose. I approached her the next day in the nearby shop I frequented to purchase fresh bread and salami and cheese for my own home-made *panino.* She confirmed that, yes, she was a sculptor, and agreed to talk to me about why she comes to Pietrasanta to work. We met the next day for a brief lunch at Bar Michelangelo, on the ground floor of one of two medieval buildings in Pietrasanta, in which Michelangelo in 1518 reputedly signed a contract for marble.

"I have a small studio in Holland," she said, "but my social life there is too busy. It is hard to concentrate. I need to have a whole day, no appointments."

She has been making art for fourteen years. Now sixty-four, she started learning to be a sculptor while working as a social worker. She retired with a pension at fifty-nine and started working in marble full time.

"A sculptor in Holland told me that if I really wanted to learn I had to go to Pietrasanta. So I did." Here, another sculptor taught Doris how to use a *martello,* that hand-held pneumatic hammer. "It has a very special way of working. You have to master the vibration. For me, [using the *martello*] is kind of like drawing. I never make a model; I just start." She might make colored-pencil marks on the stone, but no paper drawings.

And what she sets out to create can suddenly shift. A piece of a project once broke off because of an undetected flaw in the stone. "Did you get rid of that stone and start over?" I asked.

She seemed startled by the question. "Of course not. I just shifted and started something new. That happens."

It occurred to me that the same happens in other forms of creating. A writer who runs up against a roadblock in trying to tell a story will bang against the idea for a while, and when it cannot be resolved, must figure out a new approach, for the story itself or for the troubling paragraph, seldom abandoning the entire story idea.

Her work can best be described, simply, as taking on shapes she perceives from nature. "I see it, and I just do it. It is natural."

This modernistic, existential style of sculpture differs from what she used to do: female torsos. But those torsos, despite selling easily, became too easy, not challenging enough. "I don't like to do it anymore. I just want to go on and on. Many people just repeat the pieces they do; I don't like that. I need always to do something new."

In her four or five months a year in Pietrasanta, she might complete seven or eight pieces. She calls in professional box makers to take measurements, and a few days later they return with wooden boxes that fit each piece perfectly. She has them trucked to her art dealer in Holland.

It is interesting to note that while Doris has been to Carrara, a few miles to the north, and has seen the quarries famous for their remarkable, pure-white marble, she does not get her marble from there.

"I don't make pieces that big, unless I have a commission. The white marble [of Carrara] works easier than colored marble, but I prefer the colored. I love the yellow marble from Siena, the pink marble from Portugal, the travertine from Iran." She usually selects stone from a dealer on the outskirts of Pietrasanta, who sells stone shipped in from all over the world, and has it trucked to her tiny studio, which she rents in a bigger studio space owned by another sculptor.

Does she make a living from her art?

"Of course not!" she says with a laugh. "Not many sculptors I know can survive on their art alone. People have to give lessons, or have a house to rent out, or studio space to rent out to another artist. For me, I have my pension, I rent out my house in Holland when I am here, and I have a small family inheritance. It is enough. I will do this forever."

American stone carver Elisabeth Page Purcell spends up to three months a year in Pietrasanta and has been doing so for fifteen years. She has a "day job," at the Art Students League on Fifty-seventh Street in Manhattan, where she manages the cafeteria for nine months of the year. She has been able to negotiate a brief yearly sabbatical, combined with vacation time, to return to Pietrasanta year after year. She has no intention of stopping these annual trips, saying she will return each summer as long as she is able. We talked during the summer of 2012. She has no plans for retirement from the art school, but when she does, her wish is to spend at least six months a year in the Città d'Arte. With a smile, she declines to disclose her age, but she appears much younger than I have deduced, through conversation, that she is.

Like Doris Pappenheim, who is a close friend, Elisabeth says she was told, word of mouth, " 'You need to go to Pietrasanta if you want to be a sculptor.' I came finally by myself and stayed a month at a carving school and fell in love with working outside."

Elisabeth maintains that she has always been a sculptor "in my heart. I was a dressmaker" before becoming a stone carver, "so I always worked three-dimensionally. The transition, for me, was natural."

Her rented space, in that cluster of studios at SEM, near the private bar CRO, is just off Vicole Porta a Lucca. She has two walls and a tin roof. The front is open to the Tuscan environment, and the studio's owner works a few feet away, in his own space. He does finishing work on architectural marble.

Elisabeth is a master at keeping her expenses low: she has a room in a home of friends who let her live with them year after year. The owner of her studio lets her store her bicycle and other possessions there; he knows she will be back the following year. And she has developed business relationships with marble suppliers, the box maker who packages up her creations for shipping them home, and the transportation com-

pany that gets those marbles from Pietrasanta to New York City.

"It's a tight budget," she says, "but it's
who I am, it's what I do, and I'll do it
forever."

A visitor approaching Elisabeth's outdoor
studio first hears the whine of the *martello*
and spots the clouds of marble dust it
throws up into the air. Then the visitor spots
a dust-covered Elisabeth, her hair wrapped
in a colorful scarf, her eyes protected with
safety glasses, a mask covering her mouth
and nose.

She is grinding and polishing a chest-size
block of black marble that she has shaped
into curves and valleys. It's a modern piece,
and it shows her versatility when compared
with photographs of her work on display in
her studio in Park Slope, Brooklyn, and in
her home in lower Manhattan. These pieces
show diversity in form and color of stone:
from literal female forms to figurative
representations. This is lovely, gentle art that
on one hand can be explicitly realistic and
on the other can leave much to the
imagination.

Across Pietrasanta, a different sculptor's
story emerges. A few dozen feet from the
city center sits a large, two-story building

94

decorated across the front of the first story with marble busts of Italian greats, including Michelangelo, Donatello, and Brunelleschi. This is home to the studio of Spartaco Palla, a fourth-generation sculptor of Pietrasantese descent who typically works with only one longtime assistant in this vast storehouse of statues and busts. Mixed in are a few pieces of his bronze art, but nearly everything is marble. There are busts, full-blown statues of ancient heroes, angels, women in Greek and Roman robes, religious figures, beautifully executed images of animals, and gods and goddesses.

Ironically, this building stands perhaps fifty feet from the rear of a building with a sign that proudly proclaims the Florentine sculptor Michelangelo was there in 1518 to sign still another contract for marble from quarries high above the town.

There are several display rooms in Spartaco's building, a structure that has been handed down through the generations. In a large storage area at the rear, there are even more examples of his work, along with hundreds of plaster models created to guide the Palla stone carvers who worked here over the various generations. Some statues, I assume, were done decades, perhaps a century, ago and, for some reason or other, never sold. There are hundreds of pieces on display, and except for the models, all are for sale.

My favorite piece here is a carving out of dark green, almost black, marble from Prato in northern Italy of a crouched leopard, *un gattopardo,* which literally translates to "dark-skinned cat." Its shoulder blades protrude from a smooth, highly polished back showing spots of lighter green strands that represent the leopard's spots. Its feet imply the creature's intent to leap off its rough, dark greenish-gray stone and capture an unsuspecting meal. I asked Spartaco what I then discovered to be a silly question: If the sculpture came out of a single piece of marble, how come the leopard is so shiny and the rock is dark gray?

"I polished it," he said simply, meaning that he spent several days hand-rubbing the cat's figure with special polishing paper. He was speaking through his daughter Lara, who generously interpreted for me. His wife, Rosanna Mazzanti, runs the retail end of the business and also speaks some English. She helped out with some of the words.

The shaping with hammer and chisel, and later with a *martello,* had only been part of the process. Polishing involves using various degrees of paper abrasives and always is done by hand. Spartaco said that some clients want finished works to reflect various degrees of polishing: from rough hammer-and-chisel finish to shiningly smooth. When those steps are completed, he then rubs in coats of wax to achieve the kind of patina he and his clients want.

Spartaco takes me into his workshop, a large cluttered room also jammed with shelves full of small plaster models and floor space taken up with large models. If a buyer wants any particular piece that he or she saw on display, say in the Louvre, or a museum elsewhere, there usually is a model here that allows Spartaco to create an identical version.

But in one corner, held slightly off the rough stone floor by a portable hydraulic lift, sits an unfinished white-marble torso of a headless, handless male, sculpted in a traditional classical motif. Spartaco said this is a commission for someone's villa.

This torso was carved out of a block of white marble that came from a quarry near Seravezza, an inland town a few miles south of Carrara. "This marble is more delicate than Carrara marble," Spartaco said. The torso is fifty-one inches long and weighs 660 pounds. It is now finished except for hours and hours of hand polishing still to come. The marble block started out at 2,200 pounds before Spartaco "pulled" the figure out of the stone, a creative process that took him three months.

Spartaco remembers visiting Carrara as a young child, when his great-grandfather, who created the family business, took him to witness the work there. As a young man, he studied at the art academy of Carrara.

He had spent the free time of his youth in his forefathers' Pietrasanta *laboratorio*. He showed me photographs of his father as a child watching teams of oxen pull giant blocks of marble on wheeled carts through the streets of Pietrasanta — a practice dating back to the times of the Romans and Greeks that persisted well into the twentieth century.

All of Spartaco's property seems too large for one person; after all, one hundred craftsmen labored here at the turn of the twentieth century. Then, it was one of the largest of dozens of studios within the historic city center. Now there are only two studios there. As Roberta had lamented to me, nearly all of the major operations have moved to the outskirts into various industrial areas along this west Tuscan coastline. A few others remain on the city's fringes, but despite Pietrasanta denizens being extraordinarily proud of their city and its past, concerns over noise and dust caused by the many operations, particularly when carving giant statues, forced the studios' relocation.

This is also why Spartaco no longer does large statues.

"The noise is too much, and we are too close," he said of his studio only a few dozen feet from the city's main piazza. "The culture of the worker, in [the historic center of] Pietrasanta, is finished."

Locals still gather in the center for the nightly *passeggiata*. The Piazza del Duomo is where children meet each other as toddlers and grow up playing together, kicking soccer balls, and learning to ride bicycles. And now restaurants and bars surround it. Fifteen years ago, I was told by a couple of lifelong Pietrasantesi, there were three restaurants in the center; today there are at least thirty-five.

Pietrasanta, of course, still clings with great pride to its artful history. Marble and bronze art, now created on the fringes, is trucked in and put on outdoor display. Large individual pieces are placed throughout the square where people can see them up close and touch them, and where children are sometimes allowed to climb and explore smooth, highly polished surfaces. This being Italy, no one worries when fully nude statues go up in this public space — something many places in the United States would forbid. And the children do not seem to notice.

These displays are not static. Unless a major artist, such as Fernando Botero, is being featured, outdoor exhibitions are changed every few weeks. The much-beloved Botero got the square to himself for the entire month of July in 2012.

A few displayed pieces by others are judged more harshly. When an exhibition goes up, an informal *comitato d'opinione* (committee of opinion) prowls the square, passing judgment on the quality of the art. The committee is made up of elderly *pensionati* — retirees — who then sit in their usual spots, such as the long stone bench in front of a bank or on the steps of the Duomo, and heatedly discuss the pros and cons of each piece.

My friend Filippo Tofani, whose grandfather Gualtiero Coluccini claims membership on that informal committee of self-styled art critics, told me that occasionally, when a piece does not meet with the group's approval, colorful balloons will mysteriously appear tied to the sculpture. When committee members and city officials agree that an exhibition is a disaster, it can be taken down as fast as it was put up. I did not see any balloons attached to art in the half-dozen or so exhibitions installed during my nearly six months there, but I don't doubt that it happens.

Filippo laughs when he tells me that the committee's standard of excellence in statuary is the nineteenth-century statue at the east end of the Duomo square that was carved by local sculptor Vincenzo Santini (1807–1876) — a highly traditional work indeed. Santini is still viewed by Pietrasantesi — and certainly the committee members — as a hero. When he lost his leg in an accident in the 1840s and could no longer carve stone, he helped establish a school of marble in the city center, which one author believes "became a seedbed of an artisanal renaissance that is still growing today."

Gualtiero and I became good friends, often sitting together on the steps of the Duomo, but my Italian and his English were not enough for me to probe the depths of his artistic likes and dislikes.

Meanwhile, Spartaco, at age sixty in 2012, still has a lot to do. As he demonstrates polishing his nearly complete commission piece, he muses: "I already am thinking about my next work. I am thinking about the size of the next block [of marble] I will need."

So, like Doris Pappenheim and Elizabeth Page Purcell, he will go on and on.

As will Gino Barsanti, aged eighty-two. While the two women may be the first in their families to make art, Gino has a four-generation tradition to maintain.

His grandfather Martino, and then his father Amerigo, ran one of Pietrasanta's statuary *laboratori* for many decades. Martino had operated a small studio at another location, but sold the property and moved it, in 1935, when Gino was seven, to its present site between the Church and Cloister of San Francesco and what was then the city's hospital. After the move, Martino turned the property over to Amerigo; the grandfather died five years later, just as Italy's dictator, Benito Mussolini, was taking Italy into what exploded into World War II.

"Initially, Grandfather had only a few major clients, who kept the *laboratorio* very busy," Gino told me one late-spring day. It sold only statuary and marble pieces, such as altars and baptismal fonts, for Catholic churches located primarily in North, Central, and South America.

The war was brought home to Tuscany after the Italian surrender in 1943, and especially in 1944 after the Americans and English landed at Sorrento, south of Naples, and then Anzio-Nettuno, south of Rome. The Allies started pushing the Germans up the peninsula. German troops, and Italian Fascists who remained loyal to Mussolini after Italy's surrender, fought hard to stay there.

"It was not possible for us to live in Pietrasanta during this," said Gino, who turned sixteen during this period. The family's villa, located just outside the gates to the large, bustling studio, was occupied at one time by top German brass, who had made Pietrasanta a base for troops. The family fled to the mountains, living in various places away from the coast. This area had become a natural pathway for the Americans to push the Germans northward and was the scene of vicious fighting, horrific casualties, and much destruction.

It was through this part of western Tuscany, with Pietrasanta at its center, where Hitler had drawn the Gothic Line — the line at which the Germans would stop the

Allies from entering the Po Valley farther north, at whatever the cost.

"From Pietrasanta to Massa was no-man's-land," said Gino. No one could live there.

But it did end. And in 1945 the family was back in Pietrasanta. Barsanti Statuario Laboratorio reopened.

Jump ahead five years. Gino, now twenty-two, is studying business in college. He suffers a stroke, certainly unusual for his age, and is forced to drop out. When he recovers, his father tells him he does not need to return to school; he can join the family business. And that is where he has worked, almost daily, for the last sixty-one years.

Over time the family's two or three major clients began to drop away, requiring less and less statuary work. Gino persuaded his father to let him go to Canada and the United States, where he said he visited nearly every state, from New England to the West Coast, drumming up new business. It was a highly successful trip, he said, and the new business — primarily the production of altars for North America's Catholic churches — kept the *laboratorio* operating.

But that specialty would not last forever by itself. Bronze casting was becoming popular, along with commercial needs for mosaic floors and wall hangings. Gino also jumped on the opportunity to rent out studio space in the vast Barsanti complex to independent artists drawn to Pietrasanta and its art culture.

"Originally, the men in the studio worked exclusively for us. The client would tell us what they needed and provide either the designs or we would create them. Then, we would assign the work" to the employees, the *artigiani.*

As independent stone carvers and artists working in bronze moved in, Barsanti's *artigiani* then were available to help them make their art, if the artists accepted the help. Most do.

The mosaic studio is an exception: its five craftsmen work for Barsanti. They either take a client's design or create designs for a client, block those designs on heavy-duty paper, and lay out the scenes using tens of thousands of tiny pieces of colored stone — each one selected, trimmed, and placed by hand. They follow the shadings of a finished drawing showing how the mosaic should look, choosing just the right color of tiny stone for a spot on a saint's beard or the blue of the Madonna's cloak.

The mosaics are all done in reverse, glued facedown to the paper outlines. For transport, usually to churches around the world because most portray religious scenes, the larger mosaics are cut into workable sections. When the pieces are all reassembled and permanently fixed to the surface, the paper is slowly peeled away, showing the full scene in proper perspective.

Gino maintains he is not retired. He works in a small studio next to his office creating various designs, either for himself or for clients. He handles business with his lifelong contacts and helps arrange transport of finished pieces for his forty-nine-year-old son Emanuele, who took over the business a few years ago and now runs the vast enterprise. Emanuele had started working for his father in the early 1990s, just like Gino and Gino's father Amerigo had worked for theirs.

When I met father and son on that late-spring day, Emanuele was preparing for a trip to the United States to oversee the installation of a large marble altar in a Catholic church in Jackson, Mississippi. The structure had been shipped to Orlando, Florida, a few days before my visit, and Emanuele and a colleague were going to Orlando to pick it up and haul it to Jackson.

This kind of job is what the *laboratorio* has done since its start nearly eighty years ago, long before it began the bronze foundry or the mosaic studio. The Barsantis have no intention of ending the business any time soon.

"My life is this," said Gino, the octogenarian. "The only days of the week I don't like are Saturday and Sunday, when I am not here."

The memories abound. At the bottom of the stairway up to his office sits a marble bust of his grandfather, Martino. On his desk in his private office sits a black-marble bust of his father, complete with eyeglasses. In another room next door, on shelves lining all the walls, are ranks of binders, showing photographs of every statue or marble piece the *laboratorio* has ever produced. The older binders survived the destruction of wartime Pietrasanta.

The photos are organized by category: dozens of various treatments of, say, Madonna, Madonna with child, all the saints, Christ on the cross, the Last Supper, the apostles, politicians, Greek and Roman statuary, and on and on. Pore through the books and find the particular style of Madonna you want. Or come up with your own concept; Barsanti *artigiani* will make it.

On one wall, on shelves and in cabinets, are rows and rows of small boxes containing thousands of glass negatives documenting the earliest years of statuary created by this four-generation family and their craftsmen.

Gino and I return to his office. In a quiet moment I see the octogenarian gazing at the bust of his father. After a moment of silence, he draws a deep breath, lets it out slowly, and says: "Every night before I sleep I think of my father. We were together almost every day of my life; we worked together, talked together — every day. I miss him."

Four:
Versilia

The lonely and grand scenery that surrounded us . . .

> — Edward John Trelawny
> *Recollections of the Last Days*
> *of Shelley and Byron* (1858)

I met a traveler from an antique land
Who said: "Two vast and trunkless legs of
    stone
Stand in the desert. Near them, on the
    sand,
Half sunk, a shattered visage lies, whose
    frown,
And wrinkled lip, and sneer of cold
    command,
Tell that its sculptor well those passions
    read
Which yet survive, stamped on these
    lifeless things,
The hand that mocked them and the heart
    that fed.

And on the pedestal these words appear —
'My name is Ozymandias, king of kings:
Look on my works, ye Mighty, and despair!'
Nothing beside remains. Round the decay
Of that colossal wreck, boundless and bare
The lone and level sands stretch far away."
— Percy Bysshe Shelley
"Ozymandias" (1818)

I have no doubt that the western Tuscan coastline at the old Versilian town of Viareggio once offered "lonely and grand scenery." This is in a part of the area known as Versilia, named after the river that flows from marble-rich mountains and into the Ligurian Sea north of Forte dei Marmi. The river intersects a road laid out by Michelangelo in the mid-sixteenth century so he could have easier access to the marble quarries above Seravezza. And that town, along with Forte dei Marmi, Pietrasanta, Camaiore, Stazzema, and Massarosa, is one of the principal villages of this tiny enclave on Tuscany's western edge.

In Roman times, this area was called Fosse Papiriane, and it constituted a major swamp between Massa and Pisa — a distance of about twenty-eight miles.

Great swaths remain of stone pines, also known as "umbrella" pines, which humans have cultivated for their pine nuts for at least six thousand years. These Tuscan pines are packed along the sea immediately to the south of Viareggio and along its hills to the east.

The coast between Viareggio and Tuscany's boundary with Liguria to the north, while no longer isolated and lonely, remains enticing — in its own modern way. There is an almost continuous fringe of seaside resorts along the narrow plain, ending just beyond the marble-exporting ports of Massa-Carrara. This translates into miles and miles of colorful beach umbrellas belonging to dozens of privately owned establishments that rent out plots of perhaps ten square feet to sun worshipers.

These day spas, occasionally separated here and there by a public beach area, line the western edge of a coastal highway full of automobiles, semi-trailers, and blue regional buses — all following the route, more or less precisely, of ancient Roman roads that connected Western Europe to the Eternal City, located a bit more than two hundred miles south.

Along the inland edge of coastline, just a mile or so from the Tuscan Sea, the coastal shelf transforms into the gradual slope of the Apuan Alps. This is a hilly, heavily forested area between the Serchio River Valley and the Ligurian Sea, some forty miles long and roughly twelve miles wide. The western slope rises to heights from 650 feet to 1,300 feet above sea level and is peppered with numerous villages, many with origins in medieval times.

The line of mountain summits, at an average of 5,000 to 6,000 feet above sea level, hangs over and dominates these human-occupied clusters of ancient stone structures. The peaks are composed of either limestone or exposed marble that travelers on the main north–south railway line far down along the coast often mistake for alpine snowfields.

The Apuan Alps are the Italian peninsula's oldest and highest of the various ranges that lead up to the spine of Italy, the central and much higher Apennines. And because the range is no farther than ten miles from the sea, Versilia experiences heavy rainfall. The predominance of naturally porous limestone in many of the peaks means ubiquitous springs of water randomly pop up along its slopes.

In the spring and early summer, when rains can last days at a time, narrow mountain roads are often awash in runoff from these bubbling springs, destined to dry up by July and August. Locals often can be seen parked along the narrow mountain roadways, taking advantage of the short-lived free flow of pure water by filling up containers for later use.

But most travelers do not think of limestone when they view these mountains. It's the marble — the yellowish, white, and gray blocks of Massa and Seravezza and the more famous blazing whites of Carrara — that impress most newcomers.

On more than one occasion in Viareggio I sat in a bar amongst vast clusters of beach umbrellas that stretch along the sands, sipping my morning espresso while contemplating the spirit of English poet Percy Bysshe Shelley and imagining I was near the spot of his most-unusual funeral.

In midsummer of 1822, the somber event took place on a patch of then-isolated beach at Viareggio, a small town positioned at Versilia's southern edge. His fish-gnawed body, with a folded copy of his late friend John Keats's poems in an inside coat pocket, had washed up onto the shore following the sinking of his small boat, the *Don Juan,* ten days earlier. Shelley's corpse was not removed from the spot, and it was there where he was ultimately cremated. Most of his ashes and his unburned heart were carried to Rome.

The account of this event, by Shelley's close friend Edward John Trelawny, is deliciously compelling, but I suspect it's rare for a twenty-first-century visitor to know about it. To his credit, Ernest Hemingway made a brief reference to the drowning in his 1927 short story *"Che Ti Dice la Patria?"* ("What Does the Fatherland Tell You?"). His unnamed character makes an off-hand remark to a traveling companion, named Guy, as they sit in a tiny restaurant near the Ligurian town of La Spezia, several miles to the north of Tuscany's Viareggio: "They drowned Shelley somewhere along here." " 'That was down by Viareggio,' Guy said." The two comments had nothing whatsoever to do with Hemingway's story. Perhaps the then-youthful author dropped it in just to impress readers with his literary acuity.

On July 8, 1822, Shelley and his close friends Edward Williams and Charles Vivian had left Livorno, a coastal city the British in the distant past had inexplicably renamed "Leghorn," located just south of Pisa. They were en route north to Lerici, a delightful Ligurian village on the Gulf of La Spezia. Shelley and Williams, with their wives, shared a home there, the Villa Magni. Shelley and Vivian were incompetent sailors, and while Williams had experience sailing, he apparently was not skilled enough to avert disaster. The *Don Juan* also was later said to be poorly designed and unsafe.

The trio, with the wives waiting at Lerici, departed Livorno during squally weather and against the advice of Trelawny and Lord Byron, who were staying in Pisa. A sudden storm came up after they had passed the mouth of the Arno River and were halfway home. The schooner apparently was swamped and sank. It was an ignoble end to their lives and to the life of the man who gave us, among other great works, the marvelous short poem "Ozymandias" — a short poem that reminds us how fleeting fame and life can be.

Of course, conspiracy theories abound. At the time, some thought the *Don Juan* might have been rammed and deliberately sunk by people intent on doing Shelley harm. Perhaps it was someone to whom he owed money; there were many such folks in that category. Some suggested that pirates may have been responsible, or perhaps folks opposed to Shelley's controversial political views might have planned it. But the storm and overall lack of seamanship skills are the likely culprits.

Later it became clear that others in passing boats had seen the foundering craft but declined to help. In those days and in that part of Italy, anyone who rescued sailors in trouble and brought them back to shore would have to remain in quarantine for several days or be subject to customs searches before they could resume their journeys.

Shelley's body washed ashore on July 18 after the yacht and its crew had been missing for ten days. The body of Edward Williams had rolled up onto the beach south of Viareggio near the mouth of the Serchio River and the village of Migliarino, in the midst of one of those large coastal clusters of umbrella pines. Another body, believed to be that of the eighteen-year-old Charles Vivian, washed up onto a beach at Massa, north of today's Marina di Pietrasanta. The storm pushed a dinghy, thought to be from the *Don Juan,* onto the beach at Motrone, a onetime medieval port and now a tiny enclave of Marina di Pietrasanta.

Vivian's body, reduced in the sea to a skeleton, had been quickly cremated on the spot at Massa and the ashes mixed into the sand. Williams's body a few miles to the south was also cremated after several days.

Lord Byron, Byron's friend Leigh Hunt, and Trelawny handled the cremations of Williams and Shelley. They had a Livorno craftsman make a portable iron furnace — a device "of iron bars and strong sheet-iron supported on a stand."

Meanwhile, authorities at Viareggio, citing health reasons, wouldn't allow Shelley's body to be moved. It was sprinkled with lime and covered by sand while permission was being sought for cremation.

With permission finally in hand, Trelawny, Lord Byron, and a Tuscan health official attended Shelley's cremation using the portable iron furnace. Soldiers who escorted the party collected wood, and Shelley's body, unrecognizable except for his clothes, was placed on the pyre. Trelawny and others sprinkled salt and frankincense over the body and, for added accelerant, poured copious quantities of wine over it before setting the pyre ablaze.

A popular 1889 painting by Louis Edouard Fournier — created in 1889, sixty-seven years after the event — shows Lord Byron, Trelawny, and Hunt watching the cremation. In reality, Byron couldn't bear watching his friend burn. A famous swimmer known for swimming from Venice's Lido to the Grand Canal, he waded into the surf of the Ligurian Sea and swam out to his boat anchored off shore. Hunt sat out the spectacle in a nearby carriage.

Shelley's wife, Mary Shelley, creator of *Frankenstein,* wasn't there, despite being depicted in the painting as kneeling in the sand a short distance away. Some sources say her presence at a cremation would have offended pre-Victorian sensibilities. It was thought that such an event was not good for a woman's health.

Perhaps what followed was not grotesque by 1822 standards, but someone smacked Shelley's skull with a heavy object to allow the fire to consume the brain. And Trelawny, seeing Shelley's heart — some sources say it might have been his saltwater-preserved liver — untouched by fire, removed it to preserve it for Mary Shelley. After Mary Shelley's death in 1851, silk-wrapped remains of her husband's "heart" and some ashes were found in her desk drawer, reportedly wrapped in a paper copy of the Percy Shelley poem "Adonais," his elegy on the death of Keats. Eventually, they would make their way into the grave of the couple's son, Sir Percy Florence Shelley.

The poet's ashes are interred in the Protestant Cemetery in Rome, near the grave of his friend Keats, who had died a year earlier.

Trelawny's ashes — he died in 1881 — are buried next to Shelley's simple marker.

I don't know if the precise site of Shelley's "funeral" on that once-isolated beach ever was identified. There doesn't appear to be any evidence of a marker along the shoreline. One report had the body washing up just one and a half miles north of Viareggio's small harbor. Today, a spot at that distance from the harbor is awash in beach umbrellas and sunbathing Europeans. A wide pedestrian boulevard runs through Viareggio along the beach edge for nearly two miles. Piazza Shelley, with a marker noting the poet's demise at Viareggio — it does not identify where the body was cremated — is near the small port and two blocks from the sea.

Unlike that of the long-forgotten emperor Ozymandias, the spirit of the Englishman, who died a month before his thirtieth birthday, remains with us.

Viareggio lies at the southern edge of Versilia. Other villages along the coastline have their own sand and sea that draw tourists, primarily inland Italians, Europeans, Brits, and Australians. Pietrasanta, which dates back to the mid-thirteenth century, is one of the villages of the group, but sits a few miles inland. The separate town of Marina di Pietrasanta, two miles to the west of Pietrasanta's historic center, has its own resorts, hotels, and private beaches. Along with Forte dei Marmi and Lido di Camaiore, these sand strips evolved from tiny fishing villages into tourist destinations sometime around the late nineteenth century.

Inland Pietrasanta is packed with visitors during July and August. They seem to blanket the beach areas during the day, and in the evening wander, on foot or bicycle or rental car, into the town and sit in a half-dozen or so bars and nearly three dozen restaurants until well past midnight. Most of the other interior towns and villages are generally left to the locals during the hot summer months.

Beaches along the entire Tuscan shoreline from Carrara to Orbetello vary between rocky and sandy; most of Versilia's are sandy, and many are private; a visitor has to pay a fee to a concessionaire to use showers and cabanas with locks on the doors and to sit on rented recliners in the shade of uniformly colored, numbered umbrellas. These private sections, interspersed here and there by public beaches where local folks haul in their own umbrellas and spread out large towels, are often booked solid during July and August. Many vacationers return year after year to reclaim their own ten square feet of sand, hoping eventually to work their way to the front rows and unblocked views of the sea.

These beaches represent the side of Versilia sought by most tourists. There certainly is another side as well. One way for adventurous travelers to spend a few days in this area is to get noses out of guidebooks and simply wander from one village to another along narrow, postwar roads built to replace the mule tracks that for centuries were their only connection with one another. A highlight of such a journey is to occasionally stop in a village's main square to enjoy an espresso or a cold drink, sit at an outdoor table, and observe daily life in a small town.

Such visits into the coastal interior allow travelers to discover the beauty of forests blanketed with pines and chestnut and oak trees. Many of the stone villages and smaller *borghi,* or clusters of just a few houses, are true hilltop Tuscan villages without overly sandblasted pretention and trinket shops that are found more often in classical Tuscany to the east. How wonderful it is to wander through a medieval village where shopkeepers don't even sell postcards, much less touristy T-shirts and glass representations of the Leaning Tower of Pisa.

One way to experience this kind of travel is to follow, on foot or bicycle, portions of a pathway known as the Via Francigena, roughly translated as "French road" or "route of the Franks." This was considered during the Middle Ages as one of Italy's most important roads. Pilgrims from all over Europe, beginning during the eighth or ninth centuries, used the 1,180-mile trail between Canterbury in England and Rome for devotional and faith-sustaining journeys to the Holy City. Now much of the well-mapped trail has been asphalted.

Travelers through the early to late Middle Ages made the journey by crossing the English Channel, journeying through France, transiting the Alps, and dropping down into northern Italy.

First mentioned in documents from the mid-ninth century, the Francigena enters modern Tuscany high up in the northwest, following a route from Parma and Piacenza in Emilia-Romagna and down into Tuscany along the valley of the Magra River. It runs north to south through the ancient village of Pontremoli in the Tuscan province of Massa-Carrara and, when the Francigena comes within a mile or so of the modern coast at Carrara, it turns slightly southeast, moving through Massa and into the Province of Lucca at Forte dei Marmi. Then it goes directly through the historic center of Pietrasanta where it leaves the Roman road and begins its gradual shift southeast toward Tuscany's center, because travelers and pilgrims were often leery of pirates and other brigands along the more coastal route. The road goes to a point below Valdicastello di Carducci and then through rolling foothills on to Camaiore before continuing south toward Lucca. It is there where the Apuan range ends and the great plain of central Tuscany begins. The pilgrim road bypasses Pisa and heads toward Siena and beyond in eastern Tuscany before leaving Tuscany behind, a few miles north of the Lazio-region town of Aquapendente.

Today, the route is clearly marked on special maps and by small wooden signs. Each day in Pietrasanta, from early spring to late fall, modern wanderers on this road pause in Pietrasanta's main piazza for rest and relaxation.

Some adventurous souls take the entire route, starting at Canterbury and going all the way to Rome in one or two seasons. Others traverse just portions of it, such as the clearly delineated route through Tuscany. Many sections can accommodate automobiles. I traveled short stretches on foot, between Pietrasanta and Valdicastello and a few miles beyond — often finding myself surrounded in pleasant silence in the midst of Tuscan *bosci* (forests) and only greeted by a few cars.

Just a brief stretch runs along the coast, roughly following those ancient Roman-built routes through Versilia: Via Aemilia Scaura and Via Aurelia. Via Aemilia Scaura originally flanked the sea from Genoa to Pisa. There, the Via Aurelia went from Pisa to Rome. Today, the ancient name of Aemilia Scaura has been discarded, and the road, now Strada Statale 1 (SS1), is known only as Via Aurelia.

Ancient and medieval travelers could choose to split off from the Via Aurelia at Luni, that ancient Roman port just over the modern boundary of northern Tuscany, and take the Via Cassia, which turns sharply to the east and then flows south through the Serchio River Valley along the foothills of the Apennine Mountains before turning southwest toward Rome. But the Via Cassia would have been a much longer and more difficult journey for these medieval travelers and pilgrims.

The Serchio River segment might have

been preferred during hot-weather months when the mountain valley is cooler than the coastal route. Or travelers may have wanted the alternative route to avoid the malarial swamps that blanketed much of the Versilian coastline.

Either route included plenty of monasteries and churches, some built specifically to house pilgrims needing shelter for the night or for several days of respite to recover from an arduous journey that would take months to complete.

Along the Tuscan coastal route, the oldest church in Versilia, Pieve di Santi Giovanni e Felicità, sits just a mile or so from Pietrasanta and just off the narrow canyon road that leads to the suburb of Valdicastello di Carducci. This church, with its heavily illustrated bronze doors, dates back to the ninth century — around the time pilgrims first started to use the Via Francigena. A day's walk farther along the clearly marked pathway, now barely wide enough for automobiles, is the inland town of Camaiore, where pilgrims could find many hostels and inns and worship in the Church of Santo Stefano.

The Via Francigena also was the route of armies traveling down the peninsula, including, in 1096, Crusaders commanded by

Frenchman Hugh of Vermandois. He was on his way to join up, in Constantinople, with other armies called by Pope Urban II on the First Crusade. His Crusader army stopped briefly at Rome and then moved southeast through the Italian peninsula, eventually arriving in Syria and Palestine. Their goal: capturing Jerusalem from the Muslims, who had taken over the city from the Greek Christians of Byzantium, 558 years earlier in AD 638.

Deep inland, within the northwestern coastal strip of Tuscany that makes up what locals call Alta (Upper) Versilia, are numerous small villages. All are connected by a series of asphalt roads that narrowly wind their way up steep hillsides, repeatedly doubling back on themselves before topping ridgelines. It is a relatively recent phenomenon, mostly in the years following World War II, that many of the roads in this high-mountain countryside were slightly widened and paved over to accept trucks and automobiles.

Many of the hamlets, and even the larger *comune,* or municipality, of Stazzema have parking lots at their village entrances. The "streets" to businesses and homes are barely wide enough for two people to walk side by side. There is no way for motorized vehicles, except for the occasional scooter, to enter the tiny commercial center or even to park at the medieval stone houses.

On one bright summer afternoon, I drove a rental car into Stazzema and didn't see obvious signs banning vehicles. I had no inkling that the cobblestone path that extended from the parking lot would get progressively narrower. I drove a few hundred feet toward the village center before realizing that building walls were closing in on me. Backing out was awkward. Two elderly villagers saw my predicament, and with one guiding from the front and the other behind, I made it out into the parking lot with just a small (but expensive) scratch on my rear bumper. It took thirty seconds to go in and twenty minutes to back out, slowly and painfully. I sat on a bench in the tree-lined parking area overlooking a deep, wide gully and listened as the two gentlemen, with great humor, described similar motorist mistakes in their village.

Perhaps this lack of motorized access is why the town hall for the county of Stazzema is located not in the *comune* of Stazzema but closer to the main highway, several miles to the west in the more-open village of Pontestazzemese. This town is more drivable and boasts several convenient parking lots.

Sometimes, the roads connecting the fifteen tiny hamlets that are administratively tied to Stazzema drop down along fast-flowing streams and the Vezza River that, every few years in wet early springs or late falls, can overwhelm this part of mountainous Tuscany and explode out of their rocky beds. Roads and portions of some small villages, often washed away by such high water, have been repeatedly rebuilt over the decades.

This happened, on June 19, 1996, in the village of Cardoso, well east of the marble-processing center of Seravezza and north of coastal Pietrasanta.

Within six hours on that day, nearly sixteen inches of rain fell on the village and the steep slopes of the Versilia Valley. Thirteen people died in the Vezza River's rushing waters, one remained missing, and the body of a five-year-old child from Cardoso was found twenty miles away on a Ligurian beach near Portovenere, just across the Tuscany line.

Cardoso was nearly destroyed, and four other villages around Stazzema — Farnocchia, Pruno, Volegno, Pomezzana — were isolated for several days. In the wider Versilia area, the Via Aurelia along the coast between Pietrasanta and Querceta, a few miles to the north, was washed out and closed for two weeks, as was the main Genoa–Rome railway line.

Driving through Versilia Valley and along the Vezza River today, one will see a rebuilt and restored Cardoso, its buildings still holding tight against the Vezza River, its water barely a trickle in August. The village center is strung out along the narrow valley and is separated from the waterway by a slim road and a low stone wall. On the opposite bank, a couple of eating establishments and bed-and-breakfast inns sit just a few feet above the river's stones along the water's edge.

In my brief time there, I spent an hour sitting on that stone wall sampling local cheeses and the village's famous variety of mortadella, made by mixing lean pork, small cubes of pork fat, spices, and a variety of wild herbs harvested from nearby hillsides. The Vezza flowed gently at my side, and sounds of the deep Tuscan mountains swirled around me, natural sounds enhanced by the quiet life in this mountain village.

Early one August morning and on a whim,

I turned off the main road above Seravezza at the point where the Vezza River from the east joins with the Serra River (known historically as the Riomagno) from its origins in the far north, around Azzano, near the foot of Michelangelo's mountain.

Just north of Seravezza, the blue highway sign with its arrow pointing across the Vezza River beckoned me to head up the steep mountain slope to the village of Gallena. I was curious because a local historian had mentioned that Gallena might have been a starting point for one group of German soldiers, sixty-eight years earlier, to follow a narrow footpath to Sant'Anna di Stazzema on the morning the villagers there were massacred.

Gallena is slightly more than a mile up, and deep into the mountain. The steep, twisty road, overhung with giant chestnut and oak trees, makes for slow going. It took about fifteen minutes to get there. The road suddenly ends at the bottom of a cluster of stone houses planted firmly on the hillside. As in the *comune* of Stazzema, there are no streets wide enough for automobiles leading up to the houses themselves. Here, one simply parks in a large open space at the road's end, in front of a church dedicated to Saint Barbara, and hikes a few hundred

feet along paved footpaths between buildings.

The hillside below the cluster of buildings
is spotted with a few acres of grape vines
and small groves of olive trees. There appears to be no commerce here, just the
homes. This is an area rich in minerals;
mines are located near here, and an active
marble quarry sits across a gully higher up
and near the summit of the hill to the west.
The quarry is small when compared with
the giant quarries farther up the road from
Seravezza, or at Massa and Carrara well to
the north. It is stunning with its freshly
exposed slabs of white marble. The site sits
below the brow of a massive overhang of
uncut stone perhaps one hundred feet tall.
One day, if the market for marble holds,
this overhang will be gone, its stone lining
countertops and paving floors and stairways.

Standing before the church of Saint Barbara, facing south and hidden in the mountain's overgrowth, is a series of ancient
pathways, or mule trails, spilling over the
mountain and down into Sant'Anna. I can
imagine the Germans congregating at road's
end in this wide spot before the church and
then being led along those trails by Italian
supporters of the deposed Mussolini. I do
not see signs here pointing the way. This

particular trail, a Sant'Anna historian told me, is nearly lost to modern memory.

The drive back to the main highway, now all downhill, takes only a few minutes. A few miles east along the highway, at the village of Rousina — another launching point for those German soldiers seven decades ago — a road leads south into a wider Versilia Valley lined with numerous other villages I want to briefly explore: Pruno, Volegno, Cardoso, Mulina, and Farnocchia.

On the top of the steep hillside that plunges down to the Vezza River where it flows past Cardoso is a line of stone walls and the backs of buildings. This is the hamlet of Pruno, with perhaps fewer than a hundred residents and is yet another village with narrow walkways and a parking area at its base. It sits overlooking the villages strung out along the Versilia Valley, like a doting mother looking down on her children gathered around her skirts.

In medieval times, pathways were barely wide enough for carts. If today's residents don't park in the lots at the towns' lower reaches, they park along the narrow road and walk uphill using steep wooden or stone stairways to rough-stone houses high above.

Pruno's buildings — homes, a small

church, and only a shop or two, plus a small bar serving coffee — are made of raw stones, from light yellow to dark gray in color. The exterior stone walls of only a few houses are plastered. And most buildings are joined together like unique, one-of-a-kind medieval condominiums. During my midday visit, which corresponded to the usual hours of siesta, a couple of housewives swept the stoops and the stone walkways of their homes while engaged in intense conversation. My ear, attuned to school Italian, could make no sense of the overheard conversations; a local dialect is used here.

A shirtless man sat on one stoop, smoking a short, black Tuscan cigar, nodding with a welcoming smile as I passed by; a woman watering numerous plants placed around her stoop, in her alcove, and on windowsills quietly sang to herself. It is August, and windows are open. It seems, from the lack of compressor noise, that there is very little, if any, air-conditioning here, just fans rustling window curtains.

While cars were parked in the small lot below the town, light Vespas were stowed in tiny alcoves next to most houses. Occasionally, a gap appeared between the joined buildings, offering spectacular views of the mountains and the Vezza River below and the faraway cluster of Cardoso's buildings strung out along the now-placid stream.

In the other direction, and perhaps just fifteen hundred feet along the road into Pruno, sits an even smaller village, Volegno. Home to perhaps fifty people, it is only half as large as its bigger sister higher up. And like so many of these small villages, Volegno is simply a neighborhood — just a cluster of interconnected buildings well over a century old. There are no stores, post offices, or banks.

I head back toward Pontestazzemese, but before that larger town is a junction that leads to two other villages on my list. I turn sharply south, and within a few miles come to Mulina, named for a medieval mill that still stands. This is the village where the first victims of the German massacre associated with Sant'Anna were killed — a priest and members of his family. Soldiers moved on from here to Farnocchia to join colleagues who had burned the town four days before, scattering those residents to the nearby hillsides. Some of those Farnocchia residents, including their priest, had followed a *mulattiere,* or mule trail, through the mountains and over the ridge to take what would be a disastrous refuge in Sant'Anna, just a few miles away.

The company of SS troopers, led by local Italian Fascists and with the smoldering village at their backs, started early in the morning of August 12, 1944, along that same narrow ancient mule track.

The road from Mulina to Farnocchia is narrow and curvy, requiring the liberal use of the car horn to warn out-of-sight drivers heading downhill. The village, which has a parking area in front of the local church, Pieve di San Michele, like most of the others in the area, is not drivable. Cars are tucked here and there amongst stone buildings that look like they have been there for centuries. Following the German-torched fire, residents must have cleaned the stone and rebuilt as it was before.

It took perhaps fifteen minutes to walk around the tiny center, up and down stairs that make up the pedestrian lanes. A few have signs proclaiming VENDITA — for sale. There seems to be only one business: a combination tobacco shop–bar–tiny restaurant. Outside the door with large hanging beads gently swaying in the entrance is an outdoor seating area with umbrellas and plastic chairs. Here I sat, enjoying a fresh homemade cream-filled pastry and a double espresso.

Just up the road, perhaps fifty feet away, I

noticed the start of a narrow trail, first cresting a concrete retaining wall and then disappearing into the deep woods beyond. The bar's owner, Roberto, confirmed my suspicions: this was the trail to Sant'Anna.

"Everyone here knows about the Germans. A long time ago, it was horrible," he said, speaking of the burning of Farnocchia. "And then," he paused, "of course there was Sant'Anna." The Farnocchia refugees who made it there were caught up in the massacre, along with their priest, Don Innocenzo Lazzeri.

Despite these depressing thoughts, I sat outside the Farnocchia bar, appreciating the well-made espresso and watching a young family at another table enjoying the afternoon. The temperature, despite it being a blistering Tuscan August along the coast, was quite comfortable in the mountains. The mother was pointing to the different colors of her son and daughter's clothing, giving them the colors' names in English. "Yellow!" the boy would happily shout. "Red!" repeated his sister. "Pink." "Blue."

Ahead, at the start of the trail over the mountain, I saw a twentysomething couple, her in a sundress and him in slacks and a golf shirt. They had no packs, no apparent bottles of water, and were wearing street shoes. Perhaps there is a house farther along, I thought. The couple, talking and laughing quietly, disappeared into the deep hardwood forest.

I remained in that spot for about an hour, enjoying the afternoon and its sounds of birds high in the surrounding forest. The family had left, and a group of friendly older men, smoking those stubby Tuscan cigars, was sitting on a bench outside the bar door. I bought a small box of Toscanello cigars and asked if I could join them. *"Si, si,"* they said. But we could not engage in deep conversation; their mountain dialect and my basic Italian quashed all my efforts at communication. Still, we smoked the traditional cigars and smiled at one another a lot, as the comfortable afternoon passed slowly. My mind wandered: Was the apartment I saw for sale in the gray-stone building in the town center affordable? Did Farnocchia have any Internet access? What a great place this would be to settle down and work without many distractions.

Five:
The Great Loop

He was inclined toward mobility, he tended to sink deeper and deeper, to look ever more closely, lingering on the details: "I would like to be a plane tree," he used to say, "standing still, extending my roots."
— Bruna Cordati, writing about her father, Tuscan painter Bruno Cordati

My friend Filippo Tofani and I slide out of Pietrasanta on a bright, cloudless day with temperatures finally warm enough for us to shed light jackets and vests. Since my arrival in Pietrasanta two weeks earlier, it has rained almost daily and maintained, for coastal western Tuscany in late April, an unseasonal chill that mocked my decision to turn off the heat in my apartment.

But I got by, and on this day, basking in the warmth, Filippo and I will make a great loop, from Pietrasanta to Lucca and then into the mountains through the valley of the

Serchio River. This valley, which in medieval times provided Rome-bound pilgrims an alternative, more-inland stretch of the Via Francigena by following the Via Cassia, separates the coastal Apuan range from the Apennine Mountains. The Apuan range ends just before Pisa, while the Apennine, referred to as the "spine" of Italy, runs nearly the length of the peninsula, north to south, ending when it drops into the Ionian Sea where the Aspromonte massif dominates Italy's toe.

Our route for this daylong journey avoids going east into the Apennines where we could have continued on to Modena and Bologna on narrow provincial roads that follow tracks first carved by medieval travelers. That's for another time. My focus is western Tuscany, and the eastern slope of the Apuan Alps is as far as I want to go.

We are traveling "blue" highways and staying off the *autostrada,* Italy's version of the U.S. interstate highway system. It is possible, I believe in nearly all cases throughout Italy, to avoid the *autostrada,* and its occasional tolls, for a more leisurely drive from village to village, town to town, city to city on roads marked with signs painted blue. With the marvelous valley carved by the Serchio, we have no other option but slate and provincial roads.

We leave Pietrasanta and roll onto a provincial road numbered SS439. This narrow, two-lane byway through coastal foothills follows the original medieval route to Lucca, the provincial capital of those who long ago ruled the area around Pietrasanta. Of course, at various times Pietrasanta and its surrounding villages that make up Versilia also were ruled from Florence, farther to the east, and others from the north had their shot at control as well — until Italy's unification in 1861 changed all that.

At Lucca we turn toward the north on SS12 and, within a few miles, stop at the village of Borgo a Mozzano.

We want to see an ancient bridge over the Serchio. It was commissioned in early AD 1100 by Countess Matilda of Tuscany for merchants and pilgrims traveling to Rome via the eastern route of the Via Francigena, to provide them an easier way to cross the river.

Built of rough, gray-stone blocks carved from the nearby mountains, the bridge's unusual design features a high arch, flanked on the east side by three lesser arches, and on the west by an arch added in the early 1900s to strengthen the ancient bridge against potential flooding and to accommodate a railroad line. There is a definite shift in the light gray hue of the stones used to extend the bridge over the rails and the older, darker stones of the twelfth-century bridge.

The bridge, with its footpath of medium-size pavers, was wide enough for the donkey, mule, and horse carts of Matilda's time. Today, it is a footbridge. It must make for a thrilling bicycle ride down the highest arch over the slippery stones. A crash on damp, weathered pavers would be painful indeed; there are no soft spots here.

The river is deep at this point, backed up by a low-slung power-generating dam perhaps five hundred yards downstream. There are many such dams on this river, all operated and maintained by Italy's power consortium, INEL.

The bridge has stood for nearly a millennium; it is beautiful, and, with its combination of high and low arches, it remains an engineering marvel, particularly when you consider it was constructed in the early 1100s by a society just emerging from Europe's Dark Ages.

Officially, Matilda's bridge is the Ponte della Maddalena. But people commonly refer to it as the Devil's Bridge, *ponte di diavolo*. As the local legend goes, the medieval engineers were stymied over how to build the highest arch, which bulges upward at least two times higher than the other arches in order to allow for unimpeded river traffic. The builders reputedly appealed to the devil for his help; he agreed, but with the demand that he get the soul of the first to cross the structure. They agreed, finished the bridge and its tall arch overnight, and then sent a pig across. (A Cadogan guide published in 2010 claims the villagers sent over a dog. Either way, the deception was well played.) The devil was so frustrated that he jumped into the fast-flowing deep waters of the Serchio and disappeared.

Leaving the bridge, we take a short stroll through Borgo a Mozzano on the river's west bank. We pass a building, now housing a doctor's office, which is identified as a former convent, likely one that would have offered Rome-bound pilgrims a place to spend the night. A short ways on, we spot a narrow, stone-paved walkway that cuts straight up the steep hillside to what appears to be an upper portion of Borgo a Mozzano. Filippo, who knows well the history of his beloved Tuscany and whose well-worn knowledge never led me astray, suggests that these walkways were actually the original medieval roads, which were replaced by what cars use today — modern paved streets that slowly wind their way upward in gentle curves and sharp switchbacks. Miraculously, these ancient "roads" were left in place.

We choose the medieval way, straight up. This pathway, no wider than four feet, is bounded on each side by a tightly fitted rock wall, holding back the edges of wide-open fields and clusters of olive trees. It is hard going but worth the journey.

We reach the top and step onto the pavement of a small neighborhood street leading us to a church that likely also was a featured stop for pilgrims. Clues inside — a high, painted ceiling and figures showing tendencies toward the Baroque — tell us it must have been heavily expanded, perhaps in the seventeenth or later centuries, from its smaller, earlier state. We never became certain of its name, but references inside and out indicated it was named after San Giovanni; the parish is Battista-Cerreto, or the Parish of Saint John the Baptist.

After admiring this little church high above the Devil's Bridge, we trace our path back down, passing on the steepest part a middle-aged woman lugging plastic bags from the shops below. Even she preferred the steep climb to the gentle, but far longer, twentieth-century paved roadway.

During World War II, Borgo a Mozzano also was, in this narrow valley, a key spot in Hitler's Gothic Line, which ran in a two-hundred-mile irregular line from coast to coast. Renamed the Green Line in early 1944, this roughly ten-mile-wide belt of fortifications — concrete tank barriers, minefields, and reinforced gun emplacements — began just north of Pietrasanta on the Ligurian Sea. It stretched through the mountains past the marble quarries of Massa and Carrara, to just north of Ravenna on the Adriatic. Remains of some concrete fortifications and tunnels constructed during 1943–44 still exist, including an anti-tank wall at Borgo a Mazzano.

These fortifications ultimately did little to stop the Allied troops from moving up the Serchio from Lucca in September 1944. Their relentless advance, and the fact that the Gothic line was breached farther east in the area around Bologna, pushed the retreating German defenders northward along the Serchio, where they destroyed the rail line and bridges as they went. The Devil's Bridge, too narrow and fragile for motorized vehicles, survived. The war ended seven months later.

■ ■ ■ ■

Moving beyond Borgo a Mazzano, we are presented with a choice: turn east into the foothills of the Apennines for a short distance to Bagni di Lucca, one of the earliest spa towns to attract members of the European upper crust in the eighteenth and nineteenth centuries, or continue north through the Serchio River Valley.

Legend tells us that the game of roulette was invented at Bagni di Lucca, and that it had one of the earliest casinos in Europe. Such visitors to the village included English poets Robert and Elizabeth Barrett Browning. They moved to Italy when they were married in 1846, first living in Pisa and then in Florence. They went to Bagni di Lucca three times between 1849 and 1857 and would stroll along a walkway, today named for them, on the bank of the Lima River — a walk I took on a later trip. But making the choice to go north or east is easy. To follow the loop we wanted and to end up back in Pietrasanta via Massa and Carrara by late afternoon, we must continue north along the Serchio.

During our drive through this verdant valley thick with chestnut trees, we see various clusters of hardwoods covered with giant vines, groves of olive trees, and the ruins of numerous castles on hillsides. Matilda or her ancestors built many of these structures, and some are long abandoned. Villages that seem to teeter high off the Apennine slopes flank some of these medieval fortifications.

The hardwood forests alternate with open spaces that in late April were flowering with broom plants, an ever-present shrub with bright yellow flowers that I have seen throughout Italy, particularly in the south, and in Sicily on the slopes of Mount Etna. The land also shows off large clusters of herbs that looked to me like rosemary and thyme. The river slides past all of this beauty, flowing from the north, where one might see the faint tips of mountains that hint of the Italian Alps farther along.

As we move toward Castelnuovo di Garfagnana and its junction with roads north, east, and west, I see the stunning medieval hill town of Barga. We decide to pass the turnoff and stay on course to Castelnuovo, but Barga from its lonely perch intrigued me. A month later with more time at my disposal, I went back to the Serchio Valley with the sole idea of visiting Barga. I was eager to wander through thousand-year-old streets with no idea of what I would find there. Aimless walks often turn into unexpected discoveries.

The walled town has three entrances. A short walk from Porta Reale, a sign on a placard next to the doorway of a stone palazzo announced its name, "Casa Cordati," the home of twentieth-century painter Bruno Cordati (1890–1979). I walked in, and sitting at a desk at the far end of the room was Giordano Martinelli, Cordati's grandson.

In impeccable English, Giordano explained that the house contains, on the second floor in seven rooms, his grandfather's paintings — all open to the public. On floors higher up, the structure holds an apartment and a few rooms available for rent.

The exhibition rooms are grouped by subject or time period: one holds his earliest work; another is dedicated to female themes, and still another shows paintings representing motherhood. Other rooms display paintings from time Cordati spent in Bulgaria, landscapes, and then self-portraits that hang on the wall across the room from paintings of his daughter Bruna, a frequent subject of his work.

I had never heard of this artist. Not well

known outside of Tuscany, he came from a poor family, was virtually self-educated, and as a child worked for a sign painter. In that role, he met the famed Tuscan poet Giovanni Pascoli, who had a home two miles to the north in what is known today as Castelvecchio Pascoli. (Tuscans have tended to add the names of famous literary figures to the towns or villages where they lived, even if they only stayed for a few years. Near Pietrasanta, for example, is the suburban village of Valdicastello Carducci, where a near contemporary of Pascoli, Giosuè Carducci, was born. Later Carducci's family moved to the southern Tuscan village of Castagneto for a few years. Now it is known as Castagneto Carducci.)

But it was in Pascoli's garden that the adolescent Cordati was commissioned to create a fresco of a stylized coat of arms on a wall. This marked the beginning of a close relationship between the elderly poet, who died in 1912, and the youthful aspiring artist. I couldn't find that coat of arms in my wanderings along the hillsides of Barga, but I understand it was poorly restored following an earthquake many years ago.

Casa Carducci in Barga was the painter's studio for many years prior to and during the early part of World War II. He rented rooms in the house, but had to escape with his family from Barga as the war surged northward along the Serchio River. Like so many other Tuscans, they became refugees, and traveled nine miles southeast to Bagni di Lucca. That historic resort town was spared much of the violent fighting along the Gothic Line.

Following the war, Cordati returned to his Barga studio, but he didn't purchase the building that now bears the family name until the end of the 1960s.

Cordati's original studio on the palazzo's ground floor is where I found, behind a large wooden desk and a computer, Cordati's grandson, Giordano. He is the keeper of everything Cordati: the paintings, furnishings, and the story. Giordano's mother, Bruna Cordati, wrote a brief history of her father called *The House of the Painter,* which Giordano sells as part of a small collection of other privately published works. Also included are treatises by Australian artist Peter Callas describing his visit to Casa Cordati, and by art historian Sandra Lischi, of the University of Pisa, who wrote an article entitled "The Rooms of the Painter."

Naturally, daughter Bruna's brief memoir is the most compelling of the three texts. She briefly outlines her father's life as a painter, from the end of World War I — he served in the Italian army for four years, winning a medal for valor along the Piave River — until his death in 1979.

Bruna writes that her father's early paintings do not leap out at you in vivid colors. They seem restrained but "the human figure prevails: he depicted a contemplative humanity, caught in moments of rest from their daily toil." I appreciated these human elements and the way they are supplemented with brief glimpses of landscape and rooftops. These images capture the town of Cordati's youth. This medieval look still remains, despite damage from World War II.

His daughter wrote that he was rarely satisfied. He would discard paintings and, while working on a new one, an assistant, armed with sandpaper, would scrape away paint to recycle the expensive canvas of Cordati's rejects.

Today, grandson Giordano has ambitions for Casa Cordati. He rents the single rooms and the apartment to tourists stopping in Barga for a few days, but he wants to turn the house into an artist retreat. "There is plenty of space for painters to work, and a garden," he explained. Then he shrugged. "It is a new idea; it will take time."

Barga, a tiny village of only eleven thousand souls, certainly is a destination for travelers looking for a place where they can enjoy Tuscan springs, summers, and autumns. Views of sienna-colored tiled rooftops and impressive mountain peaks are abundant, and there is a satisfying array of restaurants — I ate in three of them during two visits and was never disappointed.

Like elsewhere in the region, Barga boasts the traditional cathedral and its impressive square, and the old walled town is nearly devoid of automobiles; except for a very few with special permits, cars are corralled in lots flanking the town's three gates.

Long rows of medieval stone buildings flow along narrow streets that quickly widen into small piazzas filled with small fountains and restaurant tables. There often are narrow stone stairways to lead the walker higher up into the mountains. And near the top, views of the Serchio River valley are spectacular.

But for the April journey along the Serchio with Filippo, we bypassed the exit to Barga, where I would return later. Our only intention that day was to stop farther north at Castelnuovo di Garfagnana, one of the larger walled medieval towns on the east side of the Apuan range. Here, you can choose to cut east up and over the Apennines on small provincial roads that follow ancient tracks, into the Italian region of Emilia-Romagna and then on to Modena and eventually Bologna. Or you can continue north to Capanne di Sillano, a tiny village near the headwaters of the Serchio. Or you can turn west and work your way over the Alpi Apuane, into the high marble quarries of Massa, and down to the coast north of our starting point, Pietrasanta.

This last choice would cover three distinct areas of northwestern Tuscany: the coastal area around Pietrasanta that is known as Versilia, the deep mountains of Garfagnana and the Serchio River, and the area closer to the coast and north of Versilia known as Lunigiana. This third area sits high in Tuscany's northwest corner, dominated by the marble quarries of Carrara and Massa.

Castelnuovo is a busy town and is part of the mountainous area known as Garfagnana. It is an inviting stop on this Saturday morning. We enter the fortified walls of the castle that had its origins in the tenth and eleventh centuries. It was fully developed throughout the sixteenth century when it became a seat of power run by provincial administrators from Lucca. There are a lot of people wandering the medieval streets, which are jammed on both sides by interconnected original structures dating back more than five hundred years. A lot of people speak German and Dutch, likely the dominant nationalities of the tourists; the only English I hear exchanged is between Filippo and me.

We stop at a tiny shop that sells bread, various types of salami, and cheeses. The selection is vast. Because the people of this mountainous area are far from the sea, their cuisine focuses on meat and only a few species of river fish.

We sample various meats, including two types of ham: one salted and one without salt. I prefer the salted one. We also ask the friendly shop owner to make sandwiches *panini,* to have for an improvised picnic farther down the road. He recommends peppery slices from a round of salami cured locally, along with slices off a ham that had been aged for months by hanging in cool, windowless rooms. Added to this sandwich are thick chunks of a light pecorino cheese, local of course, with everything jammed between halves of rich, crunchy, and wonderfully fresh bread made in the uniquely Tuscan way, without salt. The shop also has a homemade version of short, stubby *bis-*

cotti; I buy a quarter kilo for later.

With our *panini con salame, prosciutto, al formaggio* wrapped tightly, we walk within the town's castle walls one more time before moving on, turning west on a route that would take us east to west through the Apuan range, down into Massa and Carrara, and along the coast to Pietrasanta.

About three miles west of Castelnuovo, Filippo points to a cluster of stone-gray buildings way down in the gorge below. We decide that's where we will eat our lunch. But there does not appear to be a road down to the tiny village. We stop in the parking area in front of an abandoned restaurant, nearby where the way down must be. To the side of the abandoned restaurant, however, is a level, tree-lined walkway that leads a few dozen yards to a well-kept cemetery. Next to this walkway is a narrow dirt track that drops suddenly down the side of the small gorge. Way below, we see the buildings Filippo had spotted from the road.

Before searching for the way down, we decide to eat our lunch in the shade of trees lining the cemetery walkway. Except for the occasional roar of a passing car or motorcycle, it is cool, pleasant, and quiet there. We pack what remains of our lunch back into the car and head back to the steep path to walk to the town below.

Filippo, who has traveled throughout the American West, said he thinks the village below must be a "ghost town," abandoned long ago but revisited by descendants who make use of the well-maintained cemetery. As we head down, the narrow trail opens up to a wider view, showing an abandoned church on the shore of what appears to be a man-made lake — its modern-day dam, perhaps 150 yards away, holding back the water of the stream known as Turrite Secca.

The village at the bottom of the trail has, ahead of us, what appear to be crumbling, deserted buildings. But buildings farther back, in the heart of this small cluster, seem to be occupied — laundry is hanging outside of high windows. These structures are packed onto the tip of a small peninsula that juts into the cool-looking, deep-blue water.

"This is Isola Santa," Filippo offers. I check my map. A village by that name is on it, perhaps three miles west of Castelnuovo. We then hear voices, speaking Dutch or German, as two elderly couples appear on a walkway just ahead of us. They obviously are reconnoitering the town just as we are. As I turn the corner at one building, I spot a well-maintained shop with a coffee bar and shelves of wine bottles. Off its outside

wall hangs a sign: CASA DEL PESCATORE —
ACCOGLIENZA — HOSPITALITY (House of
the Fisherman — Reception — Hospitality). It is a bed-and-breakfast. Inside the
shop are a few tables, and on the far side is
a tented structure where a man is sitting at
a table and tackling a plate of pasta. Guests
must park in the lot at the abandoned
restaurant above and then are driven down
in a vehicle capable of maneuvering the narrow, steep trail. (During a second visit, a
few months later, I discovered that guests
could no longer enter the village that way.
They must drive a few hundred feet farther
along the main road and park on the shoulder, taking a narrow stone stairway down
into the cluster of buildings.)

We go inside and are greeted by Antonella
Tardelli, one of the owners, who serves us
cold drinks and tells us that the village is
not a ghost town at all. There are forty
people who live here year-round, about ten
families, and they are slowly restoring the
village — the abandoned church, its gutted
interior once used to house sheep, has scaffolding filling the interior.

People started leaving in 1949, when a
dam was built across the stream and a lake
started backing up, threatening the buildings' stability. The restoration effort is

designed to bring life back to the tiny village that got its start nine centuries ago. It has been a stopping point for travelers since the thirteenth century — a place that offered "hospitality" then as it does now.

And, yes, many people stay in the B and B, about fifteen hundred a year, Antonella tells us. Most are Europeans, with the majority coming from the Netherlands. Even a few Americans have been guests there, she says. She provides meals, and guests can fish from the shore of the lake, or just enjoy the solitude. There are plenty of places for long walks, and, within the valley we are driving through, there are trailheads leading hikers to the tops of several Apuan peaks. This all sounds mystical, magical to me. I vow to return for a few days of Isola Santa solitude and try out Antonella's cooking.

For now, I'm content to just look around. The deconsecrated church, the one with the scaffolding, is Chiesa di San Jacobo. A sign indicates it was first mentioned in documents dated in AD 1260. Early in the seventeenth century, the villagers raised funds to expand the church, build a parsonage, and convert an ancient tower into a belfry.

■ ■ ■ ■

The afternoon is moving along. Filippo and I make the climb back to the car and head deep into the eastern flank of the Apuan range, putting the western slopes of the Apennines behind us. Within a mile or two, the landscape quickly shifts. The tree-and-vine-covered foothills disappear as the car begins to climb on an even narrower roadway. Coming into view are the jagged, treeless peaks that mark the beginning of western Tuscany's marble mountains — Michelangelo's mountains. We pass the sharply pointed pinnacle of Mount Sumbra (5,728 feet above sea level) and move deeper into the now-barren range whose uppermost peaks are turning marble white. There, near the little village of Arni, is a quarry with a French name, Henraux, that Filippo says was developed by the French during the time of Napoleon III's rule over northern Italy. It still operates today, but with Italian owners.

More small quarries appear, some operating, some not. We cut through long, dark tunnels that were bored directly through marble outcroppings. Some of the road surfaces through these tunnels, made up entirely of marble and no asphalt, are rough and broken — the result of decades of oxen-pulled carts, and eventually huge semi-trailers, hauling harvested marble blocks to ports on the coast below. In one long, narrow tunnel — we can see only a tiny speck of daylight at the other end — we are met by a roaring semi, heading uphill, its flatbed empty. It squeezes past us on the hummocky, rock-strewn surface. When we emerge into daylight, the whole series of valleys high above coastal Massa appears before us. The white of these shaved mountain peaks is dazzling.

This is the road to Massa and, beyond, to Carrara. We don't go into Massa but continue over a ridgeline that divides one town from the other, and end up on a road above Cararra, which is spread out below us. We continue a ways north and then turn onto a road heading uphill. On our right side, around a sharp curve, a major quarry appears. We stop, get out of the car, and wander toward a screened-in platform overlooking the huge operation. Heavy machinery is operating. There are fresh cuts exposing still untapped marble next to a weathered wall of decades-earlier work. A few hundred feet toward the mountain face is the opening to a large cave.

Quarries are referred to in Italian as *cave* (pronounced "cahvay" in the plural), but most do not tunnel deep into their mountains. Harvesting is usually done off marble faces out in the open. But this quarry is a man-made cavern, in the English sense of the word.

"They cut the marble from *inside* the mountain," Filippo says. "Tour groups can sign up to go there, but it is a private operation and has to be reserved in advance." Perhaps I will do that on another day. Today, the scope of what I can see on the outside of this operation is, in itself, huge. Large blocks of cut marble, some with graffiti indicating Communist sentiments, line the roadway here. I don't know if they are there as a permanent barrier or if they are waiting for the right buyer and will eventually be cut into slices for countertops, stairways, or facings for someone's villa high on a hillside, or made into a magnificent statue to be carved by a sculptor in Pietrasanta.

After we explore the quarry, we visit one or two of the smaller villages set along the steep hillsides. Eventually we drive through Carrara and into the coastal suburb of Avenza, which was the port from which Michelangelo shipped his marble to Pisa or to a port serving Rome.

Now, as was the case with Pisa and the Arno, Avenza's historic center, where Carrara's port once was located, is perhaps a mile or so from the beach of the Mar Ligure. This littoral has been filled in over the centuries by silt deposited by the Carrione, a stream with water made milky by the dust of marble quarries twelve miles away. This narrow waterway tumbles through the city and, at a point, flows parallel to the larger Magra River that enters the sea a few miles to the north. Driving along these rivers one can see scattered along their edges for miles and miles white-marble chunks brought down during spring floods from high in the mountains.

We can take the *autostrada* from here to Pietrasanta, perhaps twelve miles to the south, and avoid stoplights. But true to our plan, we stay on the blue highway. This *strada,* the Via Aurelia, is now lined with huge marble processing plants and storage yards stacked with giant blocks alongside racks of thinly sliced marble waiting to be turned into steps or countertops. It has its own history that began long before Michelangelo rode his horse up into these valleys. Nothing but the highway's name hints of Rome these days; the road is a thread that ties together Carrara, Massa, Forte dei

Marmi, and Pietrasanta in a remarkable world of marble harvesting launched long before the birth of Christ.

Six:
Sant'Anna di Stazzema

All that is solid melts into air, all that is holy is profaned, and man is at last compelled to face with sober senses his real conditions of life, and his relations with his kind.

— Karl Marx and Friedrich Engels,
The Communist Manifesto (1848)

Ares, the Greek god of war, is seemingly insatiable. He cannot stop harvesting lives. As one myth goes, the first army sprang up like rows of corn when the teeth of Ares's descendent, a dragon, were sown across a field.

Of course, myths, in the days before science, often grew out of humans' inability to explain how certain things happen: why we have seasons, what causes the sun to rise in the east day after day, why humans continue to kill fellow humans.

Such thoughts are on my mind. It is a

humid, cloudless June day, the sky appears almost white, and the sounds of unseen birds filter through abundant vegetation. At Pietrasanta station, I board a small provincial bus for its once-a-week, three-mile journey high up into the foothills to Sant'Anna di Stazzema, a place of serene beauty tagged forever by an unspeakable horror. With me are five elderly women, each carrying shopping bags overflowing with flowers. I surmise that they must make regular jaunts to the village to decorate the graves of family members and friends.

The road, not built until twenty years after the end of World War II, is full of sharp, blind twists. Before 1965, ancient *mulattiere,* or mule tracks, connected the village with the coastal area far below and its nearby clusters of houses and farms. Some of these dirt trails are widely known, while others take the form of secret paths that travel beneath the great canopy of trees, through narrow canyons, and from heavily forested hill to hill. Only those who grew up in those mountains know such paths.

The bus driver, at the sharpest curves, sounds a loud klaxon to alert oncoming traffic to our approach. The frequency of these horn bursts escalates the higher we go. His final stop, only twenty minutes out of Pietrasanta, is just short of Sant'Anna's small cluster of buildings, including a tiny church.

The large parking lot, for cars and the tour buses that bring thousands of visitors here throughout the year, is empty. Other than a few locals gathered around the doorway of the village's only business, a small bar next to the church, the five flower-bearing women and I are the village's first visitors of the day.

Sant'Anna is where director Spike Lee shot a few brief, hard-to-watch scenes for his movie *Miracle at St. Anna,* but the film is not why I am here. This, my first visit alone to the tiny village, is one of several trips I would eventually make there during five months in 2012. My plan is to spend a day, without distraction, exploring Sant'Anna, and then walk down one of the ancient *mulattiere* to the valley below.

It was in and around Sant'Anna where, on August 12, 1944, members of the German army massacred at least 560 villagers (or perhaps more) within three hours: elderly men and women, some younger men and women with children, teenagers, and infants. Most of the area's able-bodied men, tipped off the day before that the Germans were coming, had already escaped into the hills. They figured they were the ones the Germans hunted following a spate of attacks by Italians known as partisans — groups of men and women who fought the occupying Germans after Italy surrendered in September 1943.

"After all, what kind of threat are old people, mothers, children, to these Germans," one survivor said to me. In a time before anyone in these isolated villages had any inkling about what was going on elsewhere in Italy or the rest of Europe, to think these innocents would be attacked was incomprehensible to peasant farmers and sheepherders in an out-of-the-way place such as Sant'Anna.

The village sits on a heavily forested hillside with a stunning view of Pietrasanta and coastal Tuscany, just a few miles below. On a clear day, from a spot just above the village, an observer can see the sweep of the Ligurian coastline, from Pisa in the south to Portovenere in the north — a distance of fifty-three miles.

Before sunrise on what would be a hot August day, German soldiers arrived in the village. They were members of the Second Battalion of the Thirty-Fifth Regiment of the Sixteenth SS Grenadier Armored Division. It is widely believed that local Italian *fascisti,* still loyal to Mussolini and his Germany-backed breakaway government ensconced in Italy's far north, led the solders from four, perhaps five, directions through the thick forest along those narrow, hidden trails.

The soldiers were based in at least three locations, including Pietrasanta. Some were housed in the cloister where today Pietrasanta's library, or *biblioteca,* is located. In addition to the cloister, several hundred soldiers lived in houses they confiscated from Italian residents; top officers occupied luxurious villas in Pietrasanta and the surrounding area.

During the late night of August 11 and the early predawn hours of August 12, the troops had been transported in trucks to their four or five departure points. From the west one group left Valdicastello Carducci, a small enclave on the outskirts of Pietrasanta and located at the foot of the mountain, three miles downhill from Sant'Anna. They moved up a narrow, steep trail that starts at Valdicastello's northeastern end. This was the trail I would walk down twice during my time in western Tuscany.

From the northwest, a different group

traveled toward the remote village along another trail that starts at Capezzano Monte, a tiny cluster of houses, a few shops, and a church on a mountainous flank high above Pietrasanta. I took this trail to Sant'Anna once. Today, tourists sitting in Pietrasanta's Piazza del Duomo and looking uphill to the right of the castle can see and admire lovely Capezzano Monte.

From the north, the Italian Fascist–led Germans walked toward Sant'Anna from the village of Ruosina. Local historians speculate the Ruosina troopers may have split into two groups, with the second one leaving from nearby Gallena.

From the east, a squad left Farnocchia, whose residents four days earlier had been ordered to evacuate into the hills while Germans set fire to the village. Some of those residents, along with their parish priest, sought refuge in Sant'Anna, perhaps a two-hour walk away.

The soldiers were armed with .50 caliber machine guns, flame throwers, small arms, grenades, and other gear carried by local Tuscan men and boys forcibly conscripted from Valdicastello and Capezzano Monte. The soldiers targeted the village of Sant'Anna with its four hundred residents and its small clusters of houses. These clusters, separated by woods and small plots of land growing vegetables and fruit, are known as *borghi* or the even smaller *casolari*. There might be four or five families in a *borgo* and two or three families in a *casolare*. Sometimes the houses are joined together in a single large structure with each family having its own section. People would live on two or three floors, with cows and sheep housed at ground level and the families directly above.

These clusters of homes and tiny farms went by names such as Pero, Vaccareccia, Case, Moco, Coletti, Ai Franchi. All are less than a mile from Sant'Anna. One, Ai Franchi, is only fifteen hundred feet from Sant'Anna's center. A visitor standing in the square in front of Sant'Anna's church can see this *casolare* to the south, its four joined houses comfortably nestled on a hillside.

The soldiers swept through the tiny satellite clusters, either killing residents on the spot or herding the confused civilians, many in bedclothes and still rubbing sleep from their eyes, down into Sant'Anna proper.

There the elderly and the mothers; some fathers who, for a variety of reasons, had stayed when most of the other working-age men had left the day before; and the babies, toddlers, children, and teens, were packed together on the square in front of the church. There 136 of them died; the rest that made up the official tally of 560 were killed in or around their homes.

The stories about what happened that morning, told by a few survivors who were able to hide, are bone-chilling. During a subsequent visit to Sant'Anna in the summer of 2012, I met with seventy-eight-year-old Enrico Pieri, who as a ten-year-old witnessed the unimaginable — the deaths of members of three generations of his family and more than a dozen other people at his home in Ai Franchi. We talked with the help of Ilaria Violante and Cristina Zappelli, two Tuscan friends who acted as interpreters.

"*Questo é molto difficile* [this is very difficult]," Enrico said as we began the nearly four-hour conversation and tour.

About seven o'clock on the morning of August 12, 1944, a neighbor pounded on the doors of the four houses in Ai Franchi. The man alerted Enrico's family and members of a refugee family staying next door in Enrico's grandfather's house that the Germans were coming. Enrico's father, the refugee father, and the grandfather pondered whether to hide out in the hills, certain that the Germans were only after the men. But they decided to stay. Why? The day before, they had slaughtered a cow, whose carcass was hanging in a ground-floor room below the living quarters. Such a home-based slaughter of an animal was illegal at the time, Enrico explained, and they did not want the Germans to take the "crime" out on the women. So they stayed.

An hour after the neighbor pounded on the door, family members caught glimpses of soldiers coming down the hillside behind the complex. Enrico heard occasional shots and bursts of machine-gun fire in the distance. The two families quickly gathered inside the Pieri household. There were Enrico, his parents, his grandfather, and his two sisters. His mother, Irma Bartolucci, was four months pregnant. The other family, the Pierottis, included the parents, three sisters, an aunt, and at least one toddler son.

The two families sat around the table in the grandfather's kitchen, which the Pierottis also used as a communal bedroom. Without warning, a squad of German SS soldiers burst into the room, loudly ordering the families outside and forcing them down a narrow path in the direction of the church at Sant'Anna.

"We had walked — they were constantly pushing us, shouting *'Schnell! Schnell!'* — perhaps [three hundred feet] when, suddenly, they decided to take us back into the house. This all happened in maybe ten minutes."

The Germans crowded the Pieri and Pierotti families, along with other people collected from around the compound, back into the room the Pierottis had used as their bedroom and kitchen. Perhaps twenty people were crammed into the small space. The Pierotti father tried to speak to the Germans but immediately was shot in the head at close range. Then, the Germans "started firing their guns" at the group.

In the chaos, a fourteen-year-old Pierotti daughter, Maria Grazia, was able to crawl into a small walk-in cupboard under the stairs. From there, she motioned to Enrico to join her. This all happened in a few brief seconds, and the soldiers did not see them.

"She saved my life," Enrico said, dry-eyed after all these years but speaking in a voice breaking with emotion.

After a few moments, the firing stopped and the houses were set ablaze. Four or five families had been wiped out in a matter of seconds.

When the hiding children smelled smoke,

and it sounded as if the Germans had left, they crept out of the cupboard and into the smoke-filled room, which was red with slaughter. There, beneath a cluster of dead and dying, Maria Grazia found her thirteen-year-old sister Gabriella pinned beneath bodies and physically unwounded.

The girls' mother was still alive, barely, and was pleading to be taken outside, away from the smoke-filled room. With ten-year-old Enrico, they tried to move her but couldn't. Eventually, unable to breathe in the heavy smoke and emotionally devastated by the carnage of their loved ones, the three children made it outside. By then, all those left behind were dead.

Near the house, just a hundred feet away, were small terraces that were rich in carefully tended vegetables.

"We hid there among the bean plants for a few hours," Enrico said. At one point, they could hear mouth organ music being played by a nearby German soldier. They continued to muffle any sounds of their fear, their anguish, their emotions — all the while listening to the crashing sounds of roofs collapsing into the burning houses.

Finally the mouth organ music drifted away. The Germans, including those who had slaughtered the hundreds of other residents in the church square fifteen hundred feet from Ai Franchi, were long gone. Gabriella, Maria Grazia, and Enrico crept the hundred feet or so from the bean field back to the houses, hoping to find someone still alive. No one was. Three houses were destroyed, with just the outer walls still standing; strangely, the flames had already nearly died out in the house belonging to Enrico's family, leaving it fairly intact. The remnants of the fire were still generating large amounts of smoke.

Enrico could not bring himself to enter the room where the seventeen bodies were heaped in a ghastly tangle.

The three survivors, still fearing that Germans might be in the area, returned to the bean field and huddled together until early evening, when they decided to head for the tiny *borgo* Vallecava, near the top of a hill that today holds a forty-foot-high monument and the ossuary containing the bones of most of the victims. Near there, they encountered a group of people the Germans had missed. Surrounded by people they knew, the children finally let their emotions run free, crying and mourning for their families.

In the early evening, Enrico walked back

to Ai Franchi alone. He didn't enter the kitchen/bedroom, but hauled water from a spring more than fifteen hundred feet away, to make sure all the fire in his family's home was out.

Then he went to his grandfather's house. "I just grabbed something. [To this day] I don't remember what." Then he returned to Vallecava.

By this time, it was growing dark. The trio bedded down with other survivors in the nearby woods. At three o'clock in the morning, Enrico was awakened by his forty-year-old uncle — his father's brother, Duilio Pieri — who, when the Germans came, had been hiding in the mountains. He had rushed back to Ai Franchi to find his family dead and to witness the aftermath of the widespread slaughter in nearby Sant'Anna. A survivor had told Duilio about his nephew and where he was sleeping. The two, uncle and nephew, were all that remained of the immediate Pieri family.

Duilio led Enrico along the narrow trails down the mountain into Valdicastello, where members of their extended family took them in. Duilio returned a day or two later, burying the remains of his family and the Pierottis a few dozen feet from the house.

Following my first bus trip up the mountain, I walked into Sant'Anna's small bar, where a young lady sold me a bottle of water and answered my general questions about the village. I also asked her to show me the start of the footpath that leads from the village down to Valdicastello in the valley below, as one of my goals during this visit was to skip riding the bus back down the mountain. I wanted to walk the three miles to Valdicastello, down that steep, rocky trail — perhaps to confront for myself those Nazi/Fascist ghosts. From Valdicastello, it would be an easy walk of a mile or two back to my apartment in Pietrasanta.

But before I left, I visited the fully restored church, passing the holy water font badly chipped from machine-gun bullets, dropping a coin into a small box to pay for candles, and lighting one in memory of the hundreds of innocents who died just a few feet away. One of the women from the bus was placing flowers around the altar. We acknowledged each other with a quiet *"buon giorno."*

I then headed over to a wall of photographs — head-and-shoulder shots of infants to teens, complete with names, ages, and home villages. They were arranged in pairs and trios, or more, grouped together as siblings. One family, Tucci, lost eight children, ranging in age from three months to sixteen years. Most were from Sant'Anna, but I was surprised that some were from Pietrasanta. Others were from far-flung places in Tuscany and Liguria, such as Capezzano Pianore, Pontestazzemese, Piombino, La Spezia, and Castelmare di Stabbia.

Parents had sent their children to the mountains from their hometowns and villages, thinking they would be safer there. For example, La Spezia, a major seaport, was a scene of heavy bombing, and the Germans had taken over Pietrasanta. In some cases, the Germans ordered villagers to abandon their homes, while others had already left.

Pietrasanta and surrounding villages were within the cross-country sweep of the Gothic Line, Hitler's demarcation in Italy where he hoped the German army would stop Allied troops from entering the Po Valley. Many families within that zone closed up their houses and businesses and went elsewhere, becoming *sfollati,* or refugees.

The segment of the Gothic Line in western Tuscany, from the Serchio River to the

177

coast and between Pisa and Carrara, was declared *terra di nessuno,* or no-man's-land. And it is where some of the most brutal fighting in western Tuscany, between American troops and German soldiers, took place.

As I am taking all this in, looking through faded photographs into children's eyes, I felt a tug at my sleeve. The elderly woman began to tell me about the twenty-day-old infant.

"I am her aunt," she said, speaking in soft Italian. I asked her name. "Siria Pardini. Her mother was my sister." The sister was Bruna, age twenty-six when the Germans shot her.

The story spilled out of Siria. With my basic Italian, I caught only bits and pieces, but I didn't stop her. I got her full story weeks later when, on another bus ride up to Sant'Anna, I met her family, including her nephew, Claudio Lazzeri, whose excellent English helped me to fully understand the story.

During that first conversation in the church Siria's dry eyes bored directly into my eyes, which were doing their best to stay dry. She pointed to photos of two other Pardini children, her cousins, Orietta and Sara, ages fourteen and nine, killed along with their mothers, grandmothers and grandfathers, and more than five hundred others.

"I was nine years old," Siria said. Now age seventy-seven, she pays her respects by traveling up that mountain nearly every week, loaded up with bunches of flowers, to dutifully decorate the altar.

On that tragic day, with the men in her family hiding in nearby mountains, Siria, her sisters — Adele, five years old; Lilia, six or seven; Cesira, eighteen; Bruna, twenty-six — along with their mother, and Anna, Bruna's twenty-day-old baby, remained in their home in the tiny *borgo* of Coletti, a cluster of two or three buildings perhaps a ten-minute walk from the heart of Sant'Anna.

Twenty minutes before the Germans arrived, Siria had left to take food to some of the men hiding in the mountains. Her sisters, the baby, her mother, and her grandmother were there when soldiers came crashing through the doors. The Germans had gathered together other families living in or near the Coletti complex, and in all, thirty people were forced to line up against a wall of the Pardini house.

Here, Claudio expands on the story for me via a series of e-mails: His aunt Cesira stood against a door to the house, and when the shooting started, she pushed back, forcing it open. As she tumbled backward, with a bullet in her shoulder, she grabbed the hands of two of her sisters: Claudio's mother Adele and his aunt Lilia. Adele had been hit, with a grazing wound in the face, and Lilia took a bullet to the shoulder.

The shooting stopped a few moments later, with the three wounded sisters still hiding inside, behind the door. Through a gap, Cesira could see her wounded younger sister Maria, lying on top of their dead mother but still breathing. The Germans set fire to the structure and, as they were leaving, Cesira decided to take her sisters and run. On their way out, she grabbed Maria.

The Germans spotted them and began firing as the four youngsters, slowed down by their wounds, ran, a bullet hitting Cesira in the leg. But somehow they were able to keep going, disappearing into the woods while the rest of the victims lay piled against the wall of the burning building. The infant Anna, who became Sant'Anna's youngest victim, was later found in her dead mother's arms, critically wounded. The infant lingered on for a few weeks but died on September 4. Maria died from her wounds on September 20.

The brutality of the deaths of the families

and neighbors of Enrico and the Pardini sisters was just part of a three-hour, horror-filled stretch that culminated in what happened in front of Sant'Anna's tiny church.

The priest, Don Innocenzo Lazzeri, who had followed his Farnocchia parishioners to Sant'Anna the day before, had begged the soldiers not to harm the people, proclaiming they were innocent of any partisan activity. He offered his life in order to save theirs. After he was shot, the soldiers opened fire from two machine guns set up on tripods on each side of the church's front door.

This is the way Italian writer Manlio Cancogni vividly sums up the massacre: "The villagers were gathered in the small square in front of the church. . . . When the Nazis took aim against those bodies they were so close that the soldiers could see into their eyes. The villagers fell down without a chance to scream."

The Germans, he described, then piled pews from the church on top of the bodies and set them ablaze. In the Spike Lee film, soldiers pour gasoline onto the bodies, but there were no vehicles driven to the isolated, road-less village, making it doubtful large cans of gasoline were available. It is more likely that soldiers used flamethrowers, carried there by the conscripted Italians.

"At midday, all the houses in the village were burned down," Cancogni writes. Enrico, during our 2012 discussion, told me that the church remained standing, though the back of the church, which housed quarters for a priest, was badly damaged.

Cancogni also describes, in horrific detail that I will forego here, individual atrocities the troops committed on some of the people who missed the machine-gunning in the churchyard or the mass executions at their homes.

The Germans had finished their work in three hours with the help of machine guns, rifles, pistols, and flamethrowers. By noon, they were two and a half miles away, following the trails back to their four or five starting points and to the vehicles that would return them to Pietrasanta and other bases within Versilia.

Survivors say they know local *fascisti* were involved. Despite scarves covering their faces, the *fascisti* were heard speaking in local dialect. These collaborators were men who had grown up with these villagers, sat at their tables with them, herded sheep with them, played games with them as children.

The *fascisti*'s names were never officially revealed, but many locals knew who they were. Some disappeared when their cause was lost — they left before they could be tracked down at the end of the war — and never were seen again; others were sought out, a somber son of a survivor told me. Asked their fate, he merely shrugged, looking at me with a knowing smile, eyebrows raised. I got the message. Confusingly, I heard some descendants of Sant'Anna victims say that a few of the *fascisti* lived their lives out in the area and were never called to account for their roles in the tragedy.

When they reached Valdicastello, the fourteen men and boys the Germans had conscripted to carry their equipment through the hills were machine-gunned in a streambed that ran through the village. Villagers hiding in their Valdicastello homes reported hearing a couple of German soldiers playing mouth organ music, like ten-year-old Enrico heard while hidden next to his burning house at Sant'Anna.

The final killings of the day took place in Capezzano Monte. There, six Italian equipment carriers, like those in Valdicastello, were lined up against a wall and shot. The Germans simply did not need these load bearers anymore. Plus, they were witnesses to the brutal murders the Germans had committed that morning. Within a few weeks, those Germans would head a few miles north to defend against the eventual arrival of the advancing Americans. When the killing had started at Sant'Anna, American troops were stopped twenty-five miles away, at the south bank of the Arno River, near Pisa. They would not begin moving north, along the coast and in the central mountains, until late September.

Enrico, who now lives in Pietrasanta, stayed with relatives in Valdicastello until he was seventeen. He emigrated to Switzerland and became an ironworker in a foundry near Bern, returning to Valdicastello to marry a local woman. The couple returned to Switzerland, where their son was born, then moved back to Italy in 1983.

At the time of our conversation, Enrico was involved with a survivor organization. He tells his story over and over to groups of young people in the area's schools. He also carries the keys to the Museum of the Resistance in Sant'Anna. In the museum, visitors can learn about Italy's partisan movement from 1943 to 1945, its civil war between partisans and the Italian Fascists still loyal to Mussolini, as well as the massacres of thousands of Italian civilians throughout the region. Tuscany's largest massacre, the Sant'Anna massacre, involved only innocent civilians, not partisans.

Five weeks following the Sant'Anna massacre, the Waffen SS did battle with partisans in the area around Monte Sole. This battlefield, which included numerous small villages, is not located in Tuscany. It is in Emilia-Romagna to the east, near Bologna. Like Sant'Anna, the Germans carried out reprisals against civilians there. According to James Holland in *Italy's Sorrow: A Year of War, 1944–1945,* 556 civilians and 216 partisans were killed in various villages there. These deaths occurred during much of the month of September. Numbers vary. Other authors say it involved nearly two thousand civilians and partisans. Either way, Monte Sole was Western Europe's single worst massacre.

In one episode on that mountain, nearly two hundred civilians were packed into a small cemetery at the Emilia-Romagna village of Casaglia. There nearly all were machine-gunned; only a few, hidden by bodies that landed on top, survived to tell the story. Several months after my summer 2012 visits to Sant'Anna, I visited Casaglia on Monte Sole. Only broken foundations of the former town and church remain.

■ ■ ■ ■

Italian historian Paolo Pezzino points out that in Tuscany alone, the Germans conducted 210 separate episodes of their "war against civilians," killing an estimated 3,650 people. Of those killed, 75 percent were men, but only 41 percent of those episodes were *rappresaglia,* or reprisals, for partisan activity against German soldiers. The majority of the killing was done just because the Germans had the unbridled power to do it, to keep the people in line through terror.

There were perhaps one hundred survivors of the Sant'Anna tragedy, not including the men who had escaped into the hills the day before, Enrico told me. Of those men, the same number, one hundred, "returned to find that they were without their families."

Despite the horror he witnessed at a young, innocent age, Enrico's feelings about the SS soldiers and Germans in general surprised me. "There is no hate," he said. "When my son was ready for school, in Switzerland, I had a choice: a French school or a German school. I chose the German one. I am a European. Germany at that time was important to the rebuilding of Europe."

Whatever hate he ever felt, he has gotten over it.

The number of dead Sant'Anna civilians cited in reports is 560, but the exact number will never be known. A plaque at the monument high on the hill above the town lists all the known names. The remains of those villagers are gathered together within a crypt under the tower.

Enrico's family and the Pierottis had been hastily buried near the burned houses of Ai Franchi. When the ossuary was established late in the 1940s, the remains of the Pieris were moved there. The Pierottis, because they were refugees from Pietrasanta, were moved to the cemetery in that town, a few miles away.

Only a couple of the houses in Sant'Anna have been rebuilt. Enrico's family's home has not been restored, but all four homes in that one long structure have rebuilt roofs. Only one home, at the south end, was rebuilt, its light-yellow exterior standing in dramatic contrast to the stained exterior of the other three unoccupied homes. A family lives there today.

Perhaps fifteen year-round residents live in Sant'Anna proper, a woman clearing brush from below her home told me. The village now is the center of the National

Park of Peace, created in 2000 by government statute. Included in that legislation is the museum Enrico showed me. It is housed in what was once the village's school. There was no need for the school after the massacre; only a few children had survived. In addition to exhibits, it holds a center for multimedia presentations and conferences.

Outside the museum, a handful of statues represents various parts of the Sant'Anna story, plus an ironic stone-sculpted "Ode to Kesselring," referring to the German general Albert Kesselring. It was he who oversaw military operations and strategy in Italy. It drips with sarcasm:

You will get it
kamerad Kesselring
the monument you demand of us Italians
but it's our turn to decide
the stone it will be built with.
Not with the charred stones
of the defenseless villages racked by your
    slaughter
not with the ground of the cemeteries
where our young comrades
rest in serenity
not with the untouched snow of the
    mountains
which for two winters defied you

not with the spring of these valleys
which saw you run away.
But just with the silence of the tortured
harder than any stone
just with the rock of this pact
sworn amongst free men
who of their free will gathered
for dignity and not for hatred
determined to redeem
the shame and the terror of the world.
If you wish to return on these roads,
you will find us in our places
dead and alive with the same commitment
a people serried around the monument
that is called
now and forever
RESISTANCE

On August 12, 2012, the sixty-eighth anniversary of this tragic day, Siria Pardini,
the woman I had met two months earlier in
the church, offered to show her childhood
home at the *casolare,* or farmhouse complex, known as Coletti. A healthy, strong
walker in her late seventies, she easily
outpaced my wife, Connie Disney, and me
along a narrow dirt road that begins below
the museum at Sant'Anna and continues
through the rough undergrowth of beeches,
chestnut trees, and oaks.

The buildings, partially restored after the Germans set fire to them, are still owned and occasionally occupied by the family. Siria has the key and lets us inside to see the small family spaces. Outside the rebuilt door her sister had forced open during the shooting sixty-eight years earlier is a small overgrown courtyard. A marker on the wall there tells of the moment some thirty people died against that yellowish, plastered structure.

What was particularly memorable for me was meeting Siria's surviving sisters — the ones who had been wounded as they escaped — and Adele's son Claudio, who was visiting on the anniversary day from his home in England.

The Pardini sisters and Enrico Pieri do not want this story to die, to be forgotten. But nearly seventy years later, it almost has, everywhere but in this remote corner of western Tuscany.

Sant'Anna is not listed on my official map of Tuscany, not even on the more detailed, spiral-bound Italian Travel Club map; to my surprise, it is not even mentioned in several major guidebooks. Several histories of the war in Italy do not mention Sant'Anna or Monte Sole.

Spike Lee's movie *Miracle at St. Anna*

(which misspells the village's name in the title), deals with the massacre almost in passing. It is used as a plot device to explain why a small boy befriended by four American soldiers was alone in the world and miles away from Sant'Anna.

During one of my visits to the village, I spent about an hour sitting on the low wall of stone that runs along one side of the church. A young mother was sitting about fifty feet away, watching two youngsters kick a soccer ball around the grassy area in front of the church. Earlier, I had watched the smaller one struggle with his small red bike, learning how to ride without training wheels. His eyes were alight with joy and his smile wide as he successfully traveled a few feet at a time. His unbridled happiness took me away from my growing sense of sadness.

Later on, while still sitting on that low wall, something else helped lift some of the emotional load. A group of about thirty men and women, most dressed in light blue golf-type shirts proclaiming *I Vous de la Valgranda,* walked into the square, heading for the church. This, I learned later, was a choir from mountainous northern Italy. The men also were wearing alpine-style hats with long feathers protruding, typical of the type worn in the far north.

The group entered in silence and, after a few moments, I heard a united choir's voice pour forth from the church's wide-open front doors, singing to no living audience. Life stood wonderfully still. The little boys stopped kicking their soccer ball; the young mother's gaze shifted to the church. It seemed as if the birds high up in the tall, stately plane trees were silent.

The hymn lasted perhaps two minutes. Then, one by one or in clusters of two or three, the visitors quietly filed out of the church. Some stopped at the bar for their morning espresso, others began the long trudge up the stone steps leading to the memorial at the top of the hill, perhaps a half mile away. Still others went past the "Ode to Kesselring" stone, pausing, with grim smiles, to read it before entering the museum.

After they all cleared out, I got up and headed toward the edge of the bar and started down the stone pathway that led down the steep canyon and into Valdicastello. The day was incredibly hot. The moisture-laden air seemed to quiver in front of me as I slipped my way down the steepest part of the trail and through the thick clusters of chestnut trees, giant ferns, and Mediterranean pines. I crossed over a series of stone bridges and past a couple of abandoned, decaying structures destroyed in the massacre and never reoccupied, my shoes wet from dew as I trudged along the barely perceptible, little-used trail.

Knowing that a group of Germans had used this trail to climb into Sant'Anna and then desert the shattered, dying village, I wanted to be alone to confront their ghosts and the ghosts of the Italian Fascists who led them along it. I got my wish.

It took about ninety minutes to walk down to Valdicastello, including a brief stop to sit in absolute solitude and eat my lunch. Weeks later, with Filippo Tofani, my friend from Pietrasanta, I walked the mostly uphill trail from Capezzano Monte to Sant'Anna, past the deserted *casolare* of Moco with its three or four burned-out, abandoned houses, forest vines obscuring them and trees pushing up through the crumbled floors.

For good measure during this second walk, after a brief stay in Sant'Anna, we continued downhill toward Valdicastello. Filippo told me he had made the trip as a high school student, uphill, with his history class. Filippo knows the story well — lessons taught by a wise teacher who did not want the tragedy at Sant'Anna to fade from the consciences of his Tuscan students.

Seven:
The War

What the horrors of war are, no one can imagine. They are not wounds and blood and fever, spotted and low, or dysentery, chronic and acute, cold and heat and famine. They are intoxication, drunken brutality, demoralization and disorder on the part of the inferior . . . jealousies, meanness, indifference, selfish brutality on the part of the superior.

— Florence Nightingale,
letter to her family from the Crimea (1855)

The human animal, while magnificently able to do wondrous things for fellow creatures, also is capable of doing horrible, unforgivable things. Members of our species have slaughtered tens, even hundreds of millions of their kind since the earliest of times.

A visiting friend once commented that what the Germans did at Sant'Anna made them less human. I disagreed, suggesting such behavior is a human-animal trait, though it never rises in many of us.

To me, the greater mystery is how a group of men who knew they were losing a world war that likely would be over within a short time — it did end barely nine months later — could wreak such havoc on innocent people. Didn't they know that ultimately they would have to live with the horror of what they had done?

Could it be that they were so well disciplined that they would unquestionably follow such orders? ("We are here *zur Ausführung einer Befehl* — for the execution of an order!"). Had they been so thoroughly desensitized by the brutality and terror of war that life had such little meaning? Perhaps these soldiers, indoctrinated with a belief in Aryan superiority, considered such people as somehow subhuman.

For understanding this way of thinking, a friend recommended *Hitler's Army* by Omer Bartov. Many of the soldiers present at Sant'Anna and other northern Italian massacres had first served on the Russian Front. Bartov writes that such soldiers, who had served in the heady days of the unstoppable Blitzkrieg, suddenly were faced in Russia with the reality that the German army was not invincible. The army, he wrote,

> accepted Hitler's view that this was an all-or-nothing struggle for survival, a "war of ideologies" which demanded total spiritual commitment, and thus tried to compensate for the loss of its technological superiority by intensifying the troops' political indoctrination. This in turn opened the way for an ever-greater brutalization of the soldiers.

This mode of thought, exacerbated by their experiences on the Russian front, made it easy for the German soldiers to use terror against innocent men, women, and children. German military leadership saw it as a way to maintain discipline by giving its soldiers emotional release from the stress of combat.

Nearly all of the German soldiers — as well as Eastern European conscripts and some Italian Fascists wearing German uniforms — who were present at Sant'Anna have passed on, either in subsequent battles or from old age. Only two high-ranking officers, one an Austrian, were charged specifically with civilian killings committed during the German occupation of Italy.

The British, during a 1947 military tribunal in Padua, tried Maj. Gen. Max Simon, head of the Sixteenth SS-Panzergrenadier (mechanized infantry) Division that participated in the events at Sant'Anna, found him guilty, and sentenced him to death. He claimed he did not know anything about what happened there. As the war faded in the memories of European leaders eager to make Germany a full partner in a new Europe, Simon was pardoned and released in 1954. He died in Germany seven years later at age sixty-two.

In 1951 Maj. Walter Reder, an Austrian, was acquitted of what happened in Sant'Anna — prosecutors could not prove he was there. As commander of a reconnaissance battalion in Simon's division, Reder maintained that during the August 12 massacre, he was in an area along the coast, somewhere between Pietrasanta and Marina di Carrara.

Writer Paolo Pezzino, who offers the most detailed accounting written in English about the event, agrees that Reder and his regiment of young Alsatian men likely were not there. Later evidence showed another regiment of the SS division was in Sant'Anna.

However, Reder was found guilty in an Italian court in Bologna of slaughters elsewhere. As devastating as the event at Sant'Anna was, with at least 560 killed, the biggest massacre in Italy took place over several days in September 1944, in villages around Monte Sole in the Emilia-Romagna region that adjoins Tuscany on the east. There, as we have seen, an estimated nearly 800 partisans and innocent civilians were killed, and whole villages and farms burned to the ground.

Like Simon, Reder was sentenced to death for Monte Sole, but that punishment was commuted to life imprisonment. He served time in the Italian military jail in Gaeta, Italy, a small coastal town north of Naples.

Many in the German-speaking world, who believed that such actions by victors and vanquished alike have been part of warfare since ancient times, were critical of Reder's sentence. They asserted he was simply a scapegoat for various massacres. Remarkably, some even asserted that the Monte Sole massacre, which followed the August Sant'Anna event and lasted through most of September 1944, never took place.

In the mid-1960s, Reder appealed to the citizens of Marzabotto, a major village on Monte Sole, expressing regret for his role in that series of reprisals and asking them to support his bid for a pardon. Understandably, they refused. Then, in 1985, as memories faded and the number of survivors dwindled, his appeals worked. He was pardoned and, six years later, died in Austria at age seventy-six. According to some reports, he publicly proclaimed, while safely ensconced in his native Austria, that, despite what he said in his two appeals, he really had no remorse for his role in these horrors.

The man who bore ultimate responsibility for incitement to kill Italian civilians, German Field Marshal Albert Kesselring, was tried, convicted, and sentenced to death in 1947. His sentence was commuted to life in prison, but he was released in 1952 on grounds of ill health and died in 1960 at age seventy-four.

For decades, it appeared that no one would ever have to answer for the slaughter at Sant'Anna. Then, in 1995, a government employee found a long-forgotten storage cabinet with its cupboard doors turned toward a wall in a room of the Palazzo Cesi-Gaddi in Rome. In it the employee found an archive of nearly seven hundred files detailing war crimes committed against Italian civilians during Nazi occupation.

It appears that Italian government officials had long before decided to bury these records deep in a dusty archive. They needed the new West Germany as a bulwark against the rising threat of the Soviet Union and wanted to spare the country any embarrassment over Nazi war crimes that occurred fifty years earlier. I suppose we must be grateful that whoever originally handled the documents had saved them, perhaps with the hope that someday the reports might be revealed.

Those documents from what has become known as the *armadio della vergogna,* or "closet of shame," revealed the names of several men who participated in the events in Sant'Anna. Modern Germany typically does not extradite its citizens for trials in other countries. So in 2005, ten of those men were tried in absentia in Italy. They were found guilty on June 22 at trial in La Spezia, a coastal port just a few dozen miles north-west of Sant'Anna, and given life sentences. The punishments were never enforced. Those alive today remain free in Germany.

Prosecutors in Stuttgart, Germany, however, began their own inquiries during that 2005 trial. They launched a nearly decade-long investigation into the roles of seventeen former SS soldiers who were part of the unit that participated in the Sant'Anna massacre. On October 1, 2012, the Associated Press reported that prosecutors were shutting down their investigation. The report got scant attention outside of Europe, but in Tuscany it was overwhelming news.

Essentially, no charges would be brought against the eight men out of the original seventeen who were still alive. The evidence, prosecutors said, was "not sufficient." They may have been part of the unit that carried out the slaughter but, prosecutors averred, there was nothing in the record that pointed to what they, as individuals and low-ranking soldiers, may have done.

Again, there appears to be no justice for the still-living Sant'Anna survivors, now in their late seventies and eighties, or their families. An e-mail from a young friend in Pietrasanta, who alerted me to the German prosecutors' decision, was full of anger. Once again, she said, justice was being denied.

One of the survivors I had interviewed, Enrico Pieri, echoed my friend's feelings. He told a reporter from the Florence edition of *La Repubblica* dated October 1: "I cannot believe that they have decided that such a thing is not possible. It is an offense to all 560 victims and among them innocent women and children; we cannot accept such a verdict." Survivor Cesira Pardini told the same newspaper: "It is not right. All this is a decision that has no logic."

Michele Silicani, the mayor of Stazzema, which includes Sant'Anna within its political boundaries, termed the decision one of "scandalous judgment" that has undone years of judicial cooperation between Italians and Germans to bring justice to survivors and their families. "Now this work is demolished," the mayor said in the *Repubblica* article.

A German prosecutor quoted in the Florence newspaper said the prosecution "has done everything possible to clarify the responsibilities [of soldiers involved in the massacre]. Even here we feel the weight of our responsibility."

Then, in April 2013, the German media reported that authorities *might* reopen the investigation into those former Nazi soldiers and their roles in Sant'Anna. The news came out "following a study by German-Italian historian Carlo Gentile, who has unearthed some weaknesses in the work that was carried out by German prosecutors," according to an April 12 report in the Italian news agency ANSA. But this effort was for naught. The following month, the attorney general of Stuttgart rejected reopening the investigation.

There have been times when German officials attempted to rectify the Nazi history of atrocities that took place in the peninsula. In April 2002, then–German President Johannes Rau (1999–2004) went to the Monte Sole town of Marzabotto and formally apologized for the massacre along the mountain's flanks, much like when he apologized, in February 2000, to the Israeli Parliament for the Holocaust. "I bow to the dead," he told the Italians in 2004. Still, no German leader has ever apologized for Sant'Anna. There would be so many survivors and descendants in too many places, not only in Italy but throughout German-occupied Europe, that deserve such apologies.

In *Italy's Sorrow: A Year of War, 1944–1945*, James Holland puts the Italian campaign in a chilling perspective — one that underscores the brutality of war no matter who becomes the victor or the vanquished:

It was unquestionably true that more Italians were being killed by Allied bombing, shellfire, and strafing than were being slaughtered by the Germans; but impersonal deaths as a result of inaccurate fire or mistaken identity can never be viewed in the same light as lining people up against a wall and shooting them in cold blood.

During my time in Pietrasanta, through the spring and summer of 2012, I worried about how I was going to get back to Sant'Anna on Sunday, August 12, for the survivors' annual commemoration of the tragic events of 1944. The bus usually runs between Pietrasanta and Sant'Anna only on Saturdays, and I knew cars would be unable to drive there because there wasn't enough room for parking for an event of that magnitude. There was no mention at tourist offices or in event brochures of special buses or any other means to transport participants there.

I considered hiking uphill from Valdicastello, along the narrow mule track the Germans had used sixty-eight years earlier. My wife was visiting, and I wasn't sure she would agree with that plan. But then a friend at the place where I ate lunch every day told me a man named Enrico had come by looking for me. We called Enrico Pieri, the survivor I had interviewed two months earlier, and he said that a special bus would leave Pietrasanta at seven thirty on Sunday morning, the twelfth. That bus is where Siria Pardini and I reconnected.

I was particularly interested in this commemoration because, for the first time in anyone's memory, it would be marked by a speech by a high-ranking German: Martin Schulz, president of the European Parliament. Survivors and descendants alike were curious about what he had to say.

Schulz's speech was launched from the steps of the monument high atop the hill overlooking Sant'Anna and the Ligurian coast. There were at least two thousand Italians present from all over Tuscany. The day was overwhelmingly hot and there was no shade or water offered on this Tuscan hilltop. Some of the elderly survivors sat in wheelchairs, while others, like Enrico, stood stoically throughout. I glanced at Enrico frequently. His expression never changed; his straight-ahead look was of someone facing sixty-eight-year-old memories. Young people, lined along the crest of the hilltop, held long poles hung with the colorful flags of their various villages and towns. It was a lively, congested scene, but no one complained.

Schulz was greeted warmly, and his talk was powerful. As an EU official, Schulz could not speak for Germany and therefore had no apology to offer. But he spoke, through an interpreter, from his heart as a German. I have made minor changes to clarify errors in the translation to English. He said, in part:

Early 1944 Sant'Anna di Stazzema was a pleasant place, a village where the children were happily playing in the yards . . . and roaming through the narrow streets. A place where girls went to draw water at the fountain of the village and the boys were grazing their flocks on the surrounding hills. [It was] a poor community that welcomed in her womb refugees with whom she shared her meager food. Yes, Sant'Anna di Stazzema was a peaceful village.

Until August 12, 1944: On that day the war showed its most brutal [side]. This paradise became hell. On that day, sixty-eight years ago, was perpetrated a massacre of unprecedented brutality. . . .

Now I introduce myself to you as a German, deeply shocked by the inhumanity of the massacre perpetrated here in the name of my people. Today I want to commemorate the victims of the massacre. Never forget. Keep the memories alive. Ensure that never again in Europe inhuman ideologies and criminal regimes return to show their hideous grin.

This is the task that we must pass on to the generations that will follow us. It is your merit, the merit of the survivors of Sant'Anna di Stazzema, [that has] kept alive the memory of the victims of the massacre. The monument-ossuary to the martyrs of Sant'Anna di Stazzema became thus a symbol of forgiveness.

Schulz's talk was periodically broken by spontaneous applause. It is a new Europe, after all. Former enemies are now allies, tied together by a common currency and with individual interests dependent on the stability of one another. Men like Enrico — who had told me he no longer hates Germans, because together all are Europeans — and women like Siria and her sisters, despite being survivors of an unspeakable horror, recognize these ties.

I saw Enrico afterward and asked him about the speech. He could only shrug his shoulders and give a sad smile, his eyes alone betraying immense grief. The memories continue.

No matter how well I reside in the present, I can't help but look through the lens of history when I travel throughout Italy, Sicily, and Sardinia. Walking among the stones of Selinunte, that ancient Greek ruin in southwestern Sicily, I imagined the magnificence of the city that once stood here nearly three thousand years ago. I saw myself in the midst of great crowds of toga-clad citizens gathered in the various temples that dot the huge space, now one of the world's largest archaeological sites with nothing but tumbled stone and a couple of partially reconstructed temples.

In Rome, I once spent ten days in the Forum with a detailed guidebook, trying to divine the jumble of monuments, arches, and piles of stone, and place them in the context of a thousand years of Roman history.

It is not surprising then that, as I wander narrow streets of western Tuscany villages that are buried deep in the foothills of imposing mountains, walk along Ligurian and Tyrrhenian beaches, or drive the narrow, twisty roads, I imagine the impact of history's most vicious war ever to be fought here.

My discovery of Sant'Anna and learning about its past triggered those thoughts. The need to understand it all grew even stronger when, during my second visit to the village, I stood on the platform of the crypt that contains the bones of hundreds of its victims. Looking far out over a beautiful section of Tuscany's wild west, I could take in the sweep of coastline, from Pisa in the south to Portovenere in the north. It was along that coast where for centuries pilgrims walked, with heads bowed, toward Rome; where armies marched and fought; where soldiers and innocents died in violence and in sickness; and now where people live in peace and with magnificent views of a historic sea in well-scrubbed small towns and in the midst of vineyards and olive groves.

Sant'Anna survivor Enrico Pieri told me during one of my visits that as a child, in the days before the events of August 12, 1944, he and friends would stand on this same hillside, look toward Pisa and wonder, with the innocence of youth soon to be lost forever, when the Americans would come and drive out the Germans.

That took a long time — too long for the innocents living here.

On July 19, 1944, three weeks before the Sant'Anna massacre, the American Army, fresh from the June 5 liberation of Rome, had taken over the heavily bombed port city of Livorno, just a few dozen miles southwest of Pisa, and listed on most military maps of the time by the British name "Leghorn." From there, it was a quick push to the south bank of the Arno River, where American forces arrived on July 23.

This movement northward along the Italian peninsula had begun nearly a year earlier, when the Allies, on September 9, 1943, conducted a major amphibious assault at Salerno, south of Naples. That fabled city had fallen to the Allies on October 1, and the British Eighth Army began its move northward along the peninsula's east coast. The U.S. Fifth Army moved along the west coast. The two armies also protected each other's flanks in joint operations up the middle, along the slopes and through the valleys of the Apennine Mountains.

Rome had fallen to the Allies on June 5, 1944, following landings south of the Eternal City, along twelve miles of beaches north and south of Anzio and Nettuno. The impact of that effort, known as the Battle for Rome, was staggering. It cost nearly fifty-five thousand Allied casualties and twenty thousand German casualties.

Once past Rome and into Tuscany and its port city of Livorno, the Fifth Army sat for nearly a month. American and English commanders debated whether to abandon the

Italian campaign and move Fifth Army troops to France for the push into Germany from the west. That would leave the British Eighth Army and other Allied units in place to stop any German effort to head south again and retake Livorno.

Ultimately, however, the plan for a major shift to France was abandoned. A few units that had participated mightily in the Italian campaigns, from Sicily to Rome, were moved to Marseilles, but most of the Fifth Army remained along the Arno. In fact, as the Italian conflict progressed, at times some Allied units were shifted from France back into northern Italy, where the war would continue along various fronts and across the Gothic Line into the Po Valley between Milan and Venice.

Allied Army divisions representing various nationalities eventually headed north up Italy's center and east coast, liberating such major targets as Florence and, after a long winter, eventually Bologna. By spring 1945, they broke into the Po Valley. At that point, the war in the European theater was almost over. The German Army in northern Italy surrendered on May 2. Germany itself surrendered in Reims, France, on May 7, with the official end of the war early the next day. Ten days earlier Benito Mussolini and his mistress Clara Petacci had been executed by Italian partisans as the couple attempted to escape into Switzerland, with the hope of flying to Franco's Spain.

As fascinating as the battle through north-central and eastern Italy was, my interest centered on the war in western Tuscany along two routes: the coast between Pisa and Massa-Carrara and through the Serchio River Valley north of Lucca. It was in these places where the U.S. Fifth Army's Ninety-Second Division, eventually joined by the 442nd Infantry Regiment, fought the Germans. These Americans often were joined in the two sectors by British and Brazilian units.

The Ninety-Second Division, a creature of a long-segregated military, was made up of African-Americans who were typically commanded by white officers. Many of these commanders were openly racist and distrusted troops who they felt were incapable of performing under the stress of battle. The 442nd Regiment was made up of Japanese-American soldiers who volunteered despite their families being imprisoned in U.S. internment camps. These soldiers were known as Nisei, a Japanese-language term usually meaning those in the second generation of immigrants to a new country.

The black soldiers, who adopted the sobriquet of "Buffalo Soldiers" after post–Civil War black cavalry units, were trained as combat troops at various U.S. Army posts beginning in the spring of 1944. The first units of the Ninety-Second had arrived in Italy by mid-August, and by August 25 were facing the enemy across the Arno at Pontedera — today a center for manufacturing scooters — on the road between Pisa and San Miniato.

While the Buffalo Soldiers were lined up along the Arno, the Japanese-Americans were in France. The Nisei, who had landed at Salerno and Anzio-Nettuno, would not be transferred back to Italy to fight along the coast of Tuscany until April 1, 1945.

By August 31, units of Buffalo Soldiers had crossed the Arno without opposition and were en route to the hills on the northern edge of the Plain of Pisa and to Lucca. The Americans captured Pisa on September 2 and Lucca three days later. Lucca would serve as a launching point for infantry and armor to advance northward, up the Serchio River Valley and along the coast. An entry in a volume of the history of the U.S. Army in the Mediterranean theater, *Cassino to the Alps,* describes the scene well: "They moved easily as if on autumn maneuvers through countryside dotted with ocher-colored villages set amid ripening grainfields, orchards, and vineyards." This lull would not last. Germans were digging in along both routes — the western Tuscany coast and high in the Serchio River Valley. Plus, one of Italy's harshest winters in modern times was ahead.

By early September along the coast, the Germans had withdrawn fourteen miles north of the Arno to beyond Viareggio and Pietrasanta. This retreat gave Buffalo Soldiers a free ride over those fourteen miles. The Serchio Valley Campaign for the Americans was proving to be more difficult.

Various American units were barely poking their noses into the south end of the thirty-five-mile-long Serchio River Valley when they came against major Gothic Line fortifications. The official army history describes these obstacles are "almost invisible to the approaching troops. Many had been constructed of reinforced concrete or blasted into the rock. Roofed with three feet of logs and earth, each position could accommodate five men." Today, some of those Gothic Line fortifications can still be seen, especially in the area around Borgo a Mozzano where the narrow twelfth-century Devil's Bridge sits in architectural majesty. In addition, the Germans had laid mines and strung rows of barbed wire twenty-five feet deep and a foot high.

This valley was strategically important to the Germans. It protected their right flank as they retreated north along the coast. Stopping the Americans in the valley would prevent the Allies from making an end run north and then swinging northwest to a point above Massa-Carrara to cut off the Germans' coastal retreat. And the Americans wanted to control the valley to stop enemy troops being pushed north from counterattacking and heading south down the valley — an action that would put at risk Allied-held Lucca, Pisa, and the vital port of Livorno.

During the American push up the coastal route, Pietrasanta had shifted from being a German headquarters to an American command post. U.S. units based there controlled a six-mile-wide swath of land from the sea to the slopes of the Apuan Mountains.

One battalion of the Ninety-Second was arrayed west to east along a line north of Pietrasanta, another was in reserve south of Viareggio, and a third was being moved to the coast from the Serchio River Valley. The goal of these three battalions was to eventually occupy Massa and the Italian navy port of La Spezia. It would take until spring 1945 to get there, and it would require the help of other U.S. Army units to finish the job.

The Germans were well dug in, and their heavy artillery based around the Gulf of La Spezia just north of the Liguria-Tuscany line was hammering the American-controlled coastal area. This situation, as winter was setting in, was a distinct change from the relatively easy time the Americans had moving up the coast from the Arno to Viareggio and Pietrasanta.

The fighting in both the coastal and Serchio River areas was brutal. By mid-October, serious numbers of battle casualties were not being replaced with fresh troops. In the face of undermanned units, the U.S. Fifth and British Eighth armies halted; individual unit drives farther east toward Bologna and Rimini were halted as well.

During lulls in German artillery pounding their coastal positions, a few Buffalo Soldier patrols occasionally would venture out for a couple of miles north of Forte dei Marmi. When the Germans and Americans traded artillery fire, casualties on both sides would mount.

By early winter, fourteen thousand Allied combat casualties had been reported since the beginning of the Gothic Line assault. In just one six-day stretch, across the entire Mediterranean-to-Adriatic front, four infantry divisions were hit with nearly twenty-five hundred casualties.

During the fall campaign, Britain's Prime Minister Winston Churchill begged the Americans for more divisions to be diverted to Italy. But George Marshall, army chief of staff based in Washington, D.C., refused. According to army historians, Marshall and some of his commanders believed that "north-western Europe and not the Mediterranean was the main theater of operations, and a 'diversion of divisions to Italy would withhold needed fresh troops from southern France while committing those forces to the high attrition of an indecisive winter campaign in Italy.' "

Marshall was right. Given the approaching winter, most strategists felt the time had passed when the Allies could drive the enemy across the now-snow-blocked Italian Alps and back into Germany. Essentially, the military brass felt Allied forces already committed to the Italian campaign were keeping tens of thousands of German soldiers tied up in northern Italy and unable to reinforce the struggling German army in France, Belgium, and Holland.

In the midst of all this strategizing, the Buffalo Soldiers on the coast, supplemented by black soldiers who had been transferred from the Serchio River Valley, were ordered to move closer to Massa, six miles northeast of Forte dei Marmi. They were only able to reach the outskirts of Querceta, a tiny village just outside of Pietrasanta and five miles south of heavily fortified Massa.

Buffalo Soldiers were also dispatched to take control of two low mountains, Monte Cauala and Monte Castiglione. After twice winning, and then twice losing, the battle for Monte Cauala, the regiment at last gained the summit. Then, because of approaching winter weather, continued thrusts were called off near the end of October.

The Americans mostly sat, in places like Pietrasanta and Forte dei Marmi on the coast and in a handful of towns and villages along the Serchio River. The Allies controlled a fifty-mile west–east front, from Forte dei Marmi to the Reno River Valley on the east slope of the Apennines.

Soldiers from a Brazilian expeditionary force and units of the Buffalo Soldiers'

Ninety-Second Division were brought to the front and were trained to participate in small operations. The Brazilians moved northward up the Serchio against light resistance, capturing the town of Barga, home of the painter Bruno Cordati, by the end of October.

On the day after Christmas, the Germans began to attack outposts along the Serchio River. They retook Barga. The Brazilians had left, and the Buffalo Soldiers who took over there were forced to retreat. In response, two Allied brigades from India quickly won back Barga, along with villages around the medieval city.

By year's end, the status quo reached in October and November was painfully re-established. The brief thrust southward in the valley had given German troops a couple of short-lived, morale-boosting victories, forcing the Americans to move units that had been part of the drive to Bologna on the east side of the Apennines to bolster forces in the Serchio sector.

From the American point of view, it was even more damaging because it forced the Allies to wait until better weather to attack German positions in and around Bologna. Everything between the Ligurian and Adriatic Seas was ice- and snowbound. Leadership determined that the next major offensive would not occur until April 1.

Along the coast, a few patrols made progress through January and into February. They pushed a short distance beyond the Cinquale Canal, north of Forte dei Marmi, to feel out enemy defenses and reconnoiter routes for soldiers to follow in the spring. Other patrols moved a few miles northward along the main coastal highway, the ancient Via Aurelia, into the lower slopes of the Strettoia Hills, going as far as Seravezza and the terraced olive groves on the slopes of Mount Cauala.

More units left Camaiore, that small inland town a few miles southeast of Pietrasanta, and pushed northward through the rugged mountains of the Apuan range that separated the coast from the Serchio River Valley. These soldiers may have made their way through what was left of Sant'Anna after the massacre six months earlier.

Except for in the relatively flat but narrow coastal area, winter weather was making it more difficult to supply these soldiers inland in pockets that could be reached only along the treacherous mountain roads. Soon it became impossible to drive trucks on these roads. The Allies recruited locals and their mules to get that job done, in return offering food and supplies for their families.

In the hiatus that followed, leadership began a major reorganization of the Buffalo Soldiers' Ninety-Second Division. The best men from various units were brought together into one new regiment. The Japanese-American 442nd Regimental Combat team, one of the war's most highly decorated units, returned from France and was added to the Ninety-Second at the beginning of April. An infantry regiment, the 473rd, of former anti-aircraft artillerymen from all-white units, joined them. These artillerymen became ground soldiers simply because German aviation was virtually nonexistent in the dying days of the war, and anti-aircraft guns were no longer needed.

Meanwhile, the Germans' position was deteriorating. They could no longer count on Mussolini's Fascist Italian units to support them. Kesselring, the German commander in Italy, had to shift four divisions to other fronts outside of Italy. Railroads had been heavily bombed, from above by Allied planes and from the ground by Italian partisans, making it difficult to bring more German troops, motor fuel, and vehicles into the Italian theater in a timely manner. This German difficulty, plus the introduction of new American units into the fray, would lead to a shift in American progress along the coastal area.

Renewed action began on April 5. British destroyers offshore near the Gulf of La Spezia bombarded German gun emplacements that had harassed the dug-in Americans. The newly constituted regiment of Buffalo Soldiers moved back across the Strettoia Hills while the Japanese-American units now assigned to the Ninety-Second went higher up on the steep flanks of the Apuan Mountains. The artillerymen-turned-infantrymen were briefly sent into the Serchio Valley, but they quickly returned to the coast to strengthen various units that were making good progress.

The Nisei proved magnificent. They pushed around Massa and, by April 11, occupied the marble quarries above Carrara. But by April 19, the reconstituted Ninety-Second was forced to dig in seven miles north of Carrara. Despite being stopped, the division's actions forced the Germans to move soldiers from the east around Modena to the Ligurian flank, giving Allied troops in northern Italy's center easier access to the Po Valley.

Over the next several days, the Ninety-

Second's units kept pushing northward. A few battered German artillery outposts on a small peninsula just south of La Spezia pounded American-held Massa and Carrara until April 19 and 20, when the Germans destroyed those outpost guns during a hurried withdrawal north.

From April 20 onward, the operation was to become a pursuit for the Allies, driving the Germans across the Po Valley. There, soldiers of the Third Reich would be halted on the south bank of the Po. Bridges had been destroyed by American aviators intent on denying the Germans an easy route home, and, ironically, by German gunners intent on not allowing Allied troops across.

The day is, again, hot and incredibly humid, perhaps in the nineties, maybe pushing one hundred. I am riding the bicycle the owner of my apartment generously loaned me and am heading to Marina di Pietrasanta along the Ligurian Sea, some two miles west. My once freshly laundered T-shirt is now soaked as I pedal along village streets that nearly seventy years ago were full of German military trucks and tanks.

Just across from my apartment, I pass a group of modern buildings that had replaced the rubble left in 1944, after American gunners shattered the relative calm of this tiny town. On this small block only a seventeenth- or eighteenth-century bell tower was still standing in the midst of rebuilt modernity. It was then a convent's elementary school and remains so today.

With the village at my back, I turn off the Via Aurelia and onto Viale Apua, a straight shot to the tiny beach community. Just a few hundred yards past that turn and a row of modern apartment houses, my wandering eye catches a glimpse of a statue set a few dozen feet off the Viale Apua's bike path. I make a right turn, then another, and find myself in front of a bronze statue of what appears to be an American soldier wearing a World War II helmet and battle uniform. He is a short, slight figure and clearly Japanese. His right hand holds a rifle at his side. His left rests on his hip. I read the inscription, entirely in Italian. The statue was placed here on April 25, 2000, by the *commune* of Pietrasanta in honor of Sadeo Munemori, a Nisei and member of America's famed 442nd Regiment. His unit had been assigned on April 1, 1945, to the Ninety-Second Division during the American drive northward along the Tuscan coast.

He had been in Italy nearly a year earlier on the beaches at Anzio-Nettuno and eventually in the northward assault toward Rome. He had then been transferred with the regiment to southern France before it returned to the Italian coast on April 1 and immediately pitched into battle alongside the Buffalo Soldiers of the Ninety-Second, those British units, and that group of white American anti-aircraft gunners who overnight had became infantrymen. Individual units of the Ninety-Second, however, were still segregated.

On April 5, in a firefight north of Pietrasanta and near the marble-processing town of Seravezza just a few miles away, Sadeo and a few of his comrades were hunkered down in a shell crater firing against German machine-gun nests. Sadeo was a private first class. He took charge when his squad leader was wounded. He advanced on the gun emplacements and knocked them out with grenades. As he scrambled back to the crater, a German grenade bounced off his helmet and landed in front of two of his companions. In a split-second move, he pounced on it, covering the blast's impact with his young, slight body, sacrificing his life to save his men. He was twenty-three years old. While Sadeo was fighting and dying in Italy, his family was imprisoned at Manzanar, California — one of ten camps where more than 110,000 Japanese-Americans were incarcerated during World War II.

Sadeo was the first Nisei to be awarded the Medal of Honor, and the only one of his regiment to receive that award in the war's immediate aftermath. It was awarded through the efforts of a U.S. senator, Elbert D. Thomas, a Utah Mormon who in the early years of the twentieth century served as a missionary in Japan. He was fluent in the language and had close ties to the Japanese-American community, which requested his help in getting the medal for Sadeo's family.

Shift ahead two and a half weeks to April 21. Nisei units had advanced just over the northern Tuscany border into southern Liguria. First Lieutenant Daniel Inouye was leading his men along a ridge above the village of San Terenzo in the province of La Spezia. This is a small village near Lerici, the home in the 1820s of ill-fated English poet Percy Shelley.

Incoming fire pinned down Inouye's men. When the young lieutenant stood up to attack, he was shot in the stomach, the bullet exiting through his back. He kept moving forward and took out one machine-gun emplacement with grenades. Then he rallied his men and led an assault on a second emplacement, which he also destroyed before collapsing from blood loss. He crawled within ten yards of a third machine-gun nest and raised his right arm to throw a grenade. An enemy rifle-fired grenade hit him in the elbow and exploded, leaving his arm hanging by shreds of skin. He reached around with his left hand, forced his grenade out of his clutched right hand and threw it, taking out that emplacement. He has no memory of what happened next — he blacked out — but witnesses said he stood up and continued one-handed firing at other German positions. He was shot in the leg.

In a video interview with the National World War II Museum on February 11, 2008, Inouye said, "Someone was looking out for me" when he threw that grenade with his left hand. "It was accurate, went right in the pocket." Several hours later, after being declared "unsavable" by Army field surgeons and a chaplain convincing them to operate anyway, he received seventeen blood transfusions. Buffalo Soldiers had donated the blood. "African-American blood saved my life," he proudly told his interviewer.

Declared "enemy aliens" after the Pearl

Harbor attack, Inouye along with other Japanese-American men had volunteered for the Army. He was seventeen. When he lost his arm, he was twenty. His family, living in Hawaii under military jurisdiction, had not been interned. Inouye survived the war and became a distinguished U.S. senator from Hawaii, dying on December 17, 2012, at age eighty-eight.

It took more than fifty years for the military to recognize that twenty Nisei and seven Buffalo Soldiers deserved the Medal of Honor. Both groups, it was discovered, had been judged by different criteria than white soldiers, marines, and sailors when the military was handing out its highest honor at the end of the war. The seven black American recipients, only one of whom was still living, were presented their medals in 1997. The twenty Nisei, including Inouye, received their Medals of Honor three years later, in 2000.

The only Buffalo Soldier still living in 1997 when President Clinton presented the medals was another first lieutenant, Vernon Baker. He was twenty-five on April 5, 1945, when he led his heavy-weapons platoon in an attack on Castle Aghinolfi, a German observation post high on a hill just south of

Massa in the Strettoia Hills overlooking the narrow plain of the Versilia coastline. With the castle in clear view, Baker destroyed German bunkers, two observation posts, a machine-gun nest, and telephone lines used by the Germans. As other soldiers were retrieving wounded men during the attack, he stood up to draw enemy fire away from their evacuation. The next night, he led a battalion through mine fields and heavy fire in another attack.

Baker survived the war and elected to remain in the army in Europe. But the military, away from the heat of battle and falling back into its rigid prewar practices of having only a college-educated officer corps, took away his commission in 1947. The reason: the former railroad porter lacked a college degree.

But that loss of rank didn't last long. He was recommissioned during the Korean Conflict, ultimately leaving the military in 1968 — still as a first lieutenant. In 2008, two years before he died, he was given an honorary doctorate and an award for moral courage and service to humankind from Wofford College in Spartanburg, South Carolina.

The story of these three men and their

comrades in their separate units — and the role of the Ninety-Second Division and 442nd Regiment in liberating this part of Tuscany — came to my attention only because I happened to look up — in the haze of sweat and labored breathing, as I pumped the pedals of my landlady's bicycle for a day at the beach — and glimpse the statue of Sadeo Munemori.

These soldiers had been untrusted by their white field officers who resented orders to command them in battle. As the war progressed and the casualties mounted, the United States needed more and more men to send overseas. They rose to the occasion, helping to push the Germans up the ancient peninsula and out of cities, towns, and villages. En route, they earned the everlasting gratitude of Italians who had never seen a black or Japanese man before and who had none of the prejudice of so many white Americans. Italians saw them only as heroic liberators. And here, in this narrow corridor along the Ligurian Sea, these American soldiers found the love and acceptance that they could not get from their country.

In 1948, President Harry Truman signed the order desegregating the military.

EIGHT:
FAR FROM THE
MADDING CROWD

Pisa became a refuge, an exotic setting,
in Shelley's words, a "Paradise of Exiles."
In truth, it is hard to point to anything
particularly paradisiacal about Pisa in the
early nineteenth century. . . . Pisa was *not*
a principal stop on the Grand Tour, something that Byron and Teresa Gamba appreciated because it enabled them to
avoid, in the poet's words, the "gossip-
loving" English who flocked to Florence,
Venice, and Rome.
— Nicholas Shrady, *Tilt: A Skewed History
of the Tower of Pisa* (2003)

Visiting Pisa never appealed to me. Visions
of stopping there just to see the Leaning
Tower in the midst of massive numbers of
tourists and overwhelmed by T-shirt and
trinket stands lined up for a quarter mile
along the square, the Campo dei Miracoli,
or Field of Miracles, kept me, over the

years, on trains passing through while en route to somewhere else.

But while living for several months just twenty minutes north by train, I reconsidered, and ended up going to the city three times. I saw the crowd-infested area around the Leaning Tower — begun in the twelfth century and completed in the thirteenth. I knew that preservation officials had determined that if the tower was left untended, it surely would come crashing down on their watch. Such a disaster happened to the bell tower in St. Mark's Square in Venice in the early twentieth century, and Pisans did not want their best tourist draw to suffer the same fate. While Venice's bell tower was rebuilt much sturdier than its twelfth-century predecessor, it is unlikely a fall-proof "leaning" tower could be raised from rubble to match its predecessor in such heroic fashion. Therefore officials spent the $30 million or so necessary to fix it, working through much of the 1990s to correct about sixteen inches of tilt. It was reopened in 2001. Work to clean and restore its stone was finished in 2010.

For my inaugural journey, I boarded a southbound train at Pietrasanta, and twenty minutes later disembarked with several hundred young people who commute daily to their classes at the University of Pisa. These students swarmed across the tracks at Pisa's San Rossore station, not bothering with the pedestrian tunnel underneath them. Over the loudspeaker, a recorded female voice was reminding them it is illegal to cross the tracks and please, stand behind the yellow line. The students paid no heed; I am sure this is a daily ritual for them, and it would be futile indeed for authorities to stand there to stop the hordes that get off each train early in the morning. I brazenly joined the masses, jumped the tracks, and headed for the Field of Miracles.

It was early, about eight o'clock on a weekday morning, and the square, thankfully, was nearly empty. Vendors' stalls along one long side were shuttered, except for one or two stands selling *caffè e cornetti.* The Duomo, the Baptistery, and the cemetery/cloister from the Middle Ages, Campo Santo, or sacred ground, were closed and not opening until ten o'clock. A small line outside the tall bronze doors of the great church was beginning to form anyway. I could see visitors high atop the Leaning Tower, so that site obviously opened early. A man standing guard near the tower's entrance was telling a group of German tourists they first must go to the nearby ticket office and purchase tickets that stipulate the time they could enter.

I went to the office and discovered the earliest entry time they were selling tickets for was somewhere past eleven o'clock. Waiting three hours to climb to the top of this fabled tower — something a million people do each year — was not for me. I moved along, out of the square and into the old city.

Pisa, of course, is significantly larger than Pietrasanta. And it has more visitors in a week than Pietrasanta likely has in a year or two, despite Pietrasanta's appeal to sunbathers and *appassionati di arte.* So it is harder in Pisa to keep streets swept clean of visitors' trash; an army of sanitary trucks, a bar waiter told me, are constantly on the move. Despite enduring a long, hot summer and unrelenting waves of tourists, the locals I met were delightfully friendly. Such massive tourism creates jobs, and with Italy facing a 12.5 percent unemployment rate, putting up with hundreds of thousands of visitors has become a way of life here. "What would I do," the waiter said, "if it wasn't for that tower?"

I walked east out of the square along Via Pietro Maffi, past a long row of tourist restaurants, their menus posted in four languages and all offering "tourist specials." I bumped into Largo del Parlascio, the site of some Roman ruins thought to be the baths of the Roman emperor Nero, and one of the original city gates, Porta Lucca. Again, except for the traffic traveling around the Largo and through the city gate, I was the only person poking through the ruins.

Nearby was a church, and while I have been in perhaps a few hundred churches in Europe throughout my travels, I never tire of going into them — for the serenity they offer away from the clamor of city life and because they sometimes hold surprises. This church and convent of San Torpè, named for an early Christian martyr and with an altar hewn out of Carrara marble, offered up a few surprises: an exquisite stained-glass window showing, in separate parallel panels, what appears to be a crusader knight and a high church official; a marvelous plaster statue of St. Anne, Mary's mother, holding a crucifix; and a nice Madonna and child. I've often wondered how many Madonna and child portraits one can absorb in a lifetime, but this one, by Francesco Vanni and executed in the late sixteenth or early seventeenth century, was worth the walk.

During this brief Pisan sojourn, increasingly in need of solitude from the rising clamor outside, I stumbled onto two other pleasant churches, the Chiesa Universitaria di San Frediano and the Church of San Martino. San Frediano is named for a sixth-century Irish pilgrim and hermit who became a bishop of Lucca. Canonized just a few years after his death, he was credited with several miracles, including changing the course of the Serchio River, which in his time flowed a lot closer to Lucca than it does today. It was reported that he used a simple rake to trace out, in the dusty ground, a new course for the river. When he was finished, the river immediately shifted to that new course, moving farther away from the city and keeping the Lucchesi safe from spring floods.

The Church of San Martino sits a short distance from the left bank of the Arno River on Via San Frediano. In an inside niche hangs a marvelous, discreetly lighted thirteenth-century crucifix, in wood, tempura, and gold, by Enrico di Tedice. Based on comparison with earlier photographs, it appears today to be heavily restored. The church's interior, with its many art-filled niches, is worth seeing when the visitor to the city gets tired of the Leaning Tower and fighting the masses.

I take a secular view of churches. They are

magnificent works of art. Craftsmen and artists devoted to their creations — and, most likely for most, devoted to their faith, whatever it was for them — made things for eternity, and we all are the better for it.

I hedge my nonsectarian bets by lighting candles for troubled family members and friends or those who have passed on. But perhaps the biggest reason I enjoy entering churches is that as an amateur historian (a university BS degree in history does not make one a professional) I want to see the artifacts of actual historical events that are kept in them — not just objects that symbolize something and came through history as an act of faith.

I found this kind of history a few moments later when I came upon the Church of Santo Stefano dei Cavalieri, located in central Pisa, a short walk from the Campo dei Miracoli. It is a lynchpin of the great Piazza dei Cavalieri.

The Medici grand duke of Tuscany had commissioned the structure in 1561 when he founded the order of Knights of Santo Stefano. To belong, a man had to be at least eighteen and have the financial means to support himself. Most important, members could not be descended from heretics. They fought in battles all over the Mediterranean against Ottoman Turks. The order's last battle was in 1719; the order evolved into an institute for educating noble Tuscans. Images of eight-pointed Maltese crosses are peppered throughout the square, on the church exterior, the façades of the surrounding buildings, as ornaments on light poles. That same cross dominates the flag of Pisa, which flutters on the tops of buildings everywhere.

The Tuscan painter, architect, and art historian Giorgio Vasari not only designed this magnificent church, which took three hundred years to finish (it was completed in 1859), but he also did the baptismal font and painted a picture of a beheaded St. Stephen being placed in his tomb. Such work is worth seeing; my favorite was a portion of the wood-carved ceiling that depicts a painted scene from the Battle of Lepanto — that pivotal sixteenth-century battle between Turks and Christians.

The Battle of Lepanto was fought on October 7, 1571, on the Adriatic, at a spot between southern Italy and the Gulf of Corinth in western Greece. The pope, Venice, and Spain had formed a Holy League to confront the Turks and stop, once and for all, their western expansion ambitions. The League succeeded but at great cost in terms of both ships and human lives. The outcome clearly divided the Mediterranean into two zones controlled by great powers: the Turks in the east — except the island of Cyprus that had been reclaimed by Venice — and Spain in the west.

Historian Fernand Braudel described the battle as "the most spectacular military event in the Mediterranean during the entire sixteenth century." In addition to the carved wooden ceiling, the captured Turkish banners taken from the ships of the vanquished ironically hang in the Church of Santo Stefano dei Cavalieri. As Abulafia said it: these banners are "daily proclaiming the faith of Islam amid the incense of Catholic ritual." These nearly 451-year-old banners, sheathed in giant glass frames, dominate the interior walls.

Now, as someone who was raised Protestant but no longer claims to practice a specific organized faith, I have my reasons for haunting churches in Europe. I have friends who have fallen away from their Catholic faith and cannot bear to enter a church, no matter how grand or famous it is or what glorious pieces of art or historical relics it may contain. One friend is furious that some churches charge entrance fees, either to enter the sanctuary itself or to go into special rooms. He would never go into the Duomo in Pisa, for example, which charges for admittance. I wouldn't go because of the wait and the overwhelming crowd. In Palermo, Sicily, I paid a few euros to see the tombs of the early Norman rulers in the cathedral there. My friend refused to go. I enjoyed touching the tomb of one of Sicily's greatest rulers and Europe's Holy Roman Emperor, Ferdinand II. I like experiencing how their memories linger on through their monuments.

Still another friend is outraged that early Catholics built churches on top of Greek and Roman temples. In Rome, this is true of just about any older church; pagan foundations and some tombs can be found beneath nearly all of them. A magnificent cathedral in Syracuse in Sicily is built on a Greek temple site, complete with the original stone pillars embedded in the walls. Of course, the Greeks there built their temples on top of the temples of their predecessors, and so it goes. The Catholic Church was just following a historic pattern.

My goal in Pisa — to make discoveries that are off the usual tourist grid — is being met. I found surprises, like the St. Anne statue and the wooden cross. The only church I visited that was mentioned in the one Tuscan guidebook on my shelf is San Stefano. Still, this book, one of the more prominent ones, misses the origin of the pennants hanging there, saying that they had been taken from Muslim pirates off the coast of North Africa. The guidebook had no idea that the banners were from the battle of Lepanto in the Adriatic Sea — one of history's most decisive moments.

I sometimes am tipped off to something via guidebooks. And I admit to buying the most recent editions before a major trip. But I refuse to depend on them. I have found that one often copies from another, repeating factual errors. I prefer to let the expectation of discovery be my guide.

So, I wandered back to the Field of Miracles and its leaning tower. What I saw astounded me. The square that had been nearly empty at eight o'clock, now, at noon, was packed elbow-to-elbow with thousands of people. Several were taking turns standing on the low, rounded marble posts around the perimeter of the grassy area so they could be photographed holding their hands up like they were propping up the tower. One would jump down and another would climb up and strike the same pose.

People, jostling for position, were actually lined up at certain key posts waiting for their chance for the quintessential tourist photograph.

That quarter mile of tiny shops stretched along the campo's stone wall was alive with hawkers selling trinkets of every description: T-shirts, soccer shirts, plastic ashtrays, plastic blow-ups of animals, key chains, and, of course, models of the Leaning Tower, ranging from keychain size to three feet tall.

It took me perhaps twenty minutes to push through this madding crowd and make my way through the gate and to the train station.

I've talked to friends in Pietrasanta about my mixed feelings about Pisa: the overwhelming, overheated crowds; the trash that must be a nightmare for crews who have to clean it up, day after day, week after week; the tourist menus that, from restaurant to restaurant, seem to offer the same uninspired fare.

This, for me, is also countered by the importance that Pisa holds in the history of Tuscany. Despite being inland today by three or four miles, Pisa was the historic mouth of the Arno River — long ago silted in where entire communities and superhighways now sit — and thus was a major maritime power throughout the Middle Ages. Also, its long-buried port was where coastal ships, loaded with marble harvested from the mountains above Carrara to the north, would transfer their cargoes to riverboats headed upstream to Florence where artists such as Michelangelo would unlock the magnificent figures those stones contained.

Today, the city of Pisa has no port. Along the modern coastline, about three miles from where it was located in Michelangelo's day, the rich tie up their yachts and sailboats at the modern Marina di Pisa, and holiday-goers fan out across stunning beaches.

My goal is to get away from all this, rent a car, and head inland on a journey of discovery. The Plain of Pisa is vast and a major agricultural area. Perhaps fifteen miles from the sea, it bumps up against a line of coastal hills that in turn, farther east, roll up into the Apennine Mountains, the spine of Italy.

Friends in Pietrasanta encouraged me to see some of these surrounding areas. I took them up on it, a four-day road trip that would take me no farther away from Pisa's *centro* than perhaps twenty miles. The result was surprising — and rewarding.

■ ■ ■ ■

A few miles north of Pisa, the exit from SS1 points toward San Giuliano Terme. This small town, which has several satellite villages in its sphere of influence, marks the beginning of the foothills that slowly rise toward the east and that then boil up into higher hills as they build toward the peaks of Monte Pisano.

I have a reservation for B and B Zia in La Gabella, a tiny hamlet less than a mile from my first village of interest, Calci. This B and B acts as my base for three days as I roam throughout the Plain of Pisa, from the hilltops to the vast plain of wheat, olive groves with centuries-old trees, sunflower fields, and vineyards.

Calci has an interesting church and friendly people sitting in the shade of a terrace outside one of the village's few bars. But what makes it unique for me is its layout. The town snakes its way along a stream, the Zambra, which flows under numerous small bridges and between houses and, a local told me, is full of fish — *trota fario,* or brown trout — along with eels and other edible creatures. In the heat of July, however, the Zambra is nearly dry.

This village was built in a narrow valley that has been dubbed in this modern era of tourism as the Val Graziosa, or Pretty Valley. It is a name like the one given to my Idaho childhood home: Treasure Valley, or another valley farther to the southeast, Magic Valley.

At Val Graziosa's eastern end, Calci is perhaps only three or four streets wide at its base and tapers to a fine point as it climbs uphill and, without transition, blends into the much smaller village of Castelmaggiore.

The village's main west–east road up Monte Serra, one of the hills of the Monti Pisani, is narrow, barely wide enough for two cars going in opposite directions to pass one another. At different points, a driver often has to pause and wait for another vehicle coming from the opposite direction to go by.

The few soft peaks of this Monti Pisani range are like foothills of the Alpi Apuane, similar to the Strettoia Hills between Seravezza and Massa east of Pietrasanta. These Pisan hills sit between the provinces of Lucca and Pisa and are bordered by the Serchio River in the west, the plain of Lucca in the north, the Lake of Bientina in the east, and the Arno River in the south. The view from Monte Serra's summit takes in the Apuan range to the northwest and, on the clear, cloudless day I experienced, all the way to islands of the Tuscan Archipelago.

My roadway, from Calci and into Castelmaggiore, twists and turns, traveling back and forth over bridges only one lane wide. Villagers walking along what little there is to the roadside simply trust you will not run them down, but still wait for enough room to slip by and hope another car isn't coming downhill at the same time.

There are several escape points from this road that take you to even smaller villages on hillsides framing Calci. I impulsively took one of these exits, driving through ancient olive groves and land sprinkled with a few small vineyards. Vineyards do not dominate here; they start to take over much farther to the south of Pisa, beyond the Plain of Pisa and more in the area of Bolgheri and even farther south, to the east of Grosseto.

Here, olive groves take up much of the real estate. I got the sense I was driving through a rolling sea of the greenish-silver trees. Periodically, I would see new swaths of young trees, planted perhaps in the last decade — or maybe last week. It is hard to tell because olive trees grow so slowly. Folks planting young trees do so for future generations — not for their own. It can take one hundred years for an olive tree to begin major production. And while the above-ground portion of the tree can survive for perhaps five or six hundred years, the root system can last a few thousand, sending up new shoots when the upper tree dies or is burned out or otherwise is trashed by the chariots or mechanized tanks of marauding armies.

With each journey in Italy, I learn more and more about olive trees. In a trip along the Calabria coast several years ago, I met an old man, as gnarled as the olive-wood limb he had slung over his shoulder and sun-beaten into indecipherable age, who told me he had trees in his grove that were planted at the time of Christ. A few years later in Sardinia I stayed in a bed-and-breakfast situated on land that once housed a sixteenth-century monastery. Five-hundred-year-old olive trees surrounded the B and B, built in the 1980s.

Ahead of me, as I make my way up a narrow road that is more hard dirt than asphalt, a church steeple pops out of nowhere. Then a few buildings swing into view as well, looking as old as the mountains that cradle the stone structures. A battered sign tells me that this is the tiny *borgo* of Tre Colli. With perhaps a dozen residents living in a handful of buildings constructed in the Middle Ages, this spot is not even recorded on my maps or listed in any English guidebook. But even Calci, a bustling town of possibly sixty-five hundred people, does not merit more than a sentence in the guidebook I sometimes use, which is one of the most detailed available for English-speaking visitors to Tuscany.

A plaque on the church in Tre Colli speculates the structure might date as far back as the eleventh century, but that the first mention in any known documents was two hundred years later. And the early notation wasn't a positive one; it says the Pisans, in AD 1288, destroyed it. The reason why is not given. I suspect it was to bring the villages of the Plain of Pisa under the city's influence.

This village is definitely not a tourist destination. There are no signs indicating places to stay and no restaurants. But driving through it, stopping for an hour to sit in a roadside olive grove with a view of the ancient church higher on the hill, and eating my lunch while leaning against a gnarled tree that was three or four hundred years old, was well worth the diversion.

There was plenty going on to keep my attention in that tiny space around my tree. Chewing on the soft local bread I picked up in a tiny market in Calci along with slices of a local salami, balancing a small tub of pickled olives on a thick root I used as an armrest, and sipping from a bottle of mineral water *con gas,* I studied bunches of soft, gray-green leaves with their silver-white bellies. And the ancient, broad trunk I was leaning against brought to mind a line I read in a book about olive trees: "Its big, gnarled old trunk hid a thousand secrets in its wrinkly bark, and the slight breeze that blew up from the mouth of the valley shivered through its branches."

Alex Dingwall-Main's passage in *The Angel Tree* could have been describing my tree in Tre Colli. The tree was a study in whorls seemingly sculptured by the hand of some great artist aiming to nourish the soul — the artist's and mine. The trunk was blackened in spots, attesting to a long-ago fire, and here and there alongside the main trunk, jutting out of a cluster of roots resembling the shape of a partially deflated basketball, were narrow, deep-green shoots, sturdy testaments that this old tree still had a vibrant future. All I could hear in the heavy summer air was the sound of birds and grasshoppers. Not a single car passed by on the road twenty feet above.

No sooner had I left Tre Colli and returned to the narrow main road out of Calci, appropriately named Via Panoramica Calci, than another surprise awaited me farther uphill. Glancing over the edge of the road into a deep valley, I spotted a couple of other ancient buildings, including one with a church steeple. This, a sign informed me, was San Bernardo.

Once a small *borgo,* San Bernardo has its legends, much like Pietrasanta's unlikely legend that Michelangelo designed the Duomo bell tower there. The French abbot Bernardo of Clairvaux reportedly visited the tiny monastery, known then as the hermitage of Santi Jacopo e Verano alla Costa d'Acqua, or the Saints James and Verano at the Water Coast. Bernardo had been in Tuscany in 1135 to meet with Bernardo di Calci, who some sources refer to as Bernardo di Pisa. The Calci Bernardo would become Pope Eugenius III ten years later. The two Bernardos had met to discuss peace terms between rivals Pisa and Genoa. While on retreat at the monastery, one of the earliest in the Pisan Hills, Bernardo of Clairvaux reportedly wrote the well-known final prayer of the Rosary, "Salve Regina" or "Hail Holy Queen." Some scholars dispute this, of course, and several possible authors have been credited, including a German monk and a pope. But folks in and around Calci believe otherwise.

Today, the deconsecrated church, declared a national monument and restored in the late 1960s, and one two-story medieval building, which probably was the monastery, are all that are left. It is now an *agritourismo,* a place for tourists to come, stay, eat local food, and experience Tuscan farm life. The church, with a porch made of local stone, is small and simple with only a belfry and no bell tower. I drove down to it. There were no vehicles present or people walking about. But the place offered a magnificent view of the Plain of Pisa to the west. I am sure that on a clearer day, I'd have been able to see Pisa and its tower.

San Bernardo is near the summit of Monte Serra. At the top, I find Italian Army soldiers on maneuvers. I stop, watch as a crew sets up a communications station, and I speak with an officer who advises me not to miss the village of Buti on the downhill side of the mountain.

"It is lovely," he said. "And if you can avoid the bicyclists, the route to there is through magnificent trees and, farther down, olive groves." My intention was to pass through en route to the more touristy town of San Miniato, then head back west to Pontedera before dipping into the southern reaches of the Plain of Pisa, ending up in Lari. But I generally follow advice such as the officer's, and Buti, tucked into the cleft of a hill, proved to be a pleasant two-hour layover in the heat of the July afternoon.

Buti's wide-open village square has a fountain at one end, on this day surrounded by preteen boys and girls playing in the water and using — nonstop, for the two hours I was there — water-filled balloons to squirt passing cars and playmates. Adults driving by and getting splashed would pause, roll down a window, and have a friendly talk with one or two of the youngsters. Everybody knows everybody here.

A nice bar, my chosen hangout, dominated the other end of the square. I sat in the shade of the bar's patio, engaged in light conversation with the usual elderly denizens taking a break from their almost-continuous hands of the card game Scopa, the Italian noun for "broom." The word is a reference to the players' attempts to "sweep" all cards from the table. These cards, forty to a deck, bear no resemblance to poker cards or typical suits Americans are used to. Decks can be based on designs from sixteen provincial areas, including Trieste, Piacenza, Naples, and the region of Sicily.

These games, ubiquitous in bars and town squares all over Italy, are a delight to watch. The players are mostly men — the only time I saw women playing was in a private workers' bar in Pietrasanta — and the game can get loud and raucous. The uninitiated might think that players in the Pietrasanta club are about to come to blows; they often get in others' faces, shouting and gesturing, but everyone always remains friends. These were, after all, people who as children had learned to ride their bicycles in the same central piazza; kicked soccer balls back and forth, bouncing them off the ancient stone fronts of banks and tobacco shops; chased one another down medieval streets; and who went to work together as *artigiani* in the marble workshops or as miners, or who became bakers, or even bar owners. Nearly every afternoon, these now-retired men continue to gather, drink their small glasses of white wine, and laugh and joke and attempt to "sweep" the cards.

Players, violently slapping down cards onto the discard piles, sling out words barely discernible to those knowing only school-taught Italian. In the late afternoon or early evenings when several players are spread out across several tables, the uproar can become deafening.

This was true in Buti, or Calci, or Pietrasanta, or just about anywhere I went in western Tuscany. Now, in Buti, one of the retired men, white-bearded, dark eyes sparkling, offered to teach me the game. The other three men sat back as this fine gentleman attempted, using Italian words I could scarcely follow, to explain the mysteries of Scopa. But I could not grasp it and quickly realized that I was out of my league. I scooted back my chair, motioned for the four to resume, and ordered a round of white wine for the gentlemen. When the drinks came, they picked them up and tipped their glasses toward me. When I left more than a hour later to resume my drive toward the hill town of San Miniato, they paused in their game, got up from their table, and walked me to my nearby car, one with his arm through my arm as many Italian men do as they walk side by side, and wished me *addio,* each shaking my hand.

Not being a drinker but knowing many, I can only guess at the feeling of warmth that a small glass of good wine can give. It must be like the feeling I had after experiencing the hospitality of those small-town Tuscan men. I carried this warmth with me while driving south out of Buti to catch the main highway east toward San Miniato, doing my best to stay off the *autostrada* to Florence. I followed the state highway through Pontedera, where most of Italy's scooters are made, along a brief stretch of the Arno River, and through smaller villages such as Castel del Bosco, translated as Castle of the Woods.

I took the turnoff to the south toward San Miniato, climbing into the Apennine foothills along a beautiful, tree-lined road that burst open every now and then with magnificent vistas to the west and south of the Plain of Pisa. San Miniato is one of the more touristy small towns in this area. Its draws, I suspect, are the vistas and its position high up as a Tuscan hill town.

Along the road to San Miniato, I saw the familiar wooden Via Francigena signs, and realized that the medieval pathway followed by pilgrims and armies to Rome swung by here and briefly bumped against the Apennines. What gave San Miniato its historic prominence was its location along the west–east route from Pisa to Florence as well as the early northwest–southeast road between Lucca and Siena. It also was where German

Holy Roman Emperor Frederick Barbarossa and his grandson Frederick II, at various times in the twelfth century, built massive fortifications to solidify their rule here.

Some sources claim that the eleventh-century Tuscan countess Matilda of Canossa was born in San Miniato. Most historical sources are uncertain about her birthplace, and San Miniato is left off the list of possibilities proffered by some. Matilda's biographer, Michele K. Spike, thinks Matilda was born in Mantua, 165 miles to the north, in the Lombardy region.

Still, the memory of Matilda is not lost on modern Tuscans. She is highly regarded because, despite her ancestral connections with the German emperors who ruled northern Italy, she favored Italians over the Germans. And much of her life was spent in Tuscany, building castles and launching public improvements, such as the so-called Devil's Bridge across the Serchio River at Borgo a Mozzano north of Lucca. Her father, Bonifacio III, used the Serchio as his route to the Mediterranean and recognized all its advantages: collecting taxes in villages along its route and using it for trade with Pisa and other merchant cities.

Matilda also was a warrior who led armies. In one instance, her forces rebuffed the army of the German emperor Henry IV when he tried to assault her castle at Canossa high in the Emilia-Romagna region. (Henry's son and successor, Henry V, did not support his father and named Matilda vice-queen of Liguria, a title, Spike tells us, that seems to have been created just for her but one she never used.)

She also is well known in Tuscany for her support of much-beleaguered Pope Gregory VII through his conflicts with Henry IV, and his hotly contested reforms of the Catholic clergy.

The ruins of many castles occupied by Matilda over her long life (1046–1115) dot the Tuscan countryside and portions of Emilia-Romagna, near its modern boundary with Tuscany. San Miniato has one tower dedicated to Matilda, but that does not necessarily mean that she was born there. Many other towns and villages have Matilda towers, including one in Viareggio, and one that still stands on the Tiber Island in Rome, her home when she was in the city visiting Pope Gregory VII.

According to Spike, throughout her life Matilda donated property to at least fifteen churches throughout Tuscany and Emilia-Romagna and gave gifts of gold and silver to Modena. This countess is remembered not only for these gifts and her support of Gregory, but how she stood up to a ruthless German king. On a social level, she fought against the dehumanizing feudal system that had kept the peasant class dependent on the nobility for centuries.

I crossed paths with Matilda many times throughout western Tuscany, realizing that her influence spread far beyond the region's boundaries. The more I learned about her, the more of a hero she became.

San Miniato's name once had the appellation *al Tedesco* (to the German) because of this early medieval influence.

The mighty castles the Germans built no longer stand guard. But while walls are mostly gone, it is obvious from the layout of the town, across three ridges with deep valleys in between, that the walls were incorporated into certain buildings. Two full towers dating to the German era also remain. One has been transformed into the bell tower for the village's thirteenth-century Duomo.

This tower that is called the "Tower of Matilda" has a giant clock on its early medieval stonework. A grander, taller tower near the town's highest point, the Tower of Frederick, refers to Frederick II (1194–1250), who followed his father Henry VI and grandfather Frederick Barbarossa as Holy Roman Emperor.

Ironically, the Germans, who returned in the twentieth century after an absence of seven hundred years, reduced Frederick's tower to rubble during World War II. They did not want the advancing Allies to have a vantage point over the sweeping Plain of Pisa, to zero in with heavy guns on the retreating German soldiers. The tower was rebuilt in the late 1950s and "looks exactly the same as the first one," a local restaurant owner told me as I ate lunch beneath a covered medieval entryway just down the main street leading uphill to San Miniato's historic center.

Following an excellent dessert of a classic *tiramisù* — actually a dessert I usually avoid in Italy because it is so common and other local specialties often seem more compelling — I joined the steady throng of tourists and marched up the street toward the Prato del Duomo.

As the afternoon wore on, the crowds grew smaller. San Miniato seems to be like Venice in the sense that the majority of visitors are day-trippers, not folks who spend nights in local hotels or pensions. Unlike most of the other villages and towns I visited in Tuscany, this one is indeed listed in guidebooks. It has the drawing card of a museum of sacred art, which holds famous works by such Renaissance painters as Filippo Lippi and Fra Bartolommeo.

I waited, on a comfortable bench in the nicely shaded Prado del Duomo, as the sun continued to work its way behind some tall buildings. The coolness of the forested hills began to seep into the square. Tourist crowds began to evaporate and, in their place, the locals came out for the *passeggiata,* or late afternoon "walkabout" so common in Italian towns and villages. Observing this daily ritual of friendship and community in village after village over the years is one of my favorite things to do. I watch locals meet and greet one another, catching up on the day's neighborhood news. Youngsters flash by on bicycles or skateboards, a few kick soccer balls back and forth or slam them against stone walls of buildings.

Eventually, I walked back down the main street to my car and began the hour-long drive back to La Gabella and my comfortable room at the Zia. The next day, I would move toward the south end of the Plain of Pisa, where a different kind of geography awaited.

■ ■ ■ ■

My destination was Lari, one of Italy's pasta production centers. The highway heads south of Pontedera, which, in addition to making scooters, sixty years ago was the Allied launching point against the German army that controlled Pisa, just twenty-one miles away, and the rest of northern Italy.

The highway passes through one ugly industrial area after another. Then, with low foothills defining the Càscina Valley in the distance, the industrial scene slowly evolves into ever-expanding fields of wheat. Most of what is grown here is *semola de grano duro,* or semolina — hard, yellow wheat that produces glutinous flour used throughout Italy and North America for pasta. In Lari, much of the pasta produced is made strictly with flour and water — no eggs or oil.

I had heard that Lari was worth a visit, but until I left the plain, entered the valley, and moved up into the foothills, I wasn't sure it would be that appealing. I was wrong. Like San Miniato and other villages in this region, the heart of the small, compact old village sits in the shape of a rough-hewn circle on a hilltop with two long, spindly "legs" emanating to the north and southeast, each only wide enough for a single street and a single row of medieval buildings on each side.

In addition to the wide clusters of chestnut and other hardwood trees blanketing the hillsides, great cherry orchards are spotted here and there. Lari is a center for more than pasta making. It also has a cherry festival every year that encompasses many of the smaller villages that surround it. This series of hilltops and valleys, with plenty of trails tying one village to another, must be a walker's paradise.

In the heart of Lari's center, still surrounded by high city walls, sits a nicely restored Medici castle, Castello dei Vicari, or Castle of the Vicars. From its ramparts, one can see the three gates into the town and the narrow main street that winds around the stone castle below and is lined with shops, houses, and a small factory that makes yellow pasta in a variety of shapes and sizes.

The earliest sections of the castle were in place by AD 900. Pisa controlled it for a while, then Florence, which greatly expanded and fortified it. For four centuries, Lari was the administrative center for much of the province of Pisa. That role ended in the early 1800s, when Tuscany became part of the Kingdom of Italy. Prominent, privileged families ran things here over the centuries; nearly one hundred different coats of arms line the walls of the castle courtyard.

The castle is reportedly haunted, something likely suggested as a way to lure tourists or turn the castle into reality show fodder. At least two of the village's residents, one teenager and one middle-aged woman I spoke with in a small restaurant, believe the ghosts exist. One ghost comes from the twentieth century in the form of John Princi, known as Rosso della Paola, or the Red of Paola. He was an anti-Fascist imprisoned within those walls by Mussolini's minions. Guards claimed the Red's death was a suicide, but few believe that explanation. There is also a room referred to as the "room of torments," where witches were put on trial and prisoners reportedly were tortured. Their tormented souls wander between the walls. I didn't come across any ghosts during my daytime sojourn, but the castle is not a place where I would want to spend a night.

It was midafternoon and I sat on the restaurant's outdoor terrace along one of the spindly streets branching out from the castle. It was too early for dinner, but the owner served drinks and *caffè*. A man sped by on a Vespa scooter with a toddler standing on the floorboard in front and a slightly older child on the seat behind him. None wore helmets — not an unusual sight in most of Italy — and when the man turned into an alleyway next to the bar, the scooter hit gravel and started to spin out, turning 180 degrees and threatening to dump all three. The father quickly got it back under control and disappeared down the narrow lane, he and his two children laughing — with relief, I suspect. The table of elderly men sitting next to me had witnessed the near disaster. They looked at the wide-eyed terror on my face, shaking their heads and chuckling quietly.

Early evening approached, and I wanted to drive back to the Zia in La Gabella with enough light to enjoy the countryside. This time, to avoid retracing my route through the ugly industrial center, I headed toward Collesalvetti, through the tiny villages of Créspina and Fauglia. This route goes through a far more beautiful portion of the Plain of Pisa, and Lari's cherry orchards give way to stunning expanses of vineyards. Signs along the roadway declare that this route is a wine highway, Strada del Vino — a designation on many such roads throughout the wine-growing areas of Tuscany. On my roadmap, this one is marked in green, suggesting that it is a *tratto panoramico,* or panoramic drive.

Several miles out of Lari, I pulled over to the side of the road and watched the sun drop down behind the low coastal range of hills along the sea twelve to fifteen miles away. The views along this "wine road" are equal in visual impact to the famed wine region of Chianti much farther to the east.

In western Tuscany, one can avoid crowds and find easy walks in places like Lari, along with leisurely, traffic-free drives through hardwood forests, cherry orchards, and vineyards that seem to stretch forever over the slightly rolling landscape.

In the heat of midsummer, the people in this delightful section of west-central Tuscany — the elderly men I talk to in local bars, the shop owners standing in their doorways catching the early-morning sun, the occasional teenager who stops to try out his English with *il Americano* — are not burned out by the hordes of visitors who blow through.

For my part, I felt like I had "discovered" a world unknown to all but those who live here. Except for in San Miniato, I saw no one I could recognize as a tourist. My rarely used guidebook had nothing to offer about this place. It was another new and wonderful day in this ancient land.

NINE:
L'ARCIPÉLAGO TOSCANO

The Mediterranean has the color of mack-
erel, changeable I mean. You don't always
know if it is green or violet, you can't even
say it's blue, because the next moment
the changing reflection has taken on a tint
of rose or gray.

— Vincent Van Gogh, letter to
brother Theo (June 1888)

Early-morning haze usually obscures the
islands off the Tuscan coast. The sea, as
changeable in shades of blue and gray as
Van Gogh described it, often merges with
the sky, making it difficult to see where one
begins and the other ends. Sometimes,
while standing on the low-lying hills above
coastal Pietrasanta, I can see the faint
outline of northern Corsica across the Mar
Ligure, or as I choose to think of it, the Tuscan Sea.

I've not made it to Napoleon's birthplace,

but I have been close. I've looked at Corsica's southern end from the northern tip of Sardinia, and I saw its outline just thirty or so miles away as the ferry I was on headed toward the port at Capraia — a Tuscan island that is closer to French Corsica than it is to the Italian mainland.

A professor of ancient history once told me that some coastal Tuscans and Ligurians believe Napoleon was not born in French territory but in his family's villa just north of Pietrasanta, near La Spezia. After all, the Bonaparte family descended from Tuscan nobles who went to Corsica in the sixteenth century. The birth name of his mother, Maria Letizia Ramolino, is Italian, and she had distant cousins who were nobles in the Republic of Genoa, just sixty miles up the coast from La Spezia. To top it off, his maternal grandmother's birth name was Angela Maria Pietrasanta. It is easy to see why some can claim the future French emperor was Italian-born despite historical evidence that gives his birthplace as Ajaccio, Corsica.

The various islands of the Tuscan Archipelago are arrayed between Corsica and Tuscany. Different islands can usually be seen from just about anywhere along the coast, rising like blue-grayish specks on the distant horizon. One of the best spots for viewing my favorite, Capraia, is a mile or so south of the Port of Livorno at the beautifully landscaped waterfront promenade, Terrazza Mascagni. It is named after the composer Pietro Mascagni, who wrote the opera *Cavalleria Rusticana* — the great, sorrowful Sicilian tale of unrequited love, religious hypocrisy, and tragic death. From the sweeping, curving *terrazza,* I could see the long line of cargo ships and tankers waiting to slide into the busy port, and beyond the vague outlines of the islands of Capraia and Gorgona, the northern-most islands of L'Arcipélago Toscano.

The seven principal islands of this archipelago stay in my line of sight as I move eighty miles to the south to the port of Piombino. Here, the more northerly Ligurian Sea becomes the Tyrrhenian Sea, which will bathe the western coast of the Italian peninsula all the way down to the toe of the boot and along Sicily's northern coast.

At Piombino, the even closer Elba pops out of Mar Tirreno. Ferries depart almost hourly for Elba from this modern, industrialized port that was nearly destroyed during World War II bombing. And still farther south, at the far end of Tuscany, just a few miles from its border with the region of

Lazio, is Isola del Giglio, a short ferry ride from Porto San Stefano, west of Orbetello.

There are three islands to the west of Giglio: Isola di Montecristo, Isola Pianosa, and Isola di Giannutri, which is opposite the village of Tarquinia on the mainland, in the region of Lazio. Despite its position, Giannutri remains under Tuscan control. At fewer than four square miles in size, Giannutri is among the smallest of the seven islands. It and Pianosa are reachable by ferry, but only sporadically, generally from Easter through August. During this summer season, boats going there leave from Elba and Piombino, but despite being in Tuscany for several months, I found it difficult to arrange transport. While staying on Capraia for several days in late August 2012, I purchased a ferry ticket to Elba with the hope of later finding a ride to Pianosa, but rough seas made getting to Elba impossible in the time I had available.

The small ferry between Capraia and Elba had canceled its service because of weather. I was in danger of being stranded on Capraia when the much larger Toremar ferries were nearly shut down as well between the island and the mainland at the port of Livorno. As it turned out, I was able to catch the last ferry, which plowed and rolled through roiling water, reminding me of my U.S. Navy days when I rode a World War II–class destroyer in a three-day North Pacific typhoon.

When we finally reached Livorno, the Toremar ticket clerk said I likely could not get to Elba for a few more days, even if I traveled the nearly fifty miles south to Piombino, from where several ferries daily make the short hop to Elba. It was the end of August; the tiny people-only ferries to the smaller islands were shutting down for the season, and the larger ferries were staying in port until the weather cleared.

My frustration at my decision to wait too long into the summer season to visit these islands brought to mind a quote I once read in Joseph Conrad's book *The Mirror of the Sea:* "The sea has never been friendly to men. At most it has been the accomplice of human restlessness." My Navy experience taught me how a great sea can suddenly become unfriendly. But my "human restlessness" has never stopped me from clambering aboard vessels large and small. I was willing to chance a ride to Elba and the smaller islands; Toremar and other private operators were not.

The northernmost island in the Tuscan group, Gorgona, which I could see from

Livorno's promenade, is a still-functioning agricultural penal colony that occupies a medieval monastery. It is impossible to visit no matter what time of year. A traveler en route to Capraia can see it up close from the deck of a Toremar ferry as it pulls into the tiny port to drop off supplies, prison personnel, and, sometimes, chained-up prisoners and their armed guards. Then, those ferries move on from this somber prison island to Capraia, a mere twenty-two miles to the southwest. It, too, was a penal colony from 1873 to 1986, but now it is the destination of vacationers, primarily mainland Italians. High on the hill above Capraia's tiny port, those solemn prison walls surround stone buildings that sit empty.

While Capraia, Elba, and Giglio are heavily visited, principally during July and August, Pianosa, Montecristo, and Giannutri remain tougher to reach. Pianosa, for example, also a former prison island, has only a handful of year-round residents. Pianosa.net states it is home to a few policemen, "the family of a former prison guard, and two or three inmates on probation." Now a nature preserve, Pianosa's prison was shut down in 1998 when the government transferred its mostly Mafia-related prisoners to mainland lockups. The Italian government requires tourists to get special permits if they want to visit.

Pianosa, at four square miles, is slightly larger than the southernmost Tuscan isle of Giannutri. A man I spoke with on Capraia told me he had been to nearly all seven of the significant Tuscan islands, but spent only one day on Pianosa. He said the number of visitors is limited — I later found out that the number was 250 per day — and they must get there on a small, privately arranged ferry from Piombino. There is no overnight lodging, only day trips. Visitors can wander, and snorkel or scuba dive in the island's crystal-clear water, but fishing is not allowed. There is no need for automobiles on Pianosa: Its highest point is about seventy feet above sea level, making it a foot traveler's dream.

I regretted not being able to get to this island. I wanted to feel the kind of solitude that I once enjoyed on a small Scottish island in the Western Hebrides. Capraia, Giglio, and Elba certainly do not provide that kind of solitude, even in the off-season, although Capraia is less crowded and more intimate than the other two.

Even more intriguing is the island of Montecristo which, along with Giglio and Giannutri, marks the southern extent of the archipelago. While it is southeast of Capraia, Montecristo swoops farther to the east, making this island the farthest from the western coast of the peninsula, because the mainland dramatically curves southeastward.

Montecristo is nearly uninhabited except for a clutch of forest rangers who spend summers there. Its wild vegetation and low trees make it an ideal bird sanctuary. The only way to the island is on government-owned or private boats. Again, intrepid visitors need special permits, but the government generally gives them only to university researchers interested in studying the flora and fauna, including the handful of wild goats whose ancestors were thought to have been brought there by the ancient Phoenicians some three thousand years ago.

With Montecristo nearly unreachable for the general traveler, visitors, meanwhile, can far more easily get to Giannutri. Shaped like a half-moon, it is only about sixteen hundred feet wide, three miles long, and has perhaps twenty residents. The island's first known inhabitants were Romans, and the ruins of a second-century Roman villa remain, along with a lighthouse from the 1800s. Local legend relates that the island is home to ghosts, including a woman who can be seen dressed in flowing white linen, flitting across the tops of cliffs and shrieking into the wind. I've read brief descriptions of this apparition in local guidebooks but never met anyone who had seen the sorrowful lady. Still, it would be worth the experience of trying to see her. She doesn't seem to mean harm to anyone.

Giannutri's mule tracks make it, like Pianosa, a good place for walkers and birders. An abundance of fish and other sea life make it another snorkeler's dream.

By the time I started learning about Tuscany's islands, it was late in the season, which made it difficult to get to the smaller ones. I did get to Giglio and Capraia in the final days of August and early September, and of those two, Capraia was my favorite.

It has only about four hundred year-round residents. That population swells mightily in July and August, as this tiny seven-and-a-half-square-mile island, with its eighteen-mile coastline defined by millennia-old lava flows, is a major summer destination for Italian tourists. Still, it does not seem to get as overrun as Giglio at the far south of the archipelago. This may be because getting to Capraia requires an hour longer on the ferry than traveling to Giglio. Giglio's port is larger, with more hotels, restaurants, and a clean sweep of sandy beach next to the ferry landing. On Capraia, sandy beaches are small and away from the port, and reaching them requires walking down steep paths or chartering a small local boat.

For this visit in early September, I travel from Pietrasanta to Livorno by train and catch a bus to the port that was so crucial to British merchants and warships beginning in the seventeenth century. During World War II the badly bombed-out port became a major re-supply hub for the Allies during the last year of the war in Italy. But the city has clearly been reclaimed by proud Tuscans and retains its Livorno name rather than the British appellation of Leghorn. Much of it has been rebuilt, particularly the area around the port, and now has well-defined neighborhoods and city center. Its historic center has been blended nicely into newer, rebuilt neighborhoods that slowly came back to life after Allied bombing in 1944.

I arrive at Livorno's port and the Toremar ticket office with a few hours to spare before the next ferry would depart for Capraia. Then it would take a few hours, on calm, deep-blue seas, to make the transit. I pass the time sitting in the hot, late-August sun at a nearby coffee shop, sipping espresso and watching tourists begin queuing up for boarding the huge ferry. Large trucks, full of supplies bound for the island, are being loaded into the large vehicle bay. This one, the ticket agent had told me, would not stop at Gorgona, but I hope to at least view, at a distance, the still-operating penal island from the giant ferry's deck.

A blast from the ferry's horn gets me moving. I board and, just minutes later, the ship gently pulls away from the dock and begins cutting its way through a crystal-like sea. As the ferry picks up speed, the sky-blue water begins splitting into cascading foam at the ferry's bow. A churning light blue wake follows the broad stern. The ride is smooth. I can barely feel the rumble of engines as Livorno slips away. Off to the northwest, Gorgona comes into clear view. We don't turn toward that island but stay steady on a course for Capraia, which is growing bigger ahead. It bolts out of the sea in gray shadow, the north end dropping down at a sharp angle from the 880-foot summit of Monte Scopa to the water's edge. As we move closer, with the midafternoon sun slipping down to the west, the island begins to change color from light gray to light green. And as we approach the tiny port, I notice its marina is festooned with the points of tiny white sails of small boats and yachts.

The sun beating down on the exposed part of the passenger decks is merciless. I retreat into the air-conditioned interior, slam down a quick espresso — my third, maybe fourth, of the day — and slump into a comfortable chair next to a large window. Despite the volume of caffeine, I doze. Then, feeling a shift in the giant ferry's engines, I jolt awake and can see Capraia just ahead. Outside, as I watch the docking from the shade of an overhang, the charm of the island's port — its small boats and vibrantly painted line of buildings — become real. The ferry executes a 180-degree turn, and the large ship backs up to a cement pier.

The line of small commercial buildings, which extends perpendicular from the water, makes up the tiny space known simply as Porto. The buildings house a ticket office, a tiny pharmacy, a diving shop, and a few small hotels and restaurants.

A van marked with the name of the island's one four-star hotel waits for the ferry to unload. There is also a passenger bus that goes to a small village on a bluff above Porto. Its name, also simple and direct, is Paese, which means "country" in Italian.

Paese is tucked in a small cleft just over the crest of a hill to the south. It is connected to Porto by the island's only paved road, just nine hundred feet long. This narrow, gently curved stretch runs slightly parallel to an ancient wide stone pathway that shoots up from the port straight to the town. Tourists should not bother to bring cars to Capraia. There are precious few places to park them and, besides, this is a place for walking.

I climb into the hotel van and am taken up the paved road and into the hotel's driveway. The facility is a nice one, and the views from the rooms, of Porto and the marina below as well as the Tuscan Sea beyond, are stunning. I foolishly had made a reservation that included two meals a day at the hotel. The food, surprisingly for Tuscan restaurants, was not outstanding, and my decision kept me from eating in some of the other more appealing places in Paese that were just a short walk away.

In addition to the large hotel, laid out like a resort on a hillside that plunges down into the sea, there are only two small guesthouses and two small hotels in Paese. Signs also indicate apartments for rent inside some houses. I was on Capraia during the last week of the summer tourist season, and not another room was to be had. The summertime population here can top three thousand visitors on any given day, compared to the three hundred to four hundred year-round Capraiesi.

My first adventure, late in the afternoon of my arrival, was a long walk on one of the many walking paths that crisscross this small island. I started outside the Church of San Nicola in Paese's main square. A dirt path that likely was once a *mulattiere,* or mule track, in the eleventh century, starts near the whitewashed building's outside wall and traverses one of the few relatively flat areas on the hilly island. From this plateau I could look far to the east across the sea at the hazy outline of the Italian mainland. If I were to continue to the southwest, in the valley between Monte Albero and Monte Forcone, and dip onto the crest of the island's western slope, I suspect I would eventually see the closer outline of Corsica's northern tip. But I didn't go that far. The late afternoon was excruciatingly hot, and I was not prepared for such a long walk. That view would have to wait until I could get to Capraia's western coastline, by boat, the following day.

Because it was near the end of summer, the high plain this trail crossed offered a

281

dun-colored landscape of low scrubs, occasional clusters of olive trees, and a few plots of irrigated grape vines. Low-riding walls of stone delineate various plots of land, and very quickly the small stone Church of Santo Stefano at Piano, long deconsecrated, pops up out of the landscape. The single-vault interior is barren; the floor is the wrinkled surface of the stone outcrop the church appears to be built on.

Its origins have been traced to the second century AD, but in the ninth century, Muslim raiders destroyed the structure — and likely the small town that surrounded it. The raiders hauled many of the locals onto their ships and off into slavery elsewhere in the Mediterranean. The church, rebuilt in the tenth and eleventh centuries, is all that remains of the original town. There is no obvious evidence — except for a large, deeply buried cistern near the church — that there ever was a village here.

Stumbling onto such structures during a casual walk is not the only reason to wander on Capraia. I had a conversation later that evening with a clerk in a small shop in Paese. She told me that the best season for walkers on this island is spring, when the landscape is blanketed in wildflowers. By late August, much of the bright colors of spring and early summer are gone. But there are other attractions.

"Did you see many birds?" she asked.

Although I do not know the names of many varieties, I did recognize ravens high in the sky. Raven is *corvo* in Italian, she said. I told her I had seen small, low-flying birds nervously flitting amongst the scattered bushes. She said these were likely warblers.

"Those with a creamy breast, black heads, and red eyes are Sardinian warblers," she said. She dug out a worn bird-watching guide from a drawer behind the counter, flipped through a few pages, and showed me a picture. "Some migrate, others stay here." She is an experienced bird watcher and spends many of her off days prowling through the brush.

"But the spring is the best time to be here for that. People who come in July and August only want to lounge on boats, swim, and do the snorkel."

Knowing what I now know about the lure of this Tuscan island, I could have found the solitude I crave here in the spring. My next trip to this place will be for several days longer. There simply wasn't enough time in two and a half days for me to really get to know Capraia and to walk the dozens of trails, all accessible from Porto or Paese.

■ ■ ■ ■

The following morning, I wandered down the hillside to Porto. As I walked along that short stretch of asphalt that is the island's only paved road, I could hear a low, breathy whistle coming up from the marina, the sound of a light wind passing through the rigging of the dozens of small boats tied up at the piers. This rather pleasing hum lasted the day and into the night, a constant soundtrack of the island. I could hear it each morning as I stood on my tiny terrace overlooking the sea and drinking coffee, or as I wandered the hillside between Paese and Porto, or as I sat along the main pier enjoying the shade of a bar umbrella. It was there at night as I watched the sky darken and stars appear or in the predawn as the night's dark-lilac sky began to shift toward light shades of pink.

One benefit of visiting Capraia in August is being able to lie back in a lounge chair and watch the star-filled sky during the Perseid meteor shower. There are only hints of lights from buildings there late at night, and when eyes adjust to the darkness the heavens erupt into the Milky Way. I saw my first meteor while sitting in the outdoor area of the hotel restaurant and, a few hours later, I climbed to the hotel's highest level and found an unoccupied terrace. One after another, streaks of meteors flashed across the sky. I stopped counting at a dozen, all the while listening to the background hum of a light breeze through boat wires. These were the stars I remember from my youth, sleeping in the summer on a cot behind my house set in the middle of Idaho farmland with nary a light to interrupt the heavens.

My usual practice of staying up late like this leads me to such experiences. I often do this in new places. Unless I am lounging on a terrace looking for shooting stars, I will often wander the cobblestones at night to get a different feeling for a small village or a large city at a time when nearly everyone else is inside. Footsteps ring hollow and bounce back at me off ancient stones; automobiles are quiet, the near silence only occasionally broken by the faraway whine of a scooter. The occasional murmurings of voices from a small restaurant or bar that caters to night owls like me lead me to my final cup of double espresso and, perhaps, a light dessert. Such late nights give me the time to plan what I will do the following day. Then I will have a reason to rise early, after five or six hours of sleep, to begin something new.

Rising early on my first morning, I wanted to find the ruins of a Roman villa where, local legend says, the Emperor Augustus, in AD 2, banished his daughter and only biological child, Julia. Most historians dispute that legend and believe she was banished instead to the island of Ventotene, located in the Tyrrhenian Sea much farther to the south and opposite the coastal Italian town of Gaeta located midway between Rome and Naples. Augustus definitely had issues: he banished his granddaughter, also named Julia, to a tiny island in the Adriatic Sea. Both Julias, he felt, had been guilty of promiscuity.

Whether the daughter, named by historians as Julia the Elder, had ever lived in Capraia is not important. Some Roman had, and various guidebooks for Capraia promise that Roman ruins exist. A rough map shows them located in Porto at the far end of the paved street that runs from the Toremar pier to a short distance inland. But there are no signs pointing to an archaeological site and none of the telltale piles of stones that usually are scattered around such sites.

At a small bar, I asked a young woman working there if she knew where the ruins were. She thought a moment, slightly shrugged her shoulders, and said the ruins must be in the dirt-covered parking lot next to the Church of the Assunta located at the point where the road swings left and heads up the hill toward Paese. It seemed strange that she wouldn't know for sure, especially given that she told me she had lived on the island most of her life. "They must be there," she said. "It is the only place."

Heavy undergrowth surrounded the border of the parking lot. Along one side was a small stream. No ancient stones protruded through the lot's dirt surface; the undergrowth around its fringes offered no clues. *Niente.* Nothing. I crossed the road on the other side of the church and found the same, just heavy undergrowth.

After an hour, I gave up and walked toward the marina, where I saw a woman sitting at a small table outside a nautical supply shop. She was selling tickets for a boat trip around the island. The price was reasonable, the trip would last for perhaps three hours or more, and it seemed like a great way to spend most of the day. I bought a ticket and then asked about the Roman ruins. She shrugged. "They are somewhere there," she said, pointing to the Church of the Assunta. "*Ma non lo so.* [But I do not know]."

A small dish of gelato and then a double espresso kept me occupied during the hour-long wait for the boat to return from its morning tour. Finally a small boat with a heavily tanned, white-bearded man at the tiller pulled up to the dock, and a handful of people climbed out. A small group of seven or eight tourists had gathered with me at the water's edge, and Maurizio the boatman motioned us on board. The engine roared, and we headed across the marina to another pier, where two more passengers were waiting. Fully loaded, we started our clockwise navigation of the island's eighteen-mile coastline.

Maurizio spoke in rapid-fire Italian, first pointing out a tower high atop a headland southeast from the port. I caught enough of what he said to understand the tower was built by the Genoese during their time of occupation in the Middle Ages. Genoa and Pisa often alternated in dominating this part of the Mediterranean, and when the Pisans were in control, they built their own tower on a headland north of Porto.

The eastern side of Capraia is more gently sloped than what we will see on the western shoreline, Maurizio explained. When a massive earthquake hit the island five million years ago, half of it collapsed into the sea, shearing off the western edge, resulting in steep cliffs and caves. The water is deep along the western coastline, unlike the eastern shore, which has shallow waters perfect for swimming, snorkeling, and diving.

The basins that make up the Tyrrhenian and Ligurian seas, along with the Sea of Sardinia, began to take shape twenty million years ago. Over time, perhaps as long as ten million years ago, the Strait of Gibraltar closed through tectonic action, and the Mediterranean dried up, creating massive salt-pans left by the evaporating seawater and exposing mountain ranges whose tops had been islands in the prehistoric sea. Five million years ago, over time, the strait reopened and the Atlantic poured back in, refilling the great sea in as short a time as two years. Those mountain ranges were once again submerged and tops again became islands.

Six of the seven islands of the Tuscan Archipelago are tops of mountains; Capraia is the only island of the group that was formed by volcanoes. The first volcano built it into a massive mountain with one dominant peak. Continued eruptions eventually divided that peak in two, and when the volcano became dormant, seawater, rain, and wind turned Capraia into the land of rolling hills, minor peaks, and plateaus that visitors see today.

The second, smaller volcano developed at the southeastern edge, its lava contributing to the construction of the coastline there. Maurizio the boatman steered us around that edge, bearing west and into a beautiful bay, the Cala Rosa. There were perhaps a half-dozen private boats anchored offshore, and people were swimming and snorkeling in the bay's turquoise waters.

Maurizio cut the engine and passengers peeled off their clothes, revealing swimming suits, and jumped overboard. A few of us were not prepared for such an adventure, so we sat back with Maurizio and soaked in the beauty of the place.

It was then that I first noticed, on the rocky shoreline perhaps one hundred feet away, a magnificent profusion of multicolored stone layers left by successive lava flows from the smaller volcano millions of years ago.

On the coastline at Cala Rosa, the color of the hardened lava ranged from yellow to spots of light gray. After our swimmers climbed back on board, we resumed our journey, dodging in and out of several caves on the western and northwestern shores that had been formed by various lava flows from the first volcano.

In these small enclosures, barely large enough to hold the boat, droplets of water from underground springs on the steep slopes would drip down on us from the low ceilings. Each time we pulled into a cave, our swimmers would jump into the water, and Maurizio and the rest of us would wait patiently. The sea was calm. It was cool in the shelter of these massive cliffs and the interior of the caves. Just sitting there, watching the light bounce off the lava walls that were either white or various shades of tan, was pleasure enough for me.

We eventually crested the northeastern edge of the island and turned south toward the marina at Porto. Maurizio stopped the boat one last time. Here the water was so shallow that the swimmers could stand on the rock floor with water only up to their chests. Except for the occasional splashes from a couple of the snorkelers, we sat quietly in the tiny boat, lulled into serenity by its light rocking. To the northeast, we could see the gray outline of the prison island, Gorgona. We watched as large birds swooped down, plucking small fish from just beneath the surface. In the distance, sail-boats glided past. Others were anchored as their riders lounged on deck or floated on the blue surface with snorkel gear and flippers. From the edge of the boat I could see small clusters of colorful fish in the shallow water, perhaps only three or four feet deep.

Eventually, Maurizio motioned the swimmers aboard, started his engine, and slowly headed toward the port. It had been a three-hour journey — one of the best days I had ever experienced in years of travel — and I could tell none of us wanted it to end.

From my tiny terrace early on the morning of my third and last day on the island, it was obvious the sea had changed. Where the light blue water previously had been placid, dashes of white now kicked up on the surface. The sky remained nearly cloudless, but the sea was heaving. I suspected it would be a rough journey in the much-smaller ferry I was planning to take to Elba. My cell phone rang. It was a woman from the ferry company, calling to tell me my boat to Elba was being canceled because of rough seas.

"You can go back to Livorno on Toremar and take the train to Piombino and catch one of the larger ferries to Elba — if they are sailing," she advised me. "These seas are very rough and sometimes even the bigger ferries will cancel." Then, ominously, she said, "Maybe Toremar will cancel its trip today between Livorno and Capraia. You should check."

After breakfast and a quick walk down the hill to Porto, I checked in at the Toremar office. The woman there sold me my return ticket and reassured me that the ferry would indeed arrive and then return to Livorno — "Unless," she said, "it gets much worse." Then, she added, smiling, "But of course it will not."

The ferry was scheduled to arrive mid-afternoon, so I had several more hours to spend on Capraia. I walked back to the hotel, packed, checked out, and stored my bag. I made the quick walk into Paese and found another trail to follow that took me south along the coast. I could feel the upward tick in the wind's intensity as I wandered along the short dirt path that took me to Punta della Bellavista, high on a cliff with a clear view of Elba, which was perhaps just a few dozen miles away across the open, whitecapped sea. I had a feeling that I would not make it there in the time I had left, but I would wait until arriving in Livorno before figuring out my next move.

The ferry arrived thirty minutes late. Passengers waiting to board with me said the woman in the ticket office said the tardiness was because of the rough seas. But it arrived, and it definitely was going back to Livorno. I climbed aboard, found a comfortable chair inside the cabin, and dozed off for a few minutes until being awoken by the ferry's twisting in the water, its bow rising and plunging. I am weak-kneed when it comes to seasickness. I had no sea legs as I stumbled across the shifting deck to purchase an Italian roll and a double espresso, figuring that would ease my nausea. It did, and I made the three-hour journey — the rough seas added thirty minutes to the transit — in more or less good shape. I scrambled down the ferry's ramp, walked to the ticket office at the Port of Livorno, and asked the clerk about ferries departing in the evening for Elba.

She told me what I had prepared myself to hear: I would have to take the train to Piombino, a short distance down the coast. The sea was expected to remain rough for another day, perhaps two, and she could not guarantee that ferries would be making the trip from Piombino.

That settled it. I had three days left before I had to return to my base at Pietrasanta, and I needed to decide how best to spend them. I had driven through Livorno a few months earlier and appreciated the clean look of the city and its port. It was obvious that a lot of it was postwar construction or restoration, given the major damage to the port and the city on its fringes during Allied bombing in World War II. My traveling companion Filippo Tofani had told me during that first drive through that there was a section of the city that had canals "like Venice!" That had intrigued me.

I thanked the clerk for the information, walked to the nearest bus stop, and made my way into the city. The bus stopped in front of a decent-looking hotel, the Giappone Inn, on Via Grande, the main avenue. It had a basic, reasonably priced room, including breakfast. I would explore Livorno for the next few days and head north to Pietrasanta on the third day. It was a decision that paid off, as I discovered a city full of history, explored the neighborhood connected by canals, and ate at one of the finest restaurants I had ever visited in Italy.

I knew I had to check out Livorno's canals, built, according to local legend, in the 1500s by Venetian craftsmen hired by Livorno's Medici rulers. As someone who believes the only way to really absorb Venice is to observe it from the water, I have spent a lot of time on the canals there — as a passenger on both private boats and *vaporetti,* or water buses. I wanted to see Livorno in the same way — from the water.

However, I have to admit that I am skeptical about the connection of these canals with Venetian craftsmen. The only references to this involvement in building the canals are found in guidebooks — notorious for taking some urban legends as fact and for copying one another — and from the Livornese tour guide who led a small group of visitors on a late-afternoon canal cruise. Academic studies of Livorno mention the canals but not the Venetians. These water people from Italy's northeast crescent created canals out of small streams flowing between low, muddy islands in the center of their lagoon. In Livorno, the canals and the moat around the new fort were dug out of the earth, and Tuscany had plenty of skilled people who could do the digging and line the canal walls with tightly fitting stone blocks. Meanwhile, the myth of the Venetian connection persists and remains an interesting story to pass on to tourists.

The canals are located in what is known, rightly or wrongly, as Livorno's "Venetian Quarter." They spill out in an arc along the south edge of the city's historic center.

These long, lanky bodies of water do not dominate the lives of Livornesi (or, as they are sometimes called, "Labronici") like they do Venetians'. People do not use them to get around the city, as there are plenty of streets full of cars, buses, and pedestrian walkways for that purpose.

Boats are tied up at narrow docks built along tall stone embankments where they await owners who will head out to sea for pleasure or to fish. Boat-repair shops are dug into the sides of the walls, along with an occasional coffee bar or tiny food establishment. Tourist-filled boats ply this network of waters, which connects the city's original ancient port with a fifteenth-century Fortezza Nuova, or "New" Castle, built by the then-Florentine rulers.

Pisa, in the Middle Ages, first controlled the city, building at the harbor's edge the original fortress, the "Old Fort," around an eleventh-century tower that had been constructed by Countess Matilda of Tuscany. Then, in the early 1400s, Genoa, victorious in one of its many battles with Pisa, took control of Livorno.

A few years later, Genoa sold the small port town, known then as Portus Liburni, to the Florentines. They wanted it because Livorno gave inland Florence an outlet to the sea and would contribute to its growing dominance over Pisa. It was the grand dukes of the Medici family who get credit for transforming Livorno "from a sleepy fishing village into one of the great centres of Mediterranean trade," historian David Abulafia tells us in his history of the Mediterranean, *The Great Sea.*

A succession of Medici rulers over the next century took the once-small fishing village to new heights. Today, Matilda's rebuilt tower and a few remnants of stone walls remain of the original fort, built by the Pisans. The fortress was replaced by what is known today as Fortezza Vecchia, or Old Fort.

The Medici also had a canal dredged several miles to the north that connected Livorno to the Arno River near Pisa. Just a few decades following the Old Fort's construction, a new fort was built farther inland but still within the city's walls. This is known today as Fortezza Nuova. The canal system, whether actually built by Venetian craftsmen or local craftsmen, was created to tie the new fort to the old fort, a half mile away at Livorno's harbor.

The main canal connecting the two forts opens into the original docking area where today Italian Coast Guard ships are moored, along with boats belonging to a squadron of customs police.

The name of this docking area — Darsena Vecchia, "Old Wet-docks" — shows the influence of Muslim culture along the Italian coastline. *Darsena* is an Italian-language modification of *Dār al-Sinā'a*, the Arabic word for docks. If the D is dropped and the word is further Italianized with the addition of *-le*, it becomes *arsenale*, or in English "arsenal." During the Middle Ages, the most common definition of "arsenal" was "establishment for the construction and equipment of warships."

The traveler, armed with detailed local maps, can see "Darsena" or its Italianized variant used in a variety of Italian ports. In Venice, the name "Arsenale" is used to denote the historic city's famed shipbuilding district. But "Darsena" prevails in several Italian port cities to denote their earliest dock areas, not arsenals. For example, in Siracusa, Sicily, Darsena marks the area along the ancient island of Ortigia, where ships and boats are still tied up. On its flank is Ristorante Darsena, one of Siracusa's finest seafood restaurants. Similarly named areas can likely be found in Palermo and Messina ports.

During the Middle Ages, the enlightened

Medici rule turned Livorno into an open city — a refuge for merchants and sailors of all nationalities and religions. The Medici drew up what was called the Livornine, an agreement outlining rules to be observed between them and non-Catholic subjects living within the city.

This document lasted for two centuries. Historian David Abulafia writes that it constituted a welcome to "merchants of all nations, Levantine and Poentine, Spanish and Portuguese, Greeks, Germans and Italians, Jews, Turks and Moors, Armenians, Persians and others." Also included in this melting pot were English Catholics who were exiled during Protestant rule in England. The name "Levantine" referred to eastern Jews; "Poentine" referred to western Jews, particularly those from the Iberian Peninsula who had converted to Christianity. The Medici rules required that these Poentine merchants, despite being Christian, had to declare themselves as Jews.

In Livorno, no Jewish quarter was established, although many of the Jews lived near the synagogue. The city had a variety of churches for the various religions, Christian and non-Christian, represented there. There were also three mosques and a Muslim cemetery.

Livorno certainly was an "open city." Trade was vibrant through the late sixteenth and seventeenth centuries. Because Muslim merchants were welcome, trade flourished with North Africa, particularly Morocco and Tunisia. The Dutch also were involved in trade activity with Livorno, despite being Protestant. The Medici decreed that Dutch merchants could live peaceably "with a certain amount of discretion."

This trade at Livorno was vital to the growth of Tuscany: North African wheat, wax, leather, wool, and sugar. Spain and Portugal provided tin, pine nuts, tuna fish, and anchovies. Beyond the Mediterranean side of these countries, Atlantic and North Sea ports, such as Cadiz and Lisbon, also had strong relations with Livornesi merchants.

One of the later Medici rulers, Ferdinand II, sought to create an international treaty that would turn Livorno into a neutral port. This finally happened in 1691, twenty-one years after Ferdinand's death. Napoleon Bonaparte would violate that treaty a century later.

Livorno's center is comfortable to visit on foot, but a tour by boat is well worth the time. It begins opposite the Fortezza Nuova and, almost immediately, the boat plunges into the semidarkness of a nearly 722-foot-long covered waterway that flows beneath one of Italy's largest squares, Livorno's Piazza della Repubblica.

The boat, emerging into bright sunlight from under the piazza, turns right on a narrow waterway and immediately a massive nineteenth-century building with high arched windows along the top edge appears. This structure is the Mercato Coperto, or Covered Market. I walked over to it after the canal tour ended.

Mercato Coperto is a daily market with hundreds of stalls showing off clothing; meats, kosher and otherwise; vegetables and towers of fresh fruit; a variety of fish caught early that morning; the largest selection of cheeses I have ever seen in one place anywhere in Italy; and numerous gelato, pastry, and bread stands. The aromas emanating from spice stands mix into this harmony of smells, and the sellers' barks and calls raise the din to a pleasant cacophony.

Leaving was hard; the things I wanted to buy would never fit into my bag. I've walked through a lot of markets — some rough and unkempt, others sparkling and magical — and I liked them all. This one, with sunlight filtering through a vast array of windows, including a long, narrow skylight in the ceiling high above, had my full attention for at least two hours.

I finished my day with a walk across the Piazza della Repubblica that earlier I had floated beneath during the boat ride. It is a vast open space, oval in shape, similar in magnitude to the fan-shaped Piazza del Campo in Siena. Many of the original streets of Livorno's historic center lead to the Piazza della Repubblica. The waterway below, known as the Royal Canal, came first, and then in the mid-1800s the square was built over it and dedicated to Grand Dukes of Tuscany. At the ends of the piazza are giant statues dedicated to Ferdinand III and Leopold II, two of the many Medici rulers. Medici rule ended in 1737, giving way to the Austrians and then the French under Napoleon.

In the mid-1800s, the area was renamed Republic Square, but locals refer to it as the Voltone because of the vault below that holds the nearly 722-foot-long Royal Canal.

As the day flickered into late afternoon, then early evening, I wandered the length of Via Grande back toward the port. This major boulevard is lined with shops under a series of Parisian-style arcades. My hotel was midway on this street. Around the corner is the Ristorante Gennaro, where the hotel desk clerk had made a 9 P.M. reservation for me, so I still had plenty of time to explore. As I wandered around the port area, I came across a series of churches with plaques indicating that they had been badly damaged by Allied bombing during World War II. One church is the Chiesa della Virgine e di San Giuseppe. The Medici built the church for Livorno's poor residents around the turn of the eighteenth century. Despite the war being over for nearly seventy years, the church is still surrounded in construction fencing. Across the church's parking lot to the south is still another church, the Chiesa de San Fernando. Allied bombing damaged it as well. But the plaque on the front boasts that it has been "amply restored." It, too, was closed.

I walked from the port toward the New Fort and, in the Square of the Dominicans a short distance away I found the octagonal Chiesa di Santa Caterina, a church with the Renaissance painting *Coronation of the Virgin* by Giorgio Vasari, the same fellow who designed the Church of Santo Stefano dei Cavalieri in Pisa. Next to the church is Forte San Pietro, a former prison and now a wine bar. It has a small side door that's directly across the narrow street from a similar small door in the side of the church, the entrance and exit for prisoners being led to and from Mass.

A short branch of the canal runs here, sort of a builders' afterthought that plunges between medieval houses that likely once were homes to fishermen. Along the canal I came across a cluster of elderly men, likely retired fishermen, drinking from small glasses of wine and beer, at a *circolo,* or private bar. I had a membership card from the artisans' *circolo* in Pietrasanta and showed it to the man behind the bar, who greeted me warmly, took my order for a double espresso, and pointed to a table along the canal.

I sat down next to the water lined with small boats, some rigged for pleasure and others rigged with nets and other gear. I watched the sun disappear behind the church's domed roof, listened to the low conversations of the pensioners and younger, active fishermen around me, observed a couple of card games, watched the occasional boat or skiff drift by, motors set on low purr, and felt at peace after a long day.

It was late August. My time in Tuscany was

running out, and I had to choose between visiting Giglio or Elba. Giglio won because it was small enough to be seen in a day whereas Elba would require a longer journey and a car rented on the island.

Giglio is the island where, in January 2012, the cruise ship *Costa Concordia* slammed into a rock formation just a few dozen feet off the island's coast at the edge of its port. The rocks sliced the hull lengthwise, the ship tilted on his side, and water gushed in. Of the 3,200 passengers and 1,023 crew, 32 died. Islanders collected survivors, invited them into their homes, and fed and clothed them until they could be transported to the mainland.

On my trip eight months later, I saw *Concordia*'s rust-stained, battered hulk — so big that it can be seen in satellite photographs. To get to Giglio, I took a ferry from Porto Santo Stefano — a port on the one-time island of Monte Argentario now connected by three narrow strips to the southern Tuscan mainland at Orbetello. It is a short ride, perhaps an hour, and as the ferry approached Giglio, the rust-streaked, elongated white form of the tipped ship slowly came into view, surrounded by cranes and nearly a dozen service craft. In late 2012, Italy's environment minister, Andrea Orlando, told news reporters that the ship likely would be gone by the end of 2013. In reality, it took until mid-September 2013 to bring the 951-foot vessel upright. The salvage effort to get the ship off the rocks, towed to a shipyard somewhere along the coast of Italy, and cut into pieces was estimated to cost at least $795 million, up from the original estimate of $300 million. And authorities believe that the price tag could rise even further. The towing wasn't expected to begin until spring 2014.

Some say this is the biggest maritime salvage job ever undertaken. I am skeptical, given the volume of salvage operations involving giant warships following various twentieth-century wars. But reports indicate that more than one hundred divers have been working in shifts around the clock. Their plan to raise the ship, which went off like clockwork in September 2013, a year after I was there: pour eighteen thousand tons of concrete to stabilize the vessel and then attach pontoons to both sides of the hull. Pressurized, these pontoons allowed crews to roll *Concordia* onto a massive underwater platform.

Concordia is reportedly resting on top of two archaeological sites dating from 200 BC. Archaeologists said a third site, an

Etruscan shipwreck going back to 600 BC, has been destroyed by the ship's impact. The vessel also rests alongside a protected coral reef and marine park. This area is one of several around the island that has long attracted amateur snorkelers and divers who want to see the ancient underwater ruins and the area's numerous varieties of exotic fish, dolphins, and huge mussels. Fortunately, today they have the rest of Giglio's seventeen-mile coastline, and the coastlines of other islands in this archipelago, to explore.

On the August day of my visit I was overwhelmed by the immensity of the crowds of sun-soaked tourists. Most are day-trippers, eager to see the wreck, spend a few hours on the beach, and then return to mainland Italy in the afternoon. The ship's presence has significantly reduced the number of overnight visitors. But with five hundred workers and divers struggling to refloat *Concordia,* hotels are full. When the ship is finally gone, sometime in 2014, tourism officials on the island hope to recover what has been lost for two years: the presence of multi-day tourists who will explore the island and the waters along its shoreline.

We clambered off the ferry and into a tiny village that was already elbow-to-elbow with

day-trippers who had arrived on earlier ferries from Porto Santo Stefano. The crowds
were so thick it was difficult to walk along
the thin spit of land between the edge of
the bay and the row of restaurants, T-shirt
shops, and a few hotels. The village is not
deep; only a few elongated rows of houses
and narrow streets rim the bay, offering
refuge just a few blocks higher up to its
slightly more than one thousand year-round
residents.

The most striking image of that August
day was the small beach jammed with
umbrellas and prone bodies on large, colorful towels, people splashing in the warm
blue of the narrow bay, juxtaposed with
Concordia's towering hulk just a hundred or
so feet away. What could that captain have
been thinking as he guided his ship so close
to this island's outcropping of razorlike
rocks so he could "salute" the locals? This
happened in January when only island
residents and perhaps just a few tourists
were there to witness the incident. And dinner was being served aboard the ship when
it went aground. Given the time of year, the
early evening likely was growing dark.
Anyone watching the ship doing its "sail-
by" would have seen its lights suddenly go
out and would have heard the sound of its

hull as it scraped along an outcrop of submerged rock, being peeled open like a can of sardines.

I had arrived in midmorning and wandered along the beach and glanced into shops for a few hours. Restaurants were crowded and the tiny shops were jammed. Uphill, in the quieter residential areas, locals not working the concessions below gathered in front of their houses, sitting in shade and deep in conversation. Kids, like children everywhere in Italy, were kicking soccer balls, careening them off the stones of the pale yellow houses.

The midday sun was blistering. Having a few hours before the final ferry of the day would arrive to haul tourists back to the mainland, I sought out the comfort of an outdoor bar, shaded by colorful umbrellas. I enjoyed coffee, a few cold drinks, ate proffered snacks, and watched the panoply along the crowded beach.

Eventually, in the distance far to the east, the Porto Santo Stefano ferry came into view. At that first sighting, people started moving toward the pier. I went down and found myself far behind a massive jam of people. Still more people — there were several hundred of us by now — packed into the small area. The ferry backed in, dropped its stern gate, and people started crowding on.

It became clear there was not enough space for everyone, and Coast Guard personnel started pushing folks back so the stern gate could be raised. Would I have to find a way to stay the night on Giglio? I wondered. A man in front of me, fluent in Italian, listened carefully to what a Coast Guard officer was shouting several feet away. "Ah," the man said as he turned toward his wife. "A second ferry is coming." It did, and within an hour everyone was accommodated.

By then, it was late afternoon, and the beach was nearly deserted; only a few hardy souls were still in the water or under their umbrellas. The beach and town may have been drained of visitors, but there was no letdown of activity around *Concordia*'s massive bulk. All of us leaving the island crowded along the ferry's deck rail, snapping photos of the giant cranes surrounding the doomed ship and the small workboats darting around its hull. A few of us speculated about the two bodies that had yet to be recovered. When the ship was floated upright a year after my visit, the remains of Indian crewmember Russell Rebello were found; as of the end of 2013, the body of

Sicilian Maria Grazia Trecarichi remained lost.

I knew that I would return to Giglio and Capraia — and even visit giant Elba — one day soon. And perhaps I would stop at a few of the much smaller places that require patience to travel to. It would be in the off-season, not July or August, and at a time when *Concordia* would become only a distant memory for these Tuscan islanders.

TEN:
THE DEEP SOUTH

The essence of Tuscany is in its towns and cities, what Italians call *civiltà*. A dictionary will list the meaning as "civilization," but that does not even approach its Tuscan sense. *Civiltà* is something like townishness, community, a civic sense, pride, identity all wrapped up together with its tangible consequences: the great churches and the paintings and sculpture inside them . . . and a lip-curling contempt for any other town that is not our town.

— Alistair Moffat,
Tuscany: A History (2011)

There are a couple of ways to move south through western Tuscany. One is to head east from Pisa and then turn south, say at Pontedera, and then, after crossing the Pisa–Florence *autostrada* and passing through Ponsacco, head down Tuscany's middle through some uninspiring industrial areas that thankfully give way to wheat fields, rolling hills, vineyards, vast swaths of sunflowers, and olive groves that cut through small villages.

Here is a real opportunity for a tourist to become a traveler. If a cool, shady piazza in one of these villages offers respite, the traveler could spend an hour or so and enjoy a meal, or simply a coffee or cold drink at a local bar, sitting outside, soaking in the scene of a Tuscan village and its residents. Make a point to do this once or twice each day while on the road. The memories can stay with you for a long time.

Or, the traveler can choose to venture south down the coast itself, through low rolling hills that offer occasional glimpses of the Mediterranean. Somewhere along the southern Tuscan coast is the invisible dividing line between the Ligurian and Tyrrhenian seas. The name likely changes at the port town of Piombino, near the island of Elba and the coast of the French-controlled island Corsica. On sections of this coastal road between Livorno and Piombino, parked cars line up for miles, their owners carrying umbrellas, coolers, and beach towels down to the rocky shoreline far below. Sometimes, this coastal road passes through towns and villages with their own public and private beaches and pedestrian walkways with tiny shops.

The least rewarding way — unless the traveler is hell-bent to get to Rome — is along the *autostrada,* the E80. This route, like interstate highways in the United States, avoids towns and villages. Its higher speeds propel the traveler quickly from point A to B with brief glimpses, say, of castle ruins or a cluster of medieval stone houses perched on faraway hilltops. There is no incentive — and perhaps no convenient exit — to explore them. And with sections that charge tolls, the *autostrada* periodically offers self-contained rest stops, complete with gasoline stations, restrooms, and cafeteria food, never requiring the motorist to pull into a small village for such services.

The coastal route, the mostly two-lane Via Aurelia, was my choice for a major multi-day foray into the south of western Tuscany. It would be a longer journey, but I would pass through small villages and towns, places ripe for discovery and worth stopping at if the mood strikes. I began just south of Livorno, bypassing the city that I had already spent time in, and made my first stop at Quercianella, a tiny village strung out along a high ridge overlooking the Tyrrhenian Sea. The sign announcing

Quercianella promised a brief rest and lunch.

I parked next to a magnificent walled compound containing a mix of honey-stoned buildings separated by large expanses of flower gardens. The structures appeared to range in age from one hundred to three hundred years old. The oldest building, which sits in the foreground of the property, has all the appearances of a monastery. It was somber, with few arched windows, and with a short medieval tower with toothlike merlons of stone in a circle around the top. Each merlon was separated by a gap, called a crenellation, which would have allowed defenders to shoot arrows and toss spears and then dart behind a merlon for protection. The entire battlement sat on top of what medievalist scholars call machicolations, or riblike stone beams that lean out from the tower cylinder at a sharp enough angle to keep attackers from climbing to the battlement. If it was indeed built in the 1700s, I doubt anyone was shooting arrows at attackers. I suspect it was built to honor an image of Tuscany's medieval past.

Later research suggested that this former monastery could have been turned into a spa built in the late nineteenth or early twentieth century. Many Tuscan spas were created in those days to draw well-heeled English visitors. A sign next to the locked iron gate had the name Villa Jana and the date MCMXXI — 1921. This date marks the year a small brick building was converted into the two-story neo-medieval structure that dominates the property. It also has a tower, a four-story structure that looks more like a bell tower than a battlement. The expanded house and its tower look like they could have been built six hundred years ago rather than just ninety-one.

Nothing suggested that tours or visits were available; the property appeared to be in private hands.

A hundred feet down the road and atop the ridge overlooking the sea was a small bar that offered lunch. Next to the bar, a narrow, steep trail with stone steps led down to the rocky beach. There, sun seekers, snorkelers, and scuba-equipped divers had spread large towels across the bumpy surfaces of giant boulders. There was no sand down below, just a few scattered patches of pebbles among sea-battered rocks.

I sat outside, with a terrific view of the sea, and ate one of the best *pasta pomodoro* lunches I have ever had, and learned about the area from an easy conversation with the bar's owner, each of us using a comfortable combination of English and Italian.

Quercianella first appeared on maps in the mid- to late 1700s. Apparently there was a lookout tower along the coast, likely built by Pisa in the Middle Ages, and the village gradually developed around it. As roads to the area were improved, wealthy Italians constructed elegant villas here. Some still stand today.

The town once had the full name Quercianella Sonnino in honor of Baron Sidney Sonnino, a now obscure Italian politician, born in Pisa in 1847. His political career in the newly unified nation of Italy spanned the late 1800s and the early twentieth century. Sonnino apparently loved this rugged area and its stellar views, so he built a castle that still rises up above the trees that dominate the small village. He died in 1922, and his grave is in a cave on the castle grounds. The "Sonnino" part of the town's name apparently has outlived its political relevance and has been dropped.

After a few hours at the bar, I continued on south. Via Aurelia goes through a succession of beach communities that could each be a major destination for a traveler wanting camping, bed-and-breakfast accommodations, or even a multi-star hotel experience. As elsewhere in the region, July and August are the months with the most crowds, which makes it difficult to find lodging for the night. I stopped at a few places to inquire about lodging and was told that no room was to be had until early September. If I had been so inclined, I could not have even rented an umbrella on a private beach.

"We are usually booked a year in advance," one beachfront manager told me. "The same people come back year after year and demand the same spots, over and over." Most are English, but some German, French, and Dutch travelers make up the bulk of repeat business. Americans? "Not many. I do not recall any this year or last."

But the towns and villages here are so close together that if reservations can be made in advance farther inland, the drive to an appealing public beach is a quick one.

Leaving Quercianella, Via Aurelia carried me to Vada. Its five miles of appealing white-sand beaches are so unlike the steep boulder-strewn coast at Quercianella. To get to the beach area, there are many turnoffs along its five-mile stretch. I chose the first one, at the north end of a vast pine forest. It took me a few miles west to a concessions area and the beginning of white sand.

Parking is along the road or among the trees in a haphazard pattern that is somehow typically Italian: it looks confusing, but one just needs to stop, leave room for cars to get through, and not block anyone who already has squeezed their vehicle among the skinny pine trees.

The foot trail through low scrub pines is not long, perhaps a few hundred feet, and the panorama quickly opens up to a stunning expanse of white sand, pocketed here and there with umbrellas and multicolored beach blankets.

Children are in control here, reminding me of a guidebook statement read long ago that, in Italy, children are royalty. They are everywhere — exploring the line of pines along the beach, building castles in the sand, burying playmates up to their chins, splashing in the waist-deep waters on the edge of the Tyrrhenian Sea — while watchful parents sit under umbrellas, only occasionally rising to go out to the water, swim a few strokes, and come back to the shade.

Farther out toward the water, a stubby peninsula of sand, protected from erosion by a low stone wall, seems to appeal more to solitary adults and couples. The ubiquitous African sellers of everything from facial tissues, toys for the kids, cigarette lighters, floppy hats, walking sticks, gum, umbrellas, and just about anything else, it seems, work the beach as far as the eye can see. These are hardworking immigrants with temporary residence permits who live in group houses and every morning ride local buses to assigned areas. I never saw them, in any of these communities, take breaks; loaded down with goods and with prices up for negotiation, they are constantly on the move from one cluster of sunbathers to another.

I spend an hour sitting on the low wall and watch the swimmers and snorkelers packed in the blue-water bay. I do not plan to spend the afternoon planted on a beach soaking up sun. I still have a ways to go before I reach the small, nondescript but friendly twentieth-century town of Donoratico, near Castagneto Carducci. I had settled for a one-star hotel there when I discovered all the beach communities were booked solid. This small postwar town sits a mile or two from the coast and was my base for three days.

As I walked off the beach at Vada and through the pines, the high-pitched loud buzzing of cicadas in the trees overhead persisted. Every July, a campground hostess told me, when the temperature and humidity hit a certain level, they emerge from the soil and crawl into the trees, where females lay eggs. "They sometimes make for eating, a delicacy," the hostess said. "But they are not for me." "*E non mi!* [And not me!]," I replied in Italian to her excellent English.

En route to Donoratico, I decided to stop in at Bolgheri, a few miles inland and perhaps twenty miles southeast of Vada. Bolgheri, a walled village with origins in the eighth century, sits in a sea of vineyards. Friends tell me that some of the best Tuscan wines, in sharp competition with the more established Chianti region well to the east, come from around Bolgheri.

A narrow, paved road heading directly east off the Via Aurelia leads to the town, which is nestled in the low-lying hills, the Colline Metalifere. Towering over the three-mile route are six hundred cypress trees, perhaps the most famous in Tuscany, which is well known for its stretches of cypress that line roads and act as sentinel-like windbreaks along edges of fields and vineyards. Bolgheri's cypress clusters have been there since the early 1800s. They climb to heights of well over one hundred feet and are so massive and so close together that they appear as a solid wall along the narrow roadway, broken only where a crossroad slices north–south through it.

There are other well-known cypress-lined roadways in Tuscany: in the area around Pienza, at La Foce, and at Monticchiello. But these are lightly strung out, not so packed together as on the road to Bolgheri.

The cypress, with origins in Persia or Syria, is such a part of the modern traveler's image of Tuscany that the tree is often referred to as the Tuscan cypress. For Greeks and Italians, the tall, bushy, dark green tree is dedicated to Artemis, the Greek goddess of the hunt. The trees can live for at least two thousand years and likely were revered by the pre-Roman Etruscans who lived here more than three thousand years ago and populated much of what is Tuscany today. Such trees have fragrant wood, and early peoples planted them around houses. The Etruscans marked their cemeteries with them. The cypress, like olive trees, seems magical to me, whether up close or at a distance, surrounding a farm complex or a stone-sided winery high on a Tuscan hill. Paintings and photographs capture the individual beauty of these trees and give us the images of Tuscany that we all treasure.

The six hundred trees — I took a friend's word for the number and did not count them — come to a sudden stop at the large stone entryway into Bolgheri. The town's original castle was demolished and relocated to its current site in 1496.

Off to the right of the main gate sits a small shop selling wine. The most exclusive vintage in the store is the Sassicaia. It is from a local winery, Tenuta San Guido, and is priced at a thousand euros, or a little more than thirteen hundred dollars, per bottle. This specific winery opened in the late 1940s, but real expansion of the industry in this area didn't begin until the 1990s, when the wines began to win various international competitions. Bottles of various vintages were for sale at far more affordable prices, of course, along with wines from other producers in the area.

The store, in addition to wine and local meats and cheeses, sold dried pasta in shapes and colors I have not seen anywhere else in Italy. Most of the pasta was in long, thin strips colored black and white; some came in the rounded shape of hats with stripes of various colors. I asked a clerk if these pastas are modern creations developed for the tourist trade or if they are traditional in this small village. She merely shrugged. "It is ours."

I talked for a few moments with a very busy Silvia Casini at the front door of her wine shop. She said Europeans and Italians visit the town from far away, "But few Americans make it here. You can see how crowded we are today. All Europeans, I think. But in winter it is quiet. Only sixty-four people live here around the year."

A few blocks deeper into the village I came across a small cemetery, complete with a caretaker who was more than willing to speak to anyone wanting to know its history. One grave belongs to the poet Giosuè Carducci's grandmother, Nonna Lucia, who lived there for most of her life. He did, too, but only for a few years as a small child. But Bolgheri has not seen fit to add his name. The town does honor his grandmother with a small statue, if only because she was connected to the famed wordsmith and had spent most of her life there. Near the cemetery gate is her modern statue.

Giosuè Carducci and his family moved here in 1838 from Valdicastello, next to Pietrasanta, when he was three. A decade later the family moved a few miles southwest to what is today Castagneto Carducci, a hill town that, along with Valdicastello, claims Carducci's name.

Early one morning I took a small provincial road that leads directly south of Bolgheri toward Castagneto Carducci, about seven miles away. Bolgheri is on a wide plain surrounded by vineyards. Castagneto Carducci tops a high hill that doesn't quite qualify as a mountain. I decided to bypass that town and continue south along the provincial road through a wilderness of trees. Gaps in the foliage provided occasional glimpses of vineyards and olive groves on the hill's flanks. I wasn't sure where I would end up; this was a trip of exploration; I would stop as the mood struck me.

Heading up, down, and around one of many coastal hills, I passed dozens of bicyclists, all dressed in various team colors. At one spot, above the tiny village of Suverete and on a section of the road identified as La Strada del Vino, or "the Wine Highway," a van was parked alongside the road. It had bicycles attached to its roof and on its front and back ends. A man stood next to it and, one by one, bicyclists in skintight shorts and shirts would pass by and grab the bottles of water the man was handing out. They were moving uphill, sweat dripping profusely despite the early hour.

I pulled over, got out of the car, and watched the groups of riders passing by. I asked the man whom he represented. Partly because of my poor understanding of detailed Italian speech and partly because of his rapid pattern of speaking, I caught only snatches of his response. It seemed to be a regional cycling club in active training. The Giro d'Italia (the national race second only to the Tour de France, which is usually held in July) had been in May, just a few months before my drive. Training is year-round; numerous cross-country races fill the calendar in most European countries.

These Tuscan hills are perfect for training. Many of the routes through them mirror the routes of the major races in Italy, France, and Spain. "Up, up, up!" he said as he positioned himself to hand water bottles to two more racers rounding the curve a few dozen feet below. "Then, speed and confusion. Control! Discipline." He paused while a group of six riders flashed by, each biker grabbing a proffered water bottle. I thanked him and reflected on the dangers to the bike riders I had seen during my travels all over Tuscany's coastal hills. They are on narrow roads, often with tight turns where oncoming cars cannot see them. I don't know how many collisions between bike and car occur annually, but from what I have seen while driving around Italy over the years, the riders are a savvy bunch who know how to keep to the far right. I suspect crashes with automobiles are few.

The water-bottle man laughed. "In Italy, everyone makes way for the riders," he said. "It is life here."

Ahead, beyond the nondescript village of Suverete, I could see Sassetta along a steep mountainside, with the lower part of the village fronting a massive cliff that drops down into a deep gorge.

Sassetta spills over the small summit while surrounded on three sides by a deep and appealing chestnut forest, now designated as a park area of nearly two thousand acres. Interspersed among the chestnut trees are briarwood shrubs, five to six feet tall, that produce hard, bulbous growths on roots and trunks. Sassetta craftsmen have been making smoking pipes from this briarwood since the late 1800s. A young woman in the tiny tourist office near the village's entrance told me that the craft has been handed down from father to son for generations.

Sassetta is worth a visit and perhaps an overnight stay. Even when I was there in the height of the tourist season, it seemed that few visitors have discovered it and its numerous walking trails through the hills. I wandered the once-medieval stronghold, finding numerous pink-marble carvings —

made from *rosso di Sassetta* — of various animals: deer, rabbits, and dogs.

After my visit, I read that these carvings are modern, the result of an annual sculpture symposium held over ten days every July. Five sculptors are invited to create these works of art in the outdoors while townspeople and visitors watch. Anyone can vote for his or her favorite pieces, and prizes are given. All are displayed along the so-called "path of art" I was wandering along.

Near the top of the village sits the Chiesa di Sant'Andrea, with a façade and bulk that date back to at least the 1600s. No one seems to know the origins of this church beyond its expansion and remodeling five hundred years ago, only that it sits over Roman catacombs holding the bones of an anonymous martyr.

Narrow pathways between medieval buildings, made out of local limestone, shoot off from the little square in front of the church. The visitor can take several routes out of this small village center and find trails through the surrounding *bosco,* or woods. I walk perhaps a mile or two along one of them. It was moderate walking in a green wonderland; occasional views of the Tyrrhenian coast and the gray sea pop through the trees. Humidity is high. It is summer, so cicadas are in full concert in the chestnut trees. I had spent three hours in Sassetta. It was now late morning, and if I wanted to get to Populonia, I figured it was best to move on.

Many villages throughout southern Tuscany claim Etruscan origins. They make up the land known as Costa degli Etruschi, or Coast of the Etruscans. In the first century BC, long before Rome was a local power much less an empire, Etruscans dominated this landscape. They even carved a trade route through the towering Apennine Mountains, establishing a village where the city of Bologna now sits and still farther east to their trading center at today's Adria on Italy's east coast, thought by some historians to be the source of the Adriatic Sea's name. They could have been here far back into prehistory, coming from somewhere else. Or, perhaps, they were merely an amalgam of prehistoric tribes.

The Costa degli Etruschi designation likely was created to appeal to tourists, but it does include a significant portion of the Etruscan sites that dominated what was known in ancient times as Etruria. This area encompassed much of today's Tuscany, from Livorno south to the region of Lazio, all the way down to Rome. Early kings of Rome were from a people known as the Sabini, a large tribe encompassing an area to the east of Rome. The last three kings of Rome were Etruscans; their kings ruled there until 709 BC, when the Roman Republic was founded and consuls were elected.

The earliest Romans, then, were a combination of Etruscan, Sabini, and tribal people known as "Latins," drawn from around Rome's various hills and the countryside beyond. Etruscan DNA reached way down through the generations. The family line of the greatest Roman of them all, Julius Caesar, is believed to have had Etruscan origins.

So it was Etruscans who dominated the landscape before Roman civilization emerged. Their earliest maritime villages, David Abulafia writes in his book on the Mediterranean, were where "the great leap towards urban civilization first occurred. These were rich cities, well organized, with literate elites, handsome temples, and skilled craftsmen." It was their skills and the culture they created that Rome drew from as the newly unified people moved from their mud huts on Rome's Palatine Hill to a city of rough stone and brick. It would take seven hundred years after the founding of the Republic before Augustus, the first emperor, transformed it into a city of marble.

One of the southernmost early Etruscan cities in Tuscany was my next major stop: the ruins of Populonia, a pre-Roman port created around 900 BC.

Far down the mountain to the west of Sassetta, at the end of a curving mountain road still showing occasional flashes of those colorfully garbed bicyclists at full downhill tilt, is the small village of Suvereto. I stopped there, briefly, for an early-afternoon coffee and a *panino.* I sat in a small square just outside the town's old stone gate. A remarkable tree with long, narrow, leathery leaves and a blackish bark that I did not recognize shaded several tables full of friends enjoying conversation and *caffè.* Small acorns could be seen throughout its thick foliage. I asked the man at the bar about the tree. He said it was a *leccio,* which I later found out was Italian for holm oak. Sitting by that tree, observing life in this small village, and listening to conversations in Tuscan Italian, was a pleasant break.

The ancient Etruscan port of Populonia was still farther to the southwest, on a level coastal plain and perhaps less than an hour away along a nearly straight road. This now-large archaeological park has tombs dating back to pre-Roman times. A short distance away from the necropolis, or cemetery, and toward the coast overlooking the sea at the Gulf of Baratti, is the mostly unexcavated remains of the ancient city.

The park covers nearly two hundred acres, encompassing the Etruscans' only significant coastal city; their other cities are sprinkled throughout inland Tuscany and northern Lazio — some built over by the Romans and later by builders in the Middle Ages, creating the towns and villages we know today. Others, like Populonia, survive only as ruins with a scattering of twentieth-century restoration. Few Etruscan ruins are of the magnitude of this site, which had its earliest beginning in the sixth century BC. It then operated from the fifth century to first century BC as a center to process iron ore.

Archaeologist Anna Marguerite McCann, in a 1977 article from the *Journal of Field Archaeology,* writes that the "ancient city [Populonia] . . . lies still unexcavated. Material found from the tombs may go back as early at 1000 BC." Over the intervening millennia, sea level at the Gulf of Baratti has risen more than eight feet, submerging the Etruscans' coastal structures and slag from the processing of ancient iron ore. Archaeologist McCann writes:

The height of Populonia's commercial life was thus in the late Classical and Hellenistic periods when most of the cities in southern Etruria were on the decline. Her continued prosperity was undoubtedly due to the life of her port and the working of the iron ore which took place there. Her wealth during these years is reflected in her gold and silver coinage which is the oldest and richest in Etruria. While we know of no great art manufactured in this predominantly industrial city, ships could easily bring imported work to her shores.

Today, this park is wide open for the ramblings of tourists. If the traveler has time for only one Etruscan site out of the dozens preserved throughout what was ancient Etruria, this should be the one.

My goal on this trip was to spend time at Populonia's port area. A few months earlier, friends from Pietrasanta had taken me to the necropolis, a few miles away, where the ancients buried their dead. We got there late in the day — too late to also tour the ruins in the port area before the site closed for the day.

We drove into the parking area for the

Necropoli di San Cerbone and began a day of walking amongst Etruscan and, perhaps, a few Roman-era tombs. Seven tombs are spread out in an area close to the parking lot, and each is worthy of inspection. Entrances are blocked, but visitors can roam around them at will, touching the limestone blocks that were handled by Etruscan builders and put into place between three and four thousand years ago. I did not see any of the hand-carved stone caskets where bodies were placed — they have long since been removed and taken to museums — but I remembered looking at them many years ago at the Etruscan museum in Tarquinia, just north of Rome. The reclining carved figures of men and women, propped up on one elbow atop ancient, pre-Roman caskets, have always captivated me. All are wide-eyed, complete with smiles, with goblets of wine in their hands, and perhaps with one of their favorite pets carved in stone at their sides as well.

These Etruscan caskets are so different from Christian-era stone repositories with the deceased represented in a prone position, eyes closed, hands crossed over their chests. Etruscans, it seems, were all about this life, not the afterlife so valued by their Christian successors.

The challenging walk — to the Necropoli delle Grotte — begins just beyond the visitor center. The path stretches across a flat, humid plain and then heads up into a heavily oak-forested hill, where tombs were chipped out of the hill's limestone interior. Steep steps drop down from the trail into tomb after tomb, each closed off. The trail, also steep at times with weathered, slick stones underfoot, winds up and down through heavy undergrowth. One side of the hill drops down an incline and offers a panoramic view of a handful of tombs in a small valley below. Eventually, the loop led us back to where we started at the top of the hill. There, at a junction, was a different route back to the visitor center. It avoided the flat plain and took us up another series of small hills, but there were not many tombs to see during the first part of that second slog.

As we got closer to the center, more tombs came into view. And just before the final home stretch, a new trail branched off to the west, that would take us a few miles to the ruins of the ancient town, the Etrusci Acropoli. But the day was growing short, and none in my party was eager to make that long walk to the acropolis and then back again to the parking lot. Exploring it would have to wait until another time.

Now, a few months later, I returned to Populonia, this time alone, and spent a short time skirting the ground-level ruins of the acropolis. Not much remains here, however, and it is obvious that the tombs are the most enduring structures the Etruscans left behind.

Just below the ruins and hard by the Tyrrhenian Sea, the modern village of Baratti and its marina are in a cove just seven miles north of the modern port city of Piombino. This cove is one of the most beautiful along Tuscany's 180-mile coastline. Private boats and seagoing yachts are moored here, and a short beach area, showing evidence of ancient industrialization from deposits of iron ore and slag still found there, looks out over the glistening sea. Ironically, some of those two-thousand-year-old deposits were harvested and reprocessed to make badly needed iron for rebuilding bombed-out Piombino in the days after World War II.

Wanting to reach Piombino before late evening took away the last vestige of that marvelous sunset, I drove back up on that slim coastal road and made it there before darkness. Piombino is a major departure point for numerous ferries making forty-five-minute trips to Elba, just a few miles off the coast. The town has little appeal for a traveler wanting to experience medieval Tuscany. The port area, now a modern collection of ferry terminals, a train station, and docks for ferries and other large commercial ships, has been mostly reconstructed from the rubble of World War II.

Some parts of the town itself harken back to medieval times, but the site as a village is significantly older than the Middle Ages. Some think the name Piombino is a derivation of the Italian word Populino, which means "small Populonia." The Etruscans and Romans had villages near Piombino as well as at the larger Populonia, just a few miles to the north.

By now it is dark and time to head back north to my hotel at Donoratico. I would be taking a longer drive south the next day to explore the coastal area of the Tuscan Maremma, a truly wild west part of Tuscany. This would be the farthest south I would go.

The next morning, I once again made my way toward Piombino. Instead of continuing straight toward the port, I take a narrow secondary road that heads east along the northern edge of the Gulf of Follonica. Just past a large electricity-generating plant with red-and-white-striped smokestacks, I pass beach clubs, situated one after the other, along a long band of white sand known as Carbonifera Beach. This stretch of beach is broken up by a series of cabanas and coffee shops.

The first beach area within the greater Carbonifera complex is called Spiaggia Cani, or Dog Beach. The road into it follows a canal lined with a few fishermen and boats loading customers in scuba gear. These folks obviously are preparing to head out to a tiny island off the coast, Cerboli, with its piled-high landmass resembling a delicious dollop of *tiramisu.* Twentieth-century Italian writer and essayist Carlo Cassola, who died in 1987 at age sixty-nine, once owned it.

A bit farther to the west of Cerboli is the much smaller island of Palmaiola, and beyond that is the northeastern tip of the largest island of the Tuscan archipelago, Elba — its grayish bulk dominating the western horizon.

By nine o'clock and with the August heat building toward eighty degrees Fahrenheit and 90 percent humidity making it feel more like a hundred, the parking lot has more than two hundred cars. The beach is full of mothers and their children, older men in Speedos, and teens in long shorts and bikinis. It is a happy scene where I spent a couple of hours, shoes in hand, walking barefoot along the beach and feeling the warm tiny waves as they drift onto the sand, taking in the view of Elba, and wishing I had been able to make it there. By late morning, it is time to go. I want to move on to Follonica, just a few miles away along the crescent of the Gulf of Follonica and where the small provincial road to these beach areas rejoins north–south SS1.

Follonica is a pleasant city, certainly more modern in appearance than most of the villages and towns along coastal Tuscany. A friend in Pietrasanta wrinkled her nose when I told her I might go there during my trip south. "It is so ordinary; it has no character," she said. Driving through it and toward its beach area along the gulf, I had to disagree. For a casual visitor, it offers a tastefully done, more modern city — a change of pace.

Why not spend some time in a place like Follonica? It has a wide, clean, white-sand public beach and a long line of private clubs with names like Bagno Orchidea and Bagno Roma; enough shops to satisfy the most retail-oriented tourist; nice two-,three-, and four-star hotels lined up along a comfortable, shaded pedestrian walkway. It could almost pass for a Southern California beach community, but without the surfers and plastic surgery.

If, like me, you are not a beach person but someone who enjoys magnificent views of the sea, then go into a bar on the beach, sit on a shaded veranda, and order a coffee or beer. It is high season while I'm here, but prices remain reasonable: two euros for a *caffè* and a cream-filled *cornetto,* my favorite snack. And you can sit there as long as you want. This is so typically Italian: no one is trying to get you to buy more or to make room for new customers. As long as you buy something when you first sit down, you own that table, and the view, until you are ready to leave. There are plenty of such places in Follonica, bordered by tall shrubs with sweet-smelling pink and white flowers.

As if to confirm what my friend in Pietrasanta told me, but with a different spin, a middle-aged woman who served my coffee described Follonica as "very new." "It wasn't a town until 1823," she said. The concept of "old" is very different in Italy than in the United States.

Later that afternoon, after three or four pleasant hours taken up with a double espresso at a bar table with a view, a long, leisurely lunch of pasta with pancetta and Parmesan cheese mixed in, and some time spent wandering along the mile-long promenade in this "not old" nineteenth-century town, I continued down the coast, passing through Principina a Mare and its stunning cypress forest. It has two private *bagni* with a fine public beach in between. A few miles later, I came to Marina di Alberese, which offers a unique experience for beachgoers. To get to the beach, a visitor must drive through a forest dense with cypress and coastal pines. Here, the buzzing of the cicadas was at its height, with the translucent creatures scattered along tree trunks or high on the branches above. A parking warden saw me looking closely at the embedded creatures. "*Essi sono innocui* [They are harmless]," she said, adding with a smile, "You get used to the noise!"

There is a lot of dead wood scattered about from the thick forest that ends just a few dozen feet from the water and from driftwood from the Tyrrhenian Sea that piles up in great mounds. From this wood, people have crafted stick structures, including makeshift cabanas with tarps thrown over them. This quickly becomes my favorite beach of the dozens I have passed through. It is isolated, small, not crowded, and there are no entry fees. This is a place to return to — if I am with someone who wants a beach experience.

I am a day away from moving a short distance inland, into the heart of the Tuscan Maremma, once the wildest and wooliest of Tuscany's west. A special breed of cattle is raised here, the Maremmana, tended by cowboys, the *butteri,* who traditionally wore velvet jackets and black hats, and rode a local breed of horse called Maremmano. I did not see any of these cowboys. Ranching today is modern here, and the *butteri* ride vehicles, saving the horses and their gear for festivals and parades.

Bandits flourished throughout the Maremma in the late nineteenth and early twentieth centuries, much like they did in the far south of Italy. These two areas were so remote back then that they had been largely ignored in the days after northern Italians united the peninsula. These bandits preyed on travelers along the Via Aurelia and hid out in small inland villages. Storytellers and balladeers today venerate bandits' violent ways in the wild west of Tuscany, where they have now morphed into legend.

The people of this small area had things

other than bandits to worry about. Malaria was a common malady. The Italian word *maremma* variously translates to "bad water," "swamp," and "marsh." It comes from either the Latin *maritima* or the Old Castilian word *marismas.*

In the Middle Ages, the progressive Matilda, countess of Tuscany, launched public works to drain swamps that once dominated this low-lying coastal area and bred mosquitoes, the dreaded *zanzare.* A similar attempt was made in the mid-1800s. To his credit, the Italian dictator Mussolini also launched swamp-draining projects in the 1920s and 1930s to finish Matilda's efforts. This resulted in the reclamation of vast acreage now under fields of wheat, corn, and sunflowers; vineyards; and olive groves.

At one time, beginning in the 1890s, the government had combated malaria by providing inexpensive quinine to its citizens. Mussolini's land-reclamation projects, along with similar projects following World War II, ultimately did away with that dreaded disease in this part of the world.

Today the land, of course, is still low-lying and prone to flooding. In the fall of 2012, for example, great swaths of the coastal area around Grosseto, the major city of the Maremma located slightly inland between

Piombino and the lagoon city of Orbetello, were underwater in the aftermath of heavy rains, blocking roadways and rail lines for several miles. Orbetello and the nearby town of Albinia, both along the western edge of the Maremma plain, were overwhelmed with flooding, forcing more than a thousand families to temporarily relocate. Four people died in the 2012 flooding; flooding throughout coastal Maremma returned a year later, in October 2013, killing two people.

Before I turn east toward Pitigliano I still want to explore another town in the far south, Talamone, once a fishing village that the far-inland city of Siena had hoped to turn into a port in the Middle Ages. Instead, it is now a small, walled tourist town perched high on a massive rock outcropping that overlooks the sea. Most of its medieval buildings remain intact, and tucked away down a steep rock stairway is a tiny private beach that is sold out every July and August to repeat visitors.

Ottoman sea raiders wreaked havoc along this coast for years. With the aid of the French, they sacked Talamone in 1544. Forces led by the Ottoman-Turkish privateer Hayreddin Barbarossa (Red Beard) attacked coastal Tuscany repeatedly. He hit many of the towns and villages I have visited: twenty-four years before sacking Piombino, his forces captured a sailing vessel there in 1520. In addition to Talamone, he took over such towns as Castiglione della Pescaria, Orbetello, Porto Ercole, and the island of Giglio. And he didn't stop there. The Ottoman navy claimed victory after victory farther south along the coasts of Sardinia, Calabria, and Sicily, allowing the Ottoman Empire to dominate the Mediterranean during this period in history.

The Ottoman control lasted until their 1571 defeat at the Battle of Lepanto, just off the northern coast of the Gulf of Corinth in western Greece. Orchestrated by southern Mediterranean maritime states, this battle allowed places like Talamone to reclaim their roles as significant fishing ports. The battle flags of Lepanto's defeated still hang high on the walls of the church of Santo Stefano dei Cavalieri in Pisa.

Talamone is a great place to take a few days simply to relax or, perhaps, to set up a comfortable base from which to explore the Maremma region. The road to the village takes drivers through sweeping fields. Vistas of medieval grandeur sitting high on the town's outcropping over the sea come into view, growing bigger and bigger as the village draws nearer. The small marina is port for pleasure craft and fishing boats of all sizes, and the small, privately owned beach, jammed to capacity under dozens of red umbrellas during July and August, offers a shallow inlet for swimmers.

I walked the two or three narrow streets of the town, ate an early lunch of swordfish and pasta, and before the afternoon siesta took hold, sat in the shade of a medieval building that was likely seven hundred years old. There, looking out onto a small piazza, I passed time watching villagers come and go. I allowed myself a fantasy or two about buying an apartment or stone house here and escaping the heavy winter snows and cold of my hometown. As usual with these thoughts, the fantasy slipped away as quickly as it came when I remembered the crushing reality of Italian bureaucracy dealing with foreigners buying property in Italy.

Just five miles to the south of Talamone is Orbetello. It is a small Maremma town on a long, narrow peninsula that shoots out from the coastline. The Romans constructed a land bridge at its western tip to tie the mainland to the island of Monte Argentario. Two other nearly parallel land bridges on the other sides of the Orbetello peninsula were built on top of sandbars, deposited naturally by Tyrrhenian currents, between the mainland and the island.

I had been here once before, on my way to Porto Santo Stefano for that quick ferry ride to the tiny island of Giglio. Now, I could pause a bit and take in the town that has passed, like so many other parts of Italy, from one "owner" to another. The Aldobrandeschi, a family thought to have origins in Lombardy — that region of northern Italy once dominated by Germanic tribes — owned it for a time in the Middle Ages. In the 1400s, an Umbrian town far to the east, Orvieto, took possession, followed by Siena taking over for a few hundred years. In the mid-sixteenth century the Spanish, who at the time dominated much of Tuscany, took control. The Grand Duchy of Tuscany then managed it through the seventeenth and eighteenth centuries — until Italy was unified in 1870.

During a slow drive through the town, I could see the remnants of an ancient wall. The guidebook I carried for the detail of its maps said the wall dated back to the time of the Etruscans. That statement seemed wrong. I had read elsewhere that archaeologists widely believe Populonia was the only Etruscan port, while all other Etruria sites were located farther inland. Etruscans certainly had tombs in the area around Orbetello, but an Etruscan wall on the peninsula was unlikely.

I tend to believe the nineteenth-century British explorer George Dennis, who wrote that predecessors to the Etruscans put these walls along the town's edge, perhaps an early people known as the Pelasgians. Ancient Greek writers believed Pelasgians were ancestors to the Greeks and perhaps the oldest people on earth. Of course, we know they were not the earth's oldest people, but archaeologists today give them credit for being among the earliest peoples to colonize this section of Italy.

I sit for a while, looking at these remnants of prehistoric walls still protruding here and there and topped in more modern times with stone slabs to keep the walls from crumbling. Archaeologists believe they were constructed from a porous volcanic stone and clay. Their design is unlike the designs of Etruscan-built walls crafted centuries, perhaps millennia, later. Orbetello's walls could have been built anytime between the third and first millennia BC.

Spaniards, in the late 1600s, designed the city's main gate, the Medina Coeli, with its three narrow entrances for people, horses, and donkey carts. It provides a tight squeeze for buses, trucks, and cars entering the town. I am headed to Porto Ercole, on the island of Monte Argentario, considered to be one of the most heavily touristed areas along this coast.

At the end of the causeway, the road to Porto Ercole heads south. I reach the village that in modern times has spread up into two small valleys above the original village, which is laid out in a narrow strip along the marina. I find jammed streets and no parking. I should have been here in the spring.

Suddenly, the back-up lights on a car parked along the side of the main street pop on and it pulls out of a cherished spot. I pull in, beating a driver heading in the opposite direction who intended to jockey his larger vehicle into the narrow slot. Thank heavens for tiny Fiat Puntos.

Porto Ercole makes for a pleasant walk, even with the blasting August sun and intense humidity. I did not explore the newer sections of the town that push up into the two valleys, but instead braved the crowds of tourists who congregate along a couple of streets at the harbor. High on the hill above the marina area is a Spanish-era fortress, left over from the mostly peaceful days in the sixteenth and seventeenth centuries when Spain controlled this part of Tuscany. Nearby Orbetello was the headquarters for its military enclave. A narrow but high stone gate leads to a ramp that carries walkers to the Spanish fort and the church, Sant'Erasmo, where some believe the great late-Renaissance painter Michelangelo Caravaggio was entombed.

The church, a creamy soft white with a hint of Mediterranean yellow, has a wonderful view of the harbor below and the sea beyond. Its doors were shuttered.

Caravaggio's life is fascinating and was my impetus to visit Porto Ercole. Some older histories indicate that Caravaggio died of malaria in a tavern here, or maybe he died while walking along a beach on his way to the town in 1609. These early histories say he was buried in a grave with thirty others, and the jumble of bones were later unearthed and placed in Sant'Erasmo. But recent biographies dispute this version of his death.

First, the year of his death is wrong. It likely is 1610, on July 18 or 19. Andrew Graham-Dixon, one of Caravaggio's foremost modern biographers, tells a different story. He said that Caravaggio's tragic end began in Naples, where he experienced severe injuries during a fight in late 1609.

Disfigured by a series of facial cuts, he was nearly blinded in one eye. Despite these injuries and in great discomfort, he painted his last two works of art — *The Denial of St. Peter* and *The Martyrdom of St. Ursula.*

The badly injured Caravaggio left Naples for Rome in mid-1610 aboard a small, two-masted ship bound for Porto Ercole. The ship pulled into Rome's Spanish-run port. Caravaggio had planned to head into the city. But for reasons unknown, the Spanish detained Caravaggio for a couple of days. The ship, without him and with all of his possessions still on board, left for Porto Ercole, fifty miles away and a two-day sea journey. Caravaggio eventually was able to leave, and Graham-Dixon believes he rode horseback north up the coast, desperate to reclaim the paintings he had with him and his other possessions. Rome would have to wait.

It was a trip he could make in less than a day, and he arrived in Porto Ercole ahead of the ship. But the journey was too much. He quickly succumbed, either to his wounds or his ill health — perhaps malaria or a heart condition.

Whatever the circumstances, his body was tossed with others into that unmarked grave, and the local Catholic priest never recorded his death. Ironically, the priest, for unknown reasons, was "on strike" during this period, and no deaths were recorded in Porto Ercole during that entire year.

In 2001, an Italian researcher reportedly discovered a death certificate that said Caravaggio died in a hospital, but it has since been deemed a forgery.

Meanwhile, in late 2009, other more credible researchers removed from a church ossuary a collection of bones belonging to at least thirty people who died in the early seventeenth century. They studied the DNA from those bones, compared them to Caravaggio's siblings' descendants, and proclaimed a year later they were 85 percent sure that some of the remains belonged to the artist. Many historians have yet to be convinced.

Eleven:
Colli di Maremma

These sulfuric springs, which gush out of the earth at [99 degrees F°], were famous even in Roman times for their curative properties. On windy days the smell of sulfur carries all the way up to the village of Saturnia, said to be the oldest in all of Italy. It was to these springs that injured Roman soldiers were sent to be healed after battle.

— David Leavitt and Mark Mitchell,
*In Maremma: Life and a House
in Southern Tuscany* (2011)

The SS74 road to Pitigliano, along a gentle, curving stretch through the low-lying hills of the Maremma, starts at the coast. The first small town it passes through is Marsiliana, where, in 1915, a seventh century BC Etruscan tablet was uncovered. This tablet gave archaeologists a broader hint at the composition of the Etruscan alphabet, the bulk of which remains a mystery.

An area at Tuscany's southern end, Maremma is peppered with Etruscan sites, ranging from city/village ruins now barely perceptible on the rolling landscape, to tomb areas and other ruins where ovens and kilns are located along with the remains of cisterns for water storage.

The first two-thirds of this relatively short fifty-mile drive inland to Pitigliano takes us through an area known locally as the Albegna River Valley. It holds perhaps fifteen sites tied to four different historical periods. The first is prehistoric, from which no written record exists. This is followed by the protohistoric period, which refers to people who left no written record but whom ancient writers wrote about. Without those early writings, prehistoric peoples would be unknown to us except through scant archaeological ruins and rough-hewn pottery and tools. The Etruscans, for example, left no extensive writings, except for those few chiseled words on a stone slab. But the ancient Romans who followed wrote about them extensively. Then there is the Roman period when people left vast numbers of documents. Finally, we have the medieval period and all the extensive evidence it left us, including still-standing buildings, art, and writings. Many sites, in and around various modern villages built next to or on top of them, also can claim beginnings in the prehistoric, Etruscan, Roman, or medieval periods. Many, like Pitigliano, claim occupancy by all four.

The Maremma is a land ripe for exploration by travelers interested in Etruscan/Roman history. After making Pitigliano my base for the next six days, I wandered in and around some of these sites. This was in mid-August, the height of the tourist season, but I noticed there were few visitors prowling among the stones. The sign-in registers at some of the small museums often listed two months' worth of visitors on a single page, with room for more names. As I flipped through these pages, occasionally I would come across a name with an American city as home, but it was rare.

Heading inland for the first time, I had been ignorant of all this Etruscan treasure. That would come during various forays from Pitigliano. All I knew at the beginning was that I was going to a medieval city that had been recommended to me by a friend in Pietrasanta. "It's a must-see," he said. By declining to add details about what to expect there, he encouraged me to make my own discoveries.

Pitigliano hits the unsuspecting motorist like pie in the eye: suddenly and without warning for the first-timer. The village dramatically comes into focus when you swing around a sharp curve far below the town, near the Madonna delle Grazie church. Pitigliano looks much the same today as it must have to a medieval traveler riding a mule or horse around that same curve six hundred years ago.

There it is, rising out of a spur of tufa carved through geologic time by wind and water. The town and its soft-yellow and reddish stone houses and buildings piled alongside and over one another look like they are part of the mountain itself rather than built on top.

Etruscans settled at this high spot and dug tombs out of the soft tufa that rings the base of the plateau. Now those tombs, with large wooden doors and modern heavy locks, are used to store items like olive oil, casks of wine, household goods. This village, under the Etruscans, was along a commercial route that connected it with Vulci, another major center just to the north of Rome.

A nicely detailed book written by a local historian reports that the Etruscan name for Pitigliano could have been "Statnes." Under the Romans, it was called Statonia.

The final name for Pitigliano, and the names of a handful of villages throughout Italy, evolved from the name of a distinguished Roman family, the "gens Petilia."

My arrival in Pitigliano was timed well. Within an hour, as I sat across from my hotel at a small bar's outside table near the medieval town gate, drums sounded in the distance, cars in the narrow square in front of the hotel were chased away, and a procession of townsfolk in full medieval garb flowed into the newly cleared space to mark the beginning of a medieval festival.

For the next several days, a series of musical events and dance performances filled the evening hours. Still, the town was not full of tourists. An article in *The New York Times* reported that Pitigliano has only twenty-five thousand visitors a year. Like small festivals I have attended in Sicily and southern Italy, this was purely a local affair, with residents and perhaps visitors from nearby towns. Its charm has not yet been compromised by mass tourism.

The village itself has a strong Jewish background with roots in the early 1500s. Jews, until World War II and the precipitous rise of Fascism, were very much a part of town life. There was a period that lasted a little over a century in Pitigliano when they were required to wear distinctive clothing and live in a ghetto. This happened in other places at various times throughout history. But at some point in the late 1700s the requirement that the Jews of Pitigliano wear distinctive clothing was removed; they were allowed back into the daily life of the village.

Writer Abby Ellin, in the *Times* story, reported that when anti-Jewish Fascist laws came into effect in 1938, only sixty Jews were living in Pitigliano. Some were able to stay with friends throughout the area, likely in secret. Twenty-two, all born in Pitigliano, died in concentration camps during the war.

When Italy surrendered to the Allies in 1943, the town was being used as a German military headquarters, occupying the Orsini Palace just inside the town's ancient gate. Allied bombing runs targeting that headquarters missed their mark, preserving that building but destroying some of the village's medieval housing structures and killing a handful of civilians. Those buildings have been rebuilt, of course, to closely resemble the architecture of what was lost.

Today, there is a kosher delicatessen along the southernmost of the town's three narrow streets. Nearby and down steep stone steps is the village's restored synagogue, dating back to the late 1500s. This remnant is all that is left of Pitigliano's Jewish past. I walked around the old town in just a few hours, dipping into noncommercial, purely residential areas. In all, four thousand people live here today.

I spent my evenings in Pitigliano enjoying the festival activities, standing with locals cheering on a corps of costumed drummers who dazzled with their virtuosity, or spontaneously dancing to popular Italian singers and musicians. My days were occupied with trips to the countryside, visiting such places as Sorano, Sovana and its nearby Etruscan center, and Saturnia, which surprised me with a preserved section of the Roman road known as Via Clodia. These short journeys marked the end of my nearly six months in Tuscany's west.

If, from a distance, Pitigliano appears like a pile of yellow and reddish stone set high on a plateau, Sorano is a mirror. Just seven miles to the northeast, it dominates a ridge, and tumbles down the concave side of its gentle slope. Sorano is the highest village in the Maremma region — at 2,243 feet above sea level it is 200 feet higher than Pitigliano. Its walls are intact, and the few gates in the grand sweep of stone parapets reinforce the sense that one is approaching a fortress. I could almost hear medieval trumpets braying in the distance and imagine sentries in the various watchtowers.

A large parking lot outside Sorano's main gate is only partially full on this particular Sunday visit, and that is because a crafts fair is under way along a street below. I get the sense that tourists are few here as well. A desk clerk at a local hotel lamented, "We almost always have rooms available. This should be where you stay when you visit [inland Maremma]," she said. "It is more quiet here [than Pitigliano] and there is much to see."

She is correct. The fortress looms above the town. While standing on the castle's ramparts and looking downward to the north, one can see the old town spread out among narrow streets in an almost indecipherable pattern, one more complex than Pitigliano's. Sorano offers a warren of passageways and small, dead-end courtyards with clustered living spaces. Before braving the steep stone steps that lead to it, I could imagine that I was back in the Middle Ages: The buildings seem to have been plucked from that era and remain unchanged. The only hint of modernity is the satellite dishes on their rooftops.

Sorano's population is about the same as Pitigliano, about four thousand, but it is a far more sedate village with only brief flashes of activity. This is the high tourist season in Tuscany, but you wouldn't know it here.

Giovanni Feo, respected author of an excellent book about the area and its various villages, writes that in reality, the town's inaccessibility — the narrow streets within the old town were made for donkey carts hundreds of years ago and have not been widened to suit the age of motorized vehicles — has made it impossible "to expand or modernize," and this gives it "the largest proportion of inhabited medieval buildings" in inland Maremma.

Feo's description of this lesser-known part of the Tuscan south offers an accurate picture of its past and present. He tells us that Sorano, due to its position along a main route from Rome to Siena during medieval times, was "the target of repeated sieges and interminable wars" for many centuries.

But, despite the wars, Sorano's location had medicinal benefits. Its high position kept it and other highly placed hill towns above the mosquito breeding areas in the marshy plains nearer to the sea, where tens of thousands of Tuscans perished over the centuries. These coastal marshes developed around the mouths of rivers that brought silt down from the rolling hills. They were perfect incubators for the *anopheles* mosquito.

From Sorano, it is a quick six-mile drive through sparsely populated countryside to Sovana, a much smaller town to the west that has obviously been well scrubbed for this age of tourism. Not a stone seems out of place; fresh paint is everywhere; stones are cleaned to exhibit their burnt-yellow hue. I visited twice, and for a third time I went to the Etruscan sites around the village.

Sovana is built on nearly level ground in the midst of a wide valley with olive groves and hardwood forests populated by wild boars, the official symbol of Maremma. The village is far smaller than either Pitigliano or Sorano and far easier to navigate. There are two long main streets radiating from the large town square, with one road leading to one of the most delightful, unadorned, and tasteful cathedrals I have ever visited in Italy.

Feo describes the cathedral as "a rare example of a Romanesque and Gothic cathedral." It sits near the point of a small promontory, which has a commanding view of the beautiful Tuscan countryside below.

The cathedral has its origins in the ninth century. In the twelfth century, the site was modified and expanded into what one finds today.

The mid-August humidity outside vanished once I entered the church. It seems to be the ultimate in comfortable simplicity. The walls are made of light-yellow stone, and fragments of the original frescoes remain — perhaps a partial figure here and there. Natural light is drawn in through small windows along the edges of the vaulted ceiling. The light and the inherent coolness combine to make this serene, simple place a rewarding, relaxing spot. I sit for a long time on a stone bench at the back, listening to the soft recording of a Gregorian chant piped in through hidden speakers. It was a fine respite indeed.

Prehistoric peoples lived in Sovana, as did the Etruscans, who drove the early village to the peak of its growth in the fourth and third centuries BC. The Romans, according to historian Feo, apparently left the village and surrounding area alone throughout the empire's five-hundred-year history.

Christianity made its way throughout the empire following an edict in AD 380 making it the official state religion. By the fourth century AD Sovana was home to a bishop. Christian hermits and ascetics gathered here, living in caves around the village and, Feo said, their "example contributed significantly to the spread of Christianity."

The first time I had heard of Sovana was in connection with its "reliable tradition" as the birthplace of Pope Gregory VII, whom papal historian John Julius Norwich called "the greatest churchman of the Middle Ages." The dates are not precise. One source says his birth as Hildebrand of Sovana was sometime between AD 1015 and 1028. His papacy lasted from 1073 to 1085.

Pope Gregory VII began his reign in 1073 by enforcing priestly celibacy and demanding an end to simony — paying to receive sacraments. He removed bishops and priests who had been appointed by kings and emperors and not by Rome. Such action angered these rulers, who felt they had the right to name their own bishops and other churchmen.

In this battle over papal right versus royal prerogative, Gregory refused to crown King Henry IV of Germany, who was next in line to be Holy Roman Emperor. In response, Henry called together bishops faithful to him and declared Pope Gregory dethroned. Gregory ignored that declaration and excommunicated Henry. It was at Countess Matilda's castle at Canossa where, as legend has it, the king, barefoot and dressed in sackcloth, waited three days in the snow to be allowed to enter and ask Gregory for forgiveness.

At around this time, a pope's authority to name emperors, kings, and churchmen was beginning to be challenged. Henry, who had once again broken with the pope, occupied Rome in 1084, and Gregory, his papacy in ruins, was exiled to Monte Cassino, a monastery high in the mountains between Rome and Naples, and then to the castle at Salerno, south of Naples, where he died in 1085, far from his Tuscan birthplace.

Sovana still had a lot more to offer. The following day, I was back in the area for a walk through its Etruscan past. The Etruscan village likely is beneath a large portion of medieval Sovana. Ruins have been excavated in the area near the northern edge of the cathedral. This side trip took the better part of a day and covered a wide array of tombs, both grand and small. Still, I barely touched on what is there. Three streams flow through a swath of countryside that ranges east to west around Sovana. Dozens if not hundreds of tombs are spread along their three narrow valleys.

Nearly all styles of tombs found in various Etruscan sites throughout central Italy are laid out in this countryside: chamber tombs, façade tombs, niche tombs, and burial ditches. One tomb, in the area along the stream called Picciolana, is made of eight carved stone columns and a façade with twin stairways to a second level. It is one of only two found in the Etruscan world that is carved out in this way. It is called the Ildebranda tomb, named after Hildebrand of Sovana, Pope Gregory VII.

Perhaps one of the most unique sights I caught that day was La Via Cava di Poggio Prisca, an ancient roadway cut twenty to thirty feet deep through solid tufa. It is a short distance from the Ildebranda tomb. Such roadways are common in Etruscan areas. They provided a way to bring quarried rock down to tomb sites; later, in medieval times, they offered a shortcut from one part of the valley to another for travelers and farmers.

The Via Cava curves gently for perhaps five or six hundred feet, coming out at the far end onto a dirt road with a wide expanse of vineyards on either side. I walked its length, pausing to lean against the cool stone and enjoy the refreshing shade of its leaning walls and the well-developed trees that created a leafy arbor overhead.

After several hours of plodding along in severe heat and humidity and seeing tomb after tomb, my brief walk through this wide slash in a solid stone block was the highlight.

With two days left in southwestern Tuscany, I wanted enough time to visit three or four more small villages. That gave me one more full day of exploration. The second day would be for the three- or four-hour drive back to Pietrasanta.

My day started early. I plopped my finger, almost at random, on my map. It landed on a village northwest of Pitigliano, Castell'Azzara — a village that is part of a nature preserve created in the 1990s. It is positioned on woody and mountainous terrain, and the mountainside holds numerous giant "holes" called by various names that incorporate the Italian word *buca,* or mouth.

The village's castle was built here in the twelfth century for precisely the same reason this area impressed me: magnificent panoramic views of the Tuscan countryside. Whereas castle dwellers wanted to be able to see invaders arriving, travelers thrill over the beauty of the views. The first time I had ever been overwhelmed by a Tuscan panorama was in the mid-1990s, when I stood on the ramparts of Volterra. This sweep of countryside from Castell'Azzara was Volterra's equal. The warm, inviting vineyards I had driven through to climb up this mountainside now lay below me, interspersed with olive groves and shorn wheat fields with their huge machine-rolled bales of straw.

The village and the woods around it are eminently walkable. The main drag, Via Garibaldi, is full by midmorning with locals, either strolling along the narrow sidewalks or reading newspapers on terraces. Groups of older men, likely *pensionati,* played cards or engaged in conversation punctuated by loud laughter and myriad hand gestures.

A *caffè,* a cream-filled *cornetto,* and an hour of observing small-town Italian life made up a pleasant interlude — the kind of interlude I have perfected into a fine art over the years — in what would be my final full day in the Tuscan south.

My next town, Santa Fiora, exemplifies why I often slow down and observe as a way of making discoveries. As I approached Santa Fiora, I noticed a long bridge that spans a gully with homes and gardens far below. Beyond the bridge is the old town, splayed across the side of a mountain and surrounded by Tuscan pines and chestnut trees. This place, in ancient times, was likely difficult to attack. The gully is wide, and I wondered how folks here crossed it before the bridge was built. They likely went down a steep, narrow footpath carved out of stone, walked across the gully's bottom, and then endured an exhausting climb up the other side.

I parked on the far side of the bridge and walked across it. I was surprised to discover a modern elevator put in the bridge's middle to give gully residents an easy way home. At the bridge's end, the old town begins, and all the churches that would appear on a tourist office's official "points of interest" list are in plain sight. The main street is wide and boasts the customary cafes and bars, clothing shops, and food peddlers.

But the real town can be found on numerous side streets perpendicular to the main street. These narrow, medieval streets roll up and down with the gradient of the land and are lined with shops full of local products: cheese, various kinds of sausages, herbs, and fruits of all kinds. This local aspect, I suspect, is what keeps them in business with a population of fewer than three thousand people. There rarely are chain stores to drive out the local business owners in these tiny places. Produce, meat, and fruit come from farms in the valleys below and are as fresh as the same-day seafood offered in Tuscany's coastal communities.

And, despite its small size, Santa Fiore has perhaps a dozen restaurants, all specializing in cuisine that is specific to the village itself or southern Tuscany in general: wild boar, pork, and some beef, along with pasta shapes not found anywhere else on the planet.

It is before noon, and the restaurants in the old town are not yet open. I wander back across the bridge and, near where I parked my car, I see a young woman opening a door to the Ristorante al Ponte, which has a collection of outside tables under umbrellas. I ask if she is open. *"Si, prego,"* she says, pointing to table.

I sit, order a bottle of mineral water, and peruse a menu presented only in Italian — a good sign if you want a restaurant geared to serving locals. I tell the young woman I would like a meat dish of her choosing, something local, *una specialità della casa,* a specialty of the house. She likes that idea and disappears through the beaded doorway.

Ten, perhaps fifteen minutes later, she places before me a plate with thin squares of pasta, covered in a pork sauce rich with chunks of meat. Sprinkled in is a healthy dose of fennel. The pasta, she tells me, is made from chestnut flour and is called *fazzoletti,* or handkerchiefs. This particular shape and its ingredients, she claims, have been invented by her chef partner and, she assured me, are not found anywhere else. I certainly had never seen pasta like it before. The food at Ristorante al Ponte is among the best I have ever eaten during years of travel in Italy, north and south.

I eat only a first course, finish with a creamy dessert and a double *caffè,* and wander across the street to my car. The one place on my agenda that I had definitely wanted to see, Saturnia, is several miles away, and I want to enjoy the ride through the Tuscan hills with a clear head — hence my comparatively light lunch.

Saturnia's name comes from the Roman god Saturn who, according to myth, grew tired of man's constant warfare. So he sent a lightning bolt to earth. A spring erupted from the spot where it hit, and the warm waters washed over the people, making them calmer and wiser. Saturn also gave his name to the English day of the week Saturday and to our solar system's second-largest planet. Why not to a hilltop town in the Fiora Valley?

The ancient Greek historian Dionysius of Halicarnassus, writing in the time of the Roman emperor Augustus, said he believed Saturnia was one of Italy's first towns. It could initially have been settled, perhaps in the ninth century BC, by predecessors to the Etruscans, the Pelasgians — the same people we first encountered to the west, around Orbetello. The Etruscans took over the site a century later. Then, in 183 BC, Roman colonists arrived, making the village a prefecture of Rome. Historians and archaeologists generally agree that the key to Saturnia's long life, other than its prime position atop a long, broad hill of white travertine stone in the midst of classic, fertile Tuscan countryside, was the nearby hot springs and water from two rivers, the Albegna and Fiora.

Nothing in Italy's ancient history stayed mellow for long. Groups of raiders from various tribes, Goths, and Saracen pirates besieged Saturnia and the Tuscan countryside for many centuries. Bandits hid out in these hills. The Sienese eventually attacked Saturnia, built a fortress, and eventually destroyed the town. By 1500, it was abandoned and left to fall into ruin.

Today, Saturnia flourishes. The hot springs, once appealing to a cult of water worshipers, draw tourists. The town also has a variety of low-key Roman ruins, and the remnants of ancient walls exist.

When I drove into Saturnia, I didn't know any of this specific information, only that it was worth visiting. Its center is unlike most hill-town destinations tourists seek out. There is no grand piazza, for example. Instead, the center is parklike with rows of trees and green areas where locals lounge on park benches. I stopped for gelato and a *caffè* at one of the pleasant bars along this area, enjoying the coolness of a covered terrace. As I was leaving, I turned down a few random streets and found myself on a bumpy roadway made of worn stone blocks. It was in bad shape, so I decided not to head down it and go through what I thought was a medieval arch and up into the surrounding countryside.

A sign on a building a few dozen feet from the arch caught my eye. In Italian, it mentioned Via Clodia, and I realized that this bumpy roadway was part of that famous imperial Roman road. Later, when I looked at a map of Rome's roads in Italy, I realized that the Via Clodia upended the famous dictum that all roads lead to Rome. It didn't. It began off the Via Aurelia in the far northwest of modern Tuscany, near my major base at Pietrasanta, and swept inland down south through Tuscany's center, ending at Saturnia, not Rome.

Via Aurelia and Via Cassia were imperial roads designed to quickly move troops north and south through western Italy. Via Clodia, which ran between them, was a commercial road that connected the thermal areas in this part of Tuscany — Saturnia is not the only one — and facilitated trade among them. It was completed early in Roman history, by 225 BC, at a time when the Romans were the undisputed masters of road building. The high quality of their craft allows us today to see such sections of several Roman roads, such as the stretch into Saturnia.

Later I discovered that the high stone arch I first spotted — the Porta Romana — was attached to an old Sienese fortress. The walls, reused by the Sienese and made from polygonal blocks of travertine first set in place by Romans, Etruscans, and their predecessors, show the builders' advanced skills: the stones fit precisely together without mortar of any kind. This method makes walls in this part of earthquake-prone Italy resistant to such tremblers. The ancient wall builders did their work well; these structures, like portions of Via Clodia, have survived for nearly twenty-five hundred years.

That last evening in Maremma, I wandered through the brightly lit streets of Pitigliano, listening to a brief performance by a group of drummers. It was the same band who had announced, with their tom-toms and snare drums, the procession of medieval-dressed townspeople several days earlier.

Tomorrow, I would head north again, through the central part of the Maremma in Tuscany's southwestern edge, before rejoining coastal Via Aurelia somewhere north and west of Grosseto. It would be a three- or four-hour drive back to my apartment at Pietrasanta and only a few weeks before I would return to my U.S. home.

After coffee outside a bar along the town square, I found myself at a parapet on the edge of town, high on the plateau where I could look over the darkening valley below. The music in the distance was low, the evening cool, and the air rich with scents of foliage intermingled with smells from a nearby restaurant.

A small family walked up onto the parapet — mother, grandmother, perhaps an aunt, and a young boy. Slowly, behind them, the father was pushing a wheelchair with a severely disabled girl who looked to be a teenager. He leaned over her and wrapped his arms under hers, and she struggled to wrap hers around his neck. He lifted her and carried her to the edge. There he pointed out the glow of the moon and the skittering of the insects. He held her there, in his arms, for the longest time, murmuring soft words in her ear as she gazed, eyes glistening in the lunar light, at the countryside far beyond and below.

It was a scene I certainly could have witnessed anywhere on the planet. I know there are many parents, Italian or otherwise, who are like that father and daughter. But that night, in that village on a spot as old as time itself, in the presence of this multigenerational family quietly, lovingly engaged with one another, and this gentle father with his daughter struggling to respond as he pointed out all that was around her, I felt Italian graciousness sweep over me once again.

AFTERWORD

There is so much more to western Tuscany than this book, any book, can capture. I drove through dozens of small towns and villages and past ancient sites without stopping. I only had time to visit a few of the hundreds peppered along the coast and through the low hills of the coastal interior. Each site could have been a new adventure offering great memories.

Because this is not a guidebook in the strict sense of the word, only a few specific B and Bs and a couple of restaurants are mentioned. They are easily found on the Internet if the reader wants to try them as I did. I like to think of this book simply as a guide to being a traveler: pick a direction, carry a map so you know how to get back to your resting place each evening, and set out each morning with no agenda. And if you have an agenda, be willing to abandon it if something else draws your interest. If you come to a fork in the road, flip a coin to decide which one to take. And stay off the *autostrada*!

And of course traveling isn't without its mishaps. But welcome surprises outweigh minor problems — such as scratching a rental car's fender when backing into a low, unseen stone wall. Occasionally, I would see a castle high on a hill and make a snap decision to go up there, sometimes finding a closed, tumbledown place, but more often finding, within the walls, a village that did not appear on my map. I stopped in villages that spoke to me in some inaudible way, and usually found conversation, great food, a few hours of relaxation on a stone bench in a shady spot on the main square.

I left my touristy shorts in my suitcase and Hawaiian shirts back in the States and did my best to dress like a local, particularly in the villages within the coastal hills: long pants, a dress shirt, a comfortable jacket or vest, nicely shined shoes. Of course the locals knew I wasn't from there, but my show of respect for their culture made it easier to start conversations.

The exception to this dress code was in Pietrasanta. The only truly casual place for men of my age, the *pensionati,* seemed to be Pietrasanta — and then only in the hottest, most humid days of June, July, and August, when flip-flops, T-shirts, and shorts were de rigueur. Still, younger men and boys seemed more dressed up than the older guys. When there, I dressed accordingly and fit in just fine. I should mention that while the older men were casual in this art-filled town, the women, no matter what age, were always dressed fashionably. I could never get a straight answer why Pietrasanta was unique in its residents' fashion habits compared with what I experienced elsewhere in Italy, even in Sicily and Sardinia.

I made a handful of good friends in the months I lived in Pietrasanta. These were men and women I saw on a regular basis, in whose restaurants or clubs I ate, or in whose bars I enjoyed my morning coffee and *cornetto.* We would greet each other by name, and in the service establishments they knew my routine just as I knew theirs. Nearly every day I was in town, I could count on a *caffè doppio* being set before me within a few moments of sitting down at my table on the outside terrace of Bar Pietrasantese, located at the west end of the main piazza.

One of my best memories of my time in Pietrasanta was the almost daily conversation I had with the grandfather of my close friend Filippo Tofani. Gualtiero Coluccini, who is in his late seventies or early eighties, speaks no English. I had limited conversational skills in Italian, but each day as I strolled around the piazza, Gualtiero — he was originally named "Walter," but Mussolini decreed that all names had to be Italian, not foreign — would be sitting on the well-worn, white-marble steps of the Duomo, sometimes with fellow *pensionati,* sometimes alone. We would greet each other warmly, and he would ask me where I had been, what I had learned about his beloved western Tuscany, and where I was going next. Remarkably, we found a way to understand each other. We would have only basic conversation, so I did not have the opportunity to delve into his life story.

One day his grandson Filippo took me to Valdicastello Carducci on Pietrasanta's outskirts and to the house where Gualtiero lived as a child. It was just a few dozen feet from the end of the long mule track from Sant'Anna. I learned in further conversations that the day after the massacre at Sant'Anna, Gualtiero, probably only age ten or eleven, having heard the rumors, went alone up that steep path and into the tortured village and saw the aftermath of that great tragedy. I never asked Gualtiero about it — it was something I sensed he might not want to talk about — but it was an interesting bit of insight on the man's history.

On a Sunday morning in early September, just five days before I was scheduled to return to the United States, I got a call from Brad, my youngest son, with the tragic news that his brother, my oldest then at age forty-five, had died the day before from a massive heart attack. I made immediate arrangements to fly out from Pisa the next day and would be at my son's home by that evening.

Somehow, I had to face the remaining day and say goodbye to the people I had become close with in the preceding five and a half months. None were around — it was Sunday — so I left notes where I knew they would find them. I contacted Filippo, who helped me arrange a final meeting with my landlady, and then packed.

All that done, I was left alone with the emotions such a thing engenders. I walked over to the piazza and there, in his usual spot on the steps of the Duomo, sat Gualtiero. The news spilled out of me somehow in perfect Italian, and the anguish on his face indicated he understood. He immediately offered comfort that I so desperately needed, and I understood his words perfectly. We sat on those steps for quite a while, his arm around my shoulder. Eventually, I said good-bye. He gave me a long, solemn embrace, and turned toward his home just a short distance away.

People were heading into the church. I could hear through the open doors women's voices, saying prayers in unison. Inside, white-robed priests were in their confessionals listening to parishioners, one after another. Church workers were setting up the main altar for a service. I am neither Catholic nor religious, but I have often felt at peace inside Italian churches. So I stayed, sitting in the back row. I stayed through the women's prayers, the confessions, and the entire service, complete with High Mass.

Preoccupied as I was with my son's death, the surprising comfort I felt in that sanctuary prepared me for the rest of the evening, the twenty-hour series of flights beginning at 5 A.M. the next day, and the weeks that followed.

ACKNOWLEDGMENTS

These projects are never done in a vacuum. Many people make recommendations, provide information, and offer support and friendship that, in the end, help make the whole come together in what I hope is a tidy package.

Anna Camaiti Hostert, when she was helping me with certain aspects of my previous book about Sicily, spoke often about her beloved home in Tuscany's Maremma and how few Americans spend time there. That triggered thoughts about the parts of western Tuscany that are little known to non-Europeans. I am grateful to her for opening a window into this wonderful part of southwest Tuscany.

Many years ago, I met a young man visiting my hometown of Salt Lake City who grew up in Pietrasanta. Filippo Tofani and I became good friends, and when I told him of my plan for this book, his enthusiasm bubbled over. He became a major supporter and helper. Filippo, who had returned to the town of his birth, laid the groundwork for finding my apartment, helped with interpreting, and spent several days showing me around Versilia. Most important, he introduced me to the story of the village of Sant'Anna di Stazzema, which became a significant chapter in this book. Filippo's knowledge of history proved faultless, never steering me wrong as I checked and double-checked historical facts. He, more than anyone else, played a key role in shaping the outcome of this project.

Historian Leonard Chiarelli of University of Utah's Marriott Library — and my close friend — also had a great impact on my work. A tireless researcher, he kept me supplied with documents and other reference material that added immeasurably to my efforts. This is the second book of mine to which he has contributed. His friendship and support, emotional as well as in all things historical, are priceless. Also, I must recognize photographer Steven R. McCurdy who has helped me with photos for two books. He also is a filmmaker, a fellow Italophile, and good friend.

Others also stepped in when asked. Two University of Utah historians — Drs. John

Reed and Ed J. Davies — provided insight into western Tuscany's involvement in World War II. Dr. Davies helped guide my understanding of the Nazi mind-set regarding the massacres of civilians in Italy; Dr. Reed suggested sources for understanding Allied involvement in coastal Tuscany and through the Serchio River Valley, something a lot of popular World War II histories barely mention, or ignore altogether. He reviewed my chapter on the war to ensure no errors had crept in during my brief retelling of those brutal days, focusing in particular on the roles of the black soldiers — the Buffalo Soldiers — and the men of the Japanese-American Nisei regiment, who were both segregated from white units.

A University of Utah colleague of theirs, Dr. Winthrop L. Adams, enlightened me about Etruscans and their impact on ancient Rome and tipped me off to a little-known legend about Napoleon Bonaparte's family origins.

I also am grateful for the warm hospitality of the staff at the Biblioteca communale di Pietrasanta, a true library with sunny rooms and pleasant spaces where I spent most mornings and afternoons working when I was not on the road. Incidentally, the staff kept me well supplied with books in English for when I'd relax after a day's labors. It was there I "discovered" many of John le Carré's spy novels, was reintroduced to Jack Kerouac's *On the Road,* and plowed through a massive history of the World War II battle of Stalingrad.

During my five and a half months in Pietrasanta, I struggled to expand my basic Italian beyond being able to use complete sentences only to make hotel reservations and order food. My teacher, Cristina Zappelli, tailored each of my lessons to what I was discovering during my travels around the region. While I am still nowhere near fluent, my conversational skills improved markedly. Most important, she was instrumental in arranging my first interview with a survivor of the Sant'Anna massacre. She and her colleague Ilaria Violante were interpreters for that first interview. Claudio Lazzeri, who helped me to understand the story of his mother's and aunts' experiences during that tragic event, complemented their efforts.

I also thank my editors at Thomas Dunne Books/St. Martin's Press, Kathleen Gilligan and Melanie Fried. I am particularly grateful to my publisher, Thomas Dunne, who for nearly fifteen years has provided a platform that allows me to write about my many walks in the warm Italian sun.

Of course, family plays a significant role in an undertaking of this magnitude. My wife, Connie Disney, kept things running smoothly during my nearly half-year absence and offered much-needed support through the writing process. One of the best times I had during these nearly six months of travel was when she joined me for two weeks of wandering along the southwestern edge of this remarkable region, particularly during the six days in and around Pitigliano. I am grateful for her enthusiasm, observations, and insight, and to everyone else who helped make all of this possible.

— John Keahey, Salt Lake City,
March 2014

SELECTED BIBLIOGRAPHY

Abulafia, David. *The Great Sea: A Human History of the Mediterranean.* New York: Oxford University Press, 2011.

Anonymous. *The Appetite Comes Through Eating: A Brief Journey in "Gourmet" Versilia.* Viareggio: APT Versilia Tourist Board (n.d.).

Bosworth, R. J. B. *Mussolini's Italy: Life under the Fascist Dictatorship, 1915–1945.* New York: Penguin Press, 2006.

Bratchel, M. E. *Lucca 1430–1494: The Reconstruction of an Italian City-Republic.* Oxford: Clarendon Press, 1995.

Braudel, Fernand. *The Mediterranean in the Ancient World.* London: Penguin Books, 2001.

Burkert, Walter. *Greek Religion: Archaic and Classical.* Oxford: Blackwell Publishing, 1985. Malden, Mass.: Harvard University Press, reprinted 2004.

Cooperativa La Foretezza. *Etruscan and Medieval Sovana, Including Excursions to Pitigliano and Sorano.* Pitigliano: Editrice Laurum, 1996.

"Dār al-Sinā'a." *Encyclopedia of Islam,* Second Edition. Brill Online, 2013.

Dennis, George. *The Cities and Cemeteries of Etruria.* London: John Murray, 1848.

Dingwall-Main, Alex. *The Angel Tree: The Enchanting Quest for the World's Oldest Olive Tree.* New York: Arcade Publishing, 2012.

Ellin, Abby. "A 'Little Jerusalem' in the Heart of Tuscany." *The New York Times.* November 22, 2012.

Elon, Beth. *A Culinary Traveller in Tuscany: Exploring & Eating Off the Beaten Track.* New York: The Little Bookroom, 2009.

Everitt, Anthony. *Augustus.* New York: Random House, 2006.

Feo, Giovanni. *The Hilltop Towns of the Fiora Valley.* Pitigliano: Editrice Laurum, 2007.

Fisher Jr., Ernest F. *United States in World War II, Mediterranean Theater of Operations: Cassino to the Alps.* Washington, D.C.: Center of Military History, United States Army, 1976.

Goodman, Col. Paul. *A Fragment of Victory in Italy: The 92nd Infantry Division in World*

War II. Nashville: Battery Press, 1993.

Heater, James and Colleen. *The Pilgrim's Italy: A Travel Guide to the Saints.* Nevada City, Ca.: Inner Travel Books, 2003.

Johns, Pamela Sheldon. *Cucina Povera: Tuscan Peasant Cooking.* Kansas City, Mo.: Andrews McMeel Publishing, 2011.

Laghi, Anna and Carlo Bordoni. *Pietrasanta: Work of Art.* Massa: Società Editrice Apuana s.r.l.

Lamb, Richard. *War in Italy 1943–1945: A Brutal Story.* New York: Da Capo Press, 1996.

Lambertini, Marco. Designs by Rossella Faleni. *The Island of Capraia: The Wild Heart of the Tuscan Archipelago.* Pisa: Pacini Editore SpA, 2002.

Leavitt, David and Mark Mitchell. *In Maremma: Life and a House in Southern Tuscany.* Berkeley, CA: Counterpoint Press, 2001.

McCann, Anna Margaret, Joanne Burgeois, and Elizabeth Lyding Will. "Underwater Excavations at the Etruscan Port of Populonia." *Journal of Field Archaeology,* Vol. 4, No. 3 (Autumn, 1977), pp. 275–296.

Moffat, Alistair. *Tuscany: A History.* Edinburgh: Birlinn Limited, 2011.

Morpurgo, J. E. *The Last Days of Shelley*

and Byron. Garden City, N.Y.: Doubleday and Company, 1960.

Norwich, John Julius. *Absolute Monarchs: A History of the Papacy.* New York: Random House, 2011.

Olsen, Jack. *Silence on Monte Sole.* New York: G. P. Putnam's Sons, 1968.

Pezzino, Paolo. *Memory and Massacre: Revisiting Sant'Anna.* New York: Palgrave Macmillan, 2012.

Poggesi, Gabriella. *Etruscans in the Maremma of Grosseto.* Grosetto: Soprintendenza ai Beni Archeollogici della Tuscana (n.d.).

Rosenzweig, Peter. "A Short History of Marble." Campo dell'Altissimo. Azzano, Italy: www.campo-altissimo.de (n.d.).

Spike, Michele K. *Tuscan Countess: The Life and Extraordinary Times of Matilda of Canossa.* New York: Vendome Press, 2004.

Taylor, Benjamin. *Naples Declared: A Walk Around the Bay.* New York: G. P. Putnam's Sons, 2012.